The Birth and Growth
of Industrial England

1714–1867

THE HARBRACE HISTORY OF ENGLAND

I Ancient and Medieval England: Beginnings to 1509

J. R. Lander
University of Western Ontario

II Renaissance and Reformation England: 1509–1714

Charles M. Gray
University of Chicago

III The Birth and Growth of Industrial England: 1714–1867

John F. C. Harrison
University of Sussex

IV England Since 1867: Continuity and Change

Peter Stansky
Stanford University

PART III

THE HARBRACE HISTORY OF ENGLAND

John F. C. Harrison

University of Sussex

The Birth and Growth of Industrial England

1714-1867

Under the General Editorship of John Morton Blum

Yale University

Harcourt Brace Jovanovich, Inc.

New York/Chicago/San Francisco/Atlanta

41942

ISBN: 0-15-535109-5

Library of Congress Catalog Card Number: 72-97675

Printed in the United States of America

Preface

It is a truism that each generation has to rewrite its history. This is not because the "facts" of history are no longer true, or even because new facts are discovered that invalidate previous conclusions; but because each generation asks different questions of the past. We are no longer interested in some of the things that our fathers thought important, and we want to know about some aspects of the past that they ignored. History is important to us only insofar as it extends, through the dimension of time, our experience of man and society in ways that seem to us significant. To this degree, at least, history is always present-minded.

During the past twenty years, and especially in the past ten, historians have redrawn the contours of many aspects of the period covered in this volume. It is a long time now since history was thought of as a list of kings and battles, but the legacy of a narrow political and constitutional approach has not entirely disappeared. A natural reaction to these interpretations was an emphasis on economic and social history, with a resulting proliferation of texts in these areas. This was all to the good, as a necessary correction of the earlier bias. But now the need is for a total synthesis: not this or that part of history, but the history of English society viewed as a whole. The present volume is an attempt to write history from this perspective. It seeks not to leave out the political or overemphasize the social and economic, but to interpret the history of England in terms of the development of a complete society.

This approach seems likely to be the most helpful in understanding the vast changes that convulsed England in the late eighteenth and nine-teenth centuries. The world's first industrial society was unique. Its signifi-cance can be grasped only in its totality; and so we have written about the hopes and strivings of humble men as well as the politics of Whigs and Tories; we have quoted poems as well as population figures. Above all, we have tried to get close to the men and women of the Enlightenment, the Regency, and Victorian England—so close that we can hear them talking and swearing and praying. As a great British social historian, G. M. Young, once remarked, history is not so much an account of what happened in the past as what people felt about it while it was happening.

The period covered in this volume stretches from the accession of George I to the passing of the second Reform Bill, and the presentation is chronological. The material, however, is treated thematically, being grouped in five main chapters. First is an account of the structure of society in the eighteenth century, including the political system and religious and intel-lectual beliefs. Then the origins and first phase of the Industrial Revolution are described in detail, and the speculative problems that surround this topic are presented. In the third chapter we pick up the story of England's external relations with America, India, and her neighbors in Europe, and indicate the far-reaching effects of the French Revolution. The stormy period of political and industrial change after 1815 is dealt with in Chapter Four. Finally, we come to the achievements of Victorian civilization, show-ing both the material gains and the intellectual doubts of contemporaries. The panorama that thus unfolds is rich in famous names—names of persons and institutions and incidents that have become household words in England. In the history of this period we have the genesis of modern English society.

John F. C. Harrison

Contents

Preface   v

CHAPTER ONE   *Old England: 1714–1760*   2

The Oligarchy, 4
Squires and Parsons, 11
The Age of Reason, 16

CHAPTER TWO   *The First Industrial Society*   22

The Population Explosion, 26
Economic Growth: From Cottage to Factory Industry, 29
Change on the Land, 44
Why First in Britain? 48

CHAPTER THREE *Empire, War, and Revolution*   52

An Empire Lost, 54
An Empire Gained, 61
The French Revolution, 65

CHAPTER FOUR *The Forces of Change: 1815–1848*   74

Reform, 75
The Workshop of the World, 85
Protest and Revolt, 104
Church and Chapel, 116

CHAPTER FIVE *Victorian Prosperity: 1848–1867*   124

Bourgeois England, 125
Critics of Victorian Society, 137
Pax Britannica, 141

Bibliography   153

Kings and Queens of England   159

Prime Ministers of England   161

Index   162

Illustrations

Eighteenth-century politics:
    William Hogarth's *Chairing the Member*, c. 1754   5
Georgian elegance: Two doorways in Dublin   17
Georgian splendor: Lansdown Crescent, Bath   18
John Wesley: The founder of Methodism   20
Class structure, 1750–1961   24
Population of the United Kingdom, 1688–1950   25
Domestic industry:
    Sketch of a handloom weaver at work in the eighteenth century   31
The new machines: Diagram of a carding engine and a drawing frame   35
The factory system
    (1) Interior of a cotton-spinning mill, 1830s   36
    (2) New Lanark cotton mills, Scotland, as they appeared c. 1825   41
The new industrial towns: A view of Leeds, 1846   93
Rural life
    (1) A village in Dorsetshire, 1846   97
    (2) Agricultural laborers, 1846   99
Manual labor
    (1) Ballast-heavers in the London docks, 1850s   102
    (2) Coal-porters filling wagons at a London wharf, 1850s   103
The Great Exhibition, 1851: The Crystal Palace   126
A bourgeois monarchy: Queen Victoria and the Prince Consort, 1861   128
Middle-class domesticity: Bringing in the Christmas pudding, 1849   129
The ideal of self-help:
    Title page of a temperance journal, *British Workman*, January 1859   131
Changing the face of the land:
    Crimple Valley viaduct, Harrogate, 1847   143
The Crimean War, 1855   145

Maps

The American colonies and the War of Independence   59
India in 1856   63
Trade patterns in the first half of the eighteenth century
    (1) Exports from Great Britain   70
    (2) Imports from the British colonies   71

The Birth and Growth
of Industrial England

1714–1867

CHAPTER ONE

The period of the first two Georges (1714–60) has usually been regarded by historians as an almost Golden Age. After the clamor and striving and bloodshed of the seventeenth century, an Augustan calm seems to have descended on early Hanoverian England. The tone and temper of the age were quieter and more reasonable than in Stuart times: men's passions were contained, their differences tolerated, and their energies directed into peaceful, worldly pursuits. Politically, the bounds were set by the Revolution settlement of 1688–89 and the Act of Settlement of 1701: the Protestant religion, the Hanoverian succession, and constitutional guarantees of the powers of Parliament. It was also the last age before the Industrial Revolution, that great watershed between the modern world and all earlier societies. At the risk of romanticizing preindustrial Britain, it is legitimate to think of it as a preeminently stable, rural society, embodying all that is associated with the phrase Old England. In the popular mythology of the time, the Englishman regarded himself very highly and believed (with some justification) that he enjoyed more freedom and comfort than any European. English oak, English ale—above all, English roast beef—were held to be immensely superior to anything on the Continent. And the song "Oh! The Roast Beef of England" became almost a national anthem to many who in fact scarcely ever tasted it. The flattering self-caricature of the Englishman was hearty, sturdy, honest John Bull.

Old England: 1714-1760

The realities of English life as shown by statistics, however, were somewhat different. In his pioneer work on the *Natural and Political Observations and Conclusions upon the State and Condition of England,* Gregory King made estimates of population and income for the year 1688, and his calculations provide our most useful guide to the structure of English society at the end of the seventeenth and the beginning of the eighteenth centuries. At the apex of the social pyramid was a tiny group of aristocrats, less than 200 out of a total population (for England and Wales) of 5.5 million. They were members of the peerage (dukes, marquesses, earls, viscounts, barons) who sat in the House of Lords and who with their families and servants numbered about 7,000 persons. Below them were the 16,000 gentlemen, some of whom were knights and baronets (a kind of hereditary knighthood), but the majority of whom were untitled and whose households contained about 120,000 people. A middle group of merchants, professional men, farmers (some owning, others renting their farms), shopkeepers, and tradesmen amounted to some 2.3 million persons. The remainder of the population was the "laboring poor"—over three million artisans, laborers, cottagers, soldiers, seamen, and paupers. Society was made up of ranks and orders, rather than classes. Not until the 1790s, beginning with the middle ranks, did the language of class creep into general use. Instead of thinking in terms of a stratified class system, such as is

3

found in modern Western societies, we have to envisage eighteenth-century society as a vast army that had to work with its hands to make a living. This was not a class in any significant sense, for it included all the people of England except a tiny minority of gentry, industrialists, and commercial and professional men.

Distinctions in rank were closely related to differences in wealth. King estimated the yearly income of a lord to be £2,800, although a few were much richer. A gentleman had £280 to £1,000 per annum, and a merchant £400 or more. Farmers (of whom, with their families, there were 750,000) averaged £44 a year, and artisans and craftsmen (240,000) £40. In contrast, laboring men had but £15 a year, and "cottagers and paupers" only £6.10s. The gap between the upper classes and the majority of the population was very great indeed; the general level of income of the majority, although probably increasing in the first half of the eighteenth century, was by modern standards low. Old England was a Golden Age for squires and noblemen; but for small farmers, laborers, and the poor generally, life was a hard struggle against want and misery.

Most of the 5.5 million population lived in hamlets, villages, and small towns, heavily concentrated in the South. Only two provincial towns, Bristol and Norwich, had more than 20,000 inhabitants in the early eighteenth century, although Liverpool, Manchester, and Birmingham were soon to exceed them. The interests and attitudes of the great majority of Englishmen were rural; the leadership of society was firmly in the hands of the landed aristocracy and gentry. Yet the heart of the nation was in London, a unique city. With over half a million people, it was the largest city in Europe and the wonder of all who visited it. As the seat of government, the greatest port, the commercial and cultural center of the kingdom, it dominated the national life perhaps even more completely than it does today. For many generations London had stood for wealth, fortune, and opportunity to make good—the city where the streets were paved with gold. It was the only place with a distinctively urban quality to life, separate from and often opposed to the values of the countryside. But it was a city of great contrasts: extreme opulence and grandeur in the homes of merchant princes and the townhouses of the aristocracy; squalor, disease, violence, and crime among the "lower orders." Gin drinking became a mania in the 1730s and 1740s, and only a quarter of the children born in London survived to adulthood. In the prints of William Hogarth, we can still recapture something of the rumbustiousness and coarseness of popular life in this period.

The Oligarchy

The early and mid-decades of the eighteenth century were the heyday of the aristocracy. Previously, the Crown had been powerful enough to curb their ambitions and claims; later industrialization created new groups with

Eighteenth-century politics: William Hogarth's satirical painting *Chairing the Member*, c. 1754. (Sir John Soane's Museum.)

whom they had to come to terms in a long process of assimilation and adaptation. But in Old England the aristocracy were virtually unchallenged. Their numbers were very small. The peerage were less than 200, and the active members only about 130. These men were the effective rulers of England—an oligarchy in the true sense. Politics was basically the struggle of rival groups within the oligarchy for control of the machinery of government.

The basis of aristocratic power was land. From time immemorial, land had been regarded as a very special form of property. It was felt to be the most permanent of all forms of wealth; it was the foundation of the most basic of human activities, the production of food; and it was inherited from generation to generation. Landed property conferred a stability and continuity greater than any other material possessions and provided institutions and forms of authority which have lasted from feudal times to the present. To possess a landed estate has been (and still is) the ambition of generations of "successful" Englishmen; it was the surest way to recognition as a gentleman. The strength of the mystique of landed property is shown by the extent to which a social order based on land not only survived but flourished in an increasingly industrial world. Long after England had become an industrial state, the tone of English society in its upper echelons was still set by the great houses and the owners of broad acres.

Life among the aristocracy was on a grand scale. Normally, a peer could be expected to have an estate of at least 10,000 acres, with a mansion in the country and a townhouse in London, between which he divided his time. Some had much more: the Dukes of Bedford owned almost the whole of Bedfordshire, and the Duke of Newcastle had estates all over the country and an income in 1714 of £40,000 a year. By intermarriage the aristocracy was a closely knit group, based on a series of alliances between independent families, whose name and reputation were a source of jealous pride. Each family had a main "seat" in the country, and these great houses —Blenheim, Castle Howard, Wentworth Woodhouse—built or rebuilt in the baroque or classical styles became splendid monuments of their age. Filled with art treasures from all ages and nations and surrounded by magnificent landscaped gardens, they remain one of the most distinctive features of the English countryside.

A great house in the country was a complete community, which generated its own social and economic life and made its influence felt in the county for many miles around. In addition to the members of the family and their guests, a staff of forty or fifty servants was usual, and the footmen and coachmen wore a special uniform, called a livery. Nothing less than a small palace was adequate to house such numbers, and great areas of the countryside were reserved as parks for the exclusive enjoyment of noblemen and their friends. As with royalty, the normal events of life became public occasions. The birth of an heir, the marriage of children, and the death of the head of the family were observed with due ceremony by the local villagers and lesser gentry. Some of the nobility possessed several country houses and so spent the year in different parts of the country: an estate in the North or Midlands was convenient for the shooting and fox-hunting seasons, one in the milder southern counties was preferable for the winter, and a handsome townhouse was essential for the London season. An almost continual round of hospitality was observed in the great houses, with sport of various kinds providing the main entertainment. The actual management of the estates was delegated to stewards and bailiffs, leaving the nobleman himself free to devote his time to county and national affairs.

Two characteristics of the English aristocracy distinguished them from their counterparts on the Continent, and help to account for the strength of .their position. First was the system of primogeniture, by which the eldest son inherited the title and all the landed property, and the younger sons and daughters received only a small share of their father's wealth. By this device estates were kept intact and not continually divided up for each new generation. Second, English society was relatively mobile. The aristocracy was not a caste, and it was perfectly possible, although by no means easy, for new men to gain titles and estates. Wealth from trade and commerce was quite acceptable to landed society, and the daughters of rich merchants were always eligible as wives for younger sons or impecunious heirs. There was, of course, nothing new in this. The alliance between old and new wealth had been going on since Elizabethan times, and an old saying confirmed that "gentry is but ancient riches." On the one hand, a merchant who had made a great fortune by trade could reasonably hope that by judicious marriages and skillful use of resources his grandchildren might become assimilable first into the ranks of the gentry and ultimately into the highest ranks of society; on the other hand, the need of younger sons to find some means for their support provided a steady flow of recruits from the landed classes into trade and the professions. Later in the eighteenth century, when the effects of the Industrial Revolution began to appear, this fairly easy relationship between landed society and the business world was of prime importance in preserving the prosperity and privileges of the aristocracy.

The political, as distinct from the social and economic power of the aristocracy, was exercised in their role of an oligarchy. England was a constitutional or limited monarchy, which meant that although the government was still very much the king's government, and politics centered on the court, in the last resort power resided in Parliament, which was controlled by the aristocracy. Contemporaries thought of their constitution as a mixture of monarchy (the king), aristocracy (the House of Lords), and democracy (the House of Commons) and found its peculiar excellence in the balance among the various parts. In fact, the working of this constitution was by no means clear, and it was largely a theoretical justification of the distribution of political power. Such was the legacy of the great struggles of the seventeenth century; and the chief beneficiaries were those members of the Whig aristocracy who supported William III and later the Hanoverians, George I and George II.

The oligarchy's position was dependent on its relations first with the king and second with Parliament. All ministers were appointed by the king and were answerable to him as well as to Parliament. In a real sense, the king ruled as well as reigned. But the first two Georges, whose interests were strongly German, were unable to exploit their powers to the full, and the leading minister (usually First Lord of the Treasury) and his colleagues steadily increased their share in decision-making. Here, in embryo, was the ancestor of the modern system of prime minister and cabinet—although it was not until the nineteenth century that anything like responsible cabinet government could emerge. In addition to the main offices of state, the king had at his disposal a large number of minor appointments, some in the royal household, others in government services at home and abroad. Many of these were relics from the Middle Ages, such as royal winetasters or rangers of the royal parks, which carried a stipend but no duties. Such sinecures provided the basis for a vast and complicated system of government patronage, enabling the administration to reward its supporters and control Parliament. "Places" (as these jobs were called) were much sought after by the aristocracy for both themselves and their friends and relatives, and created an intricate network of obligations and vested interests.

Parliament was an integral part of this system. To understand how and why this was so, it is necessary to forget later ideas about representative democracy and political parties, for parliamentary politics in the eighteenth century were not based on such conceptions. Only men from the wealthy and educated minority of the nation sat in the House of Commons, and they went there because of the prestige which it conferred and the material benefits it produced. A seat was regarded as a piece of property, and, like all forms of property, was expected to be beneficial to its owner. Politics was an essentially practical business, whose object was to produce tangible advantages for politicians and their innumerable friends, not an idealistic avocation to do good to mankind in general. It is in this spirit that the electoral structure has to be considered.

The House of Commons had 558 members, of whom 489 were from English constituencies, 24 from Wales, and 45 from Scotland. Each of the 40 English counties returned 2 members, making a total of 80; of the remaining members, 405 represented towns (called "boroughs") and 4 the universities of Oxford and Cambridge. The Welsh and Scottish representation was also divided between counties and boroughs. Thus 88 percent of the House of Commons was elected from England, and almost 73 percent by the English boroughs. Moreover, a heavy proportion of these boroughs was in the South and West, often small, decayed seaports. Cornwall returned a total of 44 members, and the 5 southwestern counties (Cornwall, Devon, Dorset, Somerset, and Wiltshire) about a quarter of the House of Commons. More than half the house was elected in the South, including in that definition London and the neighboring counties. Towns like Manchester, Leeds, and Birmingham returned no members; but Old Sarum, a depopulated medieval site near Salisbury, had 2. The explanation of this curious distribution of seats was that it represented the economic and political state of the country 200 years earlier, but had never been brought up-to-date. The absurdities of the system were defended on the grounds that the decayed boroughs provided seats for nonlocal candidates, thus correcting the imbalance caused by the underrepresentation of London. The members who sat for the "rotten" boroughs were not local townsmen, but professional politicians, businessmen, and landed gentlemen who needed to be in the Commons. They bought themselves a seat, and they were enabled to do this by the remarkable way in which M.P.s were chosen.

The franchise was simplest in the counties. Dating from 1430, everyone who owned freehold land to the value of 40s. a year was entitled to vote. Because of the fall in the value of money since 1430 and the liberal interpretation of the term "freehold," the electorate was fairly wide, although the two county members ("knights of the shire") might be elected by a mere 600 voters in the smallest county, Rutland, or by 15,000 in the largest, Yorkshire. Voting was in public, and so pressure could be exerted on most of the electors. The result was that county elections were often not contested, the candidate being agreed on among the leading county families. The "gentlemen, clergy, and freeholders," as part of the landed "interest," identified themselves with this leadership and influenced their tenants to vote accordingly. County members in the House of Commons were sons of peers or country gentlemen. They formed a distinctive group that prided itself on being independent of the government.

In the boroughs the franchise was more complicated. At one extreme were boroughs with virtually universal suffrage: these were the "potwalloper" boroughs, in which everyone who had a hearth on which to boil a pot could vote. In other boroughs, the franchise was the right of all residents who paid the local house tax called "scot and lot." In a third type, all the freemen (that is, members of the guilds) were the voters. In some boroughs, again, only members of the corporation (the town council) were enfranchised. And, lastly, there were the burgage boroughs, where the franchise was attached to specific houses or plots of land. The size of the electorate varied considerably between the different types of borough. Westminster by 1761 had 9,000 voters and London 6,000, but these were exceptional. Only 22 of the 203 English boroughs had electorates of 1,000 or more, and 72 percent of the borough members were returned by electorates of 500 or less. The burgage and corporation boroughs had particularly small numbers of electors, sometimes only ten or a dozen and frequently less than 50. Cornwall was rich in this type of borough: 42 members were returned by 21 boroughs, with a total electorate of less than 1,400. In England as a whole, there were over 100 of these "close," "rotten," or "pocket" boroughs, as they were variously called.

These complexities and anomalies in the franchise and size of the electorate made possible a system of proprietary politics. By means of bribery, corruption, and the exertion of "influence," rich men were able to control the election of members to Parliament. This, when combined with the system of patronage outlined earlier, formed the basis of the eighteenth-century practice of government. In the middle years of the century, over half the borough seats were subject to patronage: some 111 patrons (peers and gentlemen) controlled the election to 205 seats. The government itself was very active in the business of "borough-mongering," and kept a number of seats directly under its control and many more subject to its influence. Patrons who nominated government supporters were rewarded with places for themselves and their relatives. The management of government interest was developed to a fine art under the Duke of Newcastle in the forty years before 1760. He nominated to twelve seats directly and used official pressure to influence many more. By these means, the government of the day was able to control a majority in Parliament. The modern system of disciplined parties, with the government relying on its majority in the Commons, had not yet emerged. Instead, the administration had to manipulate the representative system to ensure the necessary support from placemen. Offices, sinecures, and contracts took the place of party funds. One result of this perfection of the government machine was that the number of election contests declined. Politics became not so much a concern for rival policies as a struggle between the "ins" and the "outs" for the fruits of office. According to the political morality of the day, there was nothing reprehensible in accepting a bribe for services rendered. The voter, the borough, the member of Parliament—all expected some return on the assets they held. Self-interest or the "service of one's friends" was a legitimate goal. For, as the poet Alexander Pope proclaimed in his *Essay on Man* (1733):

> . . . reason, passion answer one great aim
> That true self-love and social are the same.

The main beneficiaries of this system after 1714 were the Whig aristocracy. In the 1670s and 1680s, the terms "Whig" and "Tory" had been used to designate the two rival groups who had divided over the issues of Church and king. The Tories favored the Church of England and supported the king and the accession of his brother, James. The Whigs were for limiting the powers of kingship, excluding James (since he was a Roman Catholic), and tolerating religious dissenters. But the Glorious Revolution of 1688 changed this alignment. Whigs and Tories had combined to effect the Revolution and thereafter struggled fiercely for the benefits they felt they deserved from it. The names "Whig" and "Tory" were terms of abuse rather than party designations, for men disliked "the spirit of faction" with which the idea of party was commonly associated. Until 1714 political life was hectic, with frequent changes and contests at all levels. But after the death of Queen Anne, the Whigs established themselves in power so strongly that for the rest of the eighteenth century the government was a coalition of various types of Whigs. They were able to do this because some of the Tory leaders had unwisely been flirting with the Jacobites (the supporters of the exiled Stuarts) in France, and thus became implicated in an armed rebellion to restore the "Old Pretender" in 1715. Henceforth, it was easy to stigmatize the Tories as Jacobites and impugn their loyalty to the Crown. The Whigs could plausibly pose as the defenders of the Hanoverian succession and the most reliable friends of the king. With the aid of the political machine described above, they ensconced themselves firmly in the seats of power.

From 1715 to 1721, two factions of the Whigs struggled for dominance, but eventually a leader emerged who for twenty years (1722–42) remained at the head of British politics. Sir Robert Walpole spent over forty years in the House of Commons and was in office for more than thirty. With his henchman, the Duke of Newcastle, he exploited the system of patronage to control Parliament more thoroughly than had ever been done before. By tremendously hard work and meticulous attention to detail, he created a political machine of unrivaled competence. He tirelessly cultivated the good graces of the king, without whose full confidence he could not have survived so long. Whereas previously patronage had been dispersed among many separate offices, Walpole reduced the whole field to one monopolistic, government-controlled operation. Episcopal appointments were so carefully controlled that twenty-four of the twenty-six bishops in the House of Lords could always be relied on to support the government. A "treasury" party in the Commons consisted of about thirty members whose seats were directly controlled by the administration. Under Newcastle's skillful direction, every office in Church and state, whether national or local, big or small, was used to support Walpole. The whole system was a brilliant demonstration of how a set of obsolete and irrelevant institutions could be made to serve new purposes, and of how, as so often in British life, outward forms masked internal changes.

Consciously, change was the last thing Walpole wanted. His motto was "Let sleeping dogs lie," and his aim was to secure stability and tranquility at home and peace abroad. He believed that the prosperity of a commercial nation could best be promoted by keeping taxation low, avoiding head-on political clashes, and restraining public excitement of all kinds. Only twice was he seriously defeated on such issues: in 1733, over an excise bill which he proposed as an alternative to increasing taxes on land; and in 1739, when he was forced into a war with Spain. Inevitably, Walpole's policy lacked glamor, and the dispensing of so much patronage created envy and discontent, with the result that his enemies among rival Whig groups were able to secure his defeat and resignation in 1742. But by then he had made England safe for the Whig oligarchy. To have developed a workable system of constitutional monarchy and aristocratic control at a time when the rest of Europe was on the eve of enlightened despotism was no mean achievement.

Squires and Parsons

For the great majority of Englishmen, life was most directly affected not by the goings-on of the oligarchy at Westminster and Whitehall, but by the government and events of their locality. The realities of daily life were experienced in the thousands of villages and hundreds of small towns that comprised Old England. As in other preindustrial societies, the local units were largely independent and autonomous, and the national state was in many respects little more than a collection of separate communities and groups, each jealous of its privileges and hostile to any suggestion of inter-ference from outside. The much-vaunted blessings of English liberty were often defined as the preservation of this independence, especially by the one group that had most to gain from it, the landed gentry. When they were returned to Parliament as members for the county, they inevitably sat as Tories, and thought themselves to be representatives of the "country" as opposed to the "court" party, which was the Whigs. The natural attitude of a Tory M.P. was deep suspicion of ministers and the central government, impatience with most of what went on in Whitehall, and a desire to return to the local affairs of his county as soon as possible.

The effective leadership of rural England was firmly in the hands of the country gentlemen, the squires. Unlike the aristocracy, they normally could not afford a townhouse and so lived on their estates the year round, occupying themselves with village and county matters. Typically, the squire lived in his hall or manor house, surrounded by a small garden and home farm managed by a bailiff. The rest of his land was subdivided into farms which were let to tenant farmers, whose rents provided the main income of the estate. In some places, the squire owned all the land in the village; in others, only a major part of it; but in either case his influence was dom-inant and virtually unchallengeable. As with the aristocracy, the estate was preserved intact from generation to generation by the custom of the eldest son or daughter inheriting it all. In a deferential society, squirearchical leadership, while it preserved the interests of a privileged minority, also provided a form of public service. The squire and his family recognized obligations towards "their" people in the village and dispensed justice and charity in a patriarchal manner. None of these duties, however, was pur-sued to the point where it might become burdensome. A landed gentle-man's life was essentially a life of leisure. Unlike the laboring man or the merchant, whose preoccupation was making a living, the country gentle-man enjoyed an inherited income and spent his time doing the things that pleased him. Since comparatively few of the gentry had any intellectual or sustained political interests, their lives fell into a routine of social enter-tainments and obligations. They visited and dined regularly with neighbor-ing families, they enjoyed a round of balls and social occasions when they met together in the county town for the quarter sessions, and they in-dulged their taste for hunting and shooting to the full. To many observers, it seemed that the English country gentleman's life was the most enviable of all.

The social leadership and economic strength of the squires was sup-ported by formidable judicial and administrative power. They effectively ran the government of rural England through the basic units of the parish and county. The office through which the squires exercised this authority was the justice of the peace. Ever since Elizabethan times, the J.P.s had been the crucial element of administration in the countryside. Sitting alone, the J.P. could try minor offenses and dispense rough-and-ready justice to his tenants and villagers. At petty sessions, two or three J.P.s could deal with a wide variety of issues; and at the quarter sessions in the local county town, the bench of J.P.s tried more serious cases, heard appeals, and undertook administrative chores.

The authoritarian nature of this regime is well illustrated by that curious English offense, "poaching." Under English law, wild animals and birds were held to belong to the owner of the land on which they were found, and a series of game laws protected these rights of ownership against anyone who tried to "poach" (that is, kill or steal) the animals. On gentlemen's estates certain creatures—foxes, hares, pheasants, trout—were deliberately encouraged and protected by gamekeepers so that there would always be a plentiful supply for hunting, shooting, and fishing by the squire and his friends. Among some villagers, the temptation to poach was too strong to be resisted, and a constant battle to outwit both the game and the gamekeepers went on in the rural areas. If caught, the poacher could expect little mercy, for he would be tried by the same squire (sitting in his capacity as J.P.) against whose rights he had offended. The squire was judge in his own cause, and there was no redress for the unfortunate prisoner.

The day-to-day government of rural England was based on the parish and supervised by the J.P.s. Originally an ecclesiastical unit, the parish also functioned as an organ of civil administration, in which the inhabitants, through a body called the "vestry," chose their own, unpaid officials. The churchwardens, overseers of the poor, highway surveyors, and constables were appointed, usually reluctantly, for a year or until a successor could be found. The vestry levied local taxes (rates) to pay for relief of the poor, maintenance of the church building and churchyard, and other public services. If the roads required mending, the inhabitants were required to undertake this work themselves. Control and enforcement of this system of administration was through the squire's judicial office. For instance, if a parish failed to carry out some of its obligations, it could be charged before the J.P.s with not doing its duty. The charge could be brought by any private citizen or by a higher administrative body or authority. The J.P.s would then declare this failure to be a "common nuisance," which was a punishable offense, and the offending parish and its officers would be ordered to remedy their default. Again, if the parish overseers of the poor refused to grant relief, the poor person concerned could appeal to the J.P., who could overrule the overseers.

To a considerable extent, the justices were not only judges and administrators; they were also legislators. They had the power to make bylaws, and their decisions in such matters as Sunday drinking, the licensing of fairs, and the enforcement or not of Elizabethan statutes regulating wages and poor relief had the effect of legislation on social questions. The J.P.'s authority in rural England was virtually unquestioned. Once appointed on the nomination of the lord lieutenant (the head of the county hierarchy), a J.P. was almost irremovable. His dominant position derived not solely from his office, but from far deeper roots. In a hierarchical and deferential society, he was accepted as the natural leader.

Only one other figure in the village could normally expect the respect due to natural authority and leadership, and that was the parson. It is impossible to generalize about the position of parish priests in the eighteenth century: some were but poor curates with £30 to £40 a year; others were the younger sons of nobility or gentry and enjoyed fat livings. The former were in no sense on the same social footing as the squire; the latter might dine and hunt with him on terms of gentlemanly equality. At the beginning of the century, many parsons farmed their own "glebe"—the land that went with their living—but later more of them preferred to let their land. Many parsons were not appointed by their bishop or by any ecclesiastical authority, but by laymen who had acquired the right of appointment by virtue of holding land originally acquired from the Church at the Reformation. Such "advowsons," as they were called, enabled many a squire to appoint his own parson. This put the priest in a position of independence in relation to the bishop or the government, but of subordination or obligation to the squire. To raise his income level to that of gentlemanly standards, a parson was allowed to hold more than one living; pluralism and nonresidence were tolerated. As the century progressed, the number of parsons who were J.P.s increased.

Whether or not the parson in a particular parish was felt to be fully a gentleman, his role as leader was second only to the squire. In birth, education, and frequently income the parson was superior to the farmers, cottagers, and craftsmen who were his flock. He was treated with respect and was usually chairman of the vestry. His clerical duties were, by later standards, light. Sunday services tended to be erratic and abbreviated, and sermons were by no means as regular as they became in the Victorian age. Communion was usually administered only three times a year, and confirmation was infrequent. But baptisms, marriages, funerals, and "churchings" of women (thanksgiving after childbirth) were held as and when required. The leisure which his office provided could be used by a parson in a variety of ways. Some took to fox-hunting and field sports; others contentedly looked after their animals and crops; an important minority devoted themselves to learning and made distinguished contributions to literature (Lawrence Sterne), philosophy (George Berkeley), natural history (Gilbert White), and archaeology (William Stukeley). A few were devout priests who tried to lead a holy life and care for the souls of their people. But the great majority showed little concern for spirituality, and at their best were wise and benevolent advisers who administered the blessings of welfare to all who needed help.

No better example of the life of a country parson can be found than the *Diary* of the Reverend James Woodforde, who lived uneventfully in his quiet parish of Weston Longeville, Norfolk. The entries are for the period after 1758, but the round of days they describe is equally typical of the earlier part of the century. One such entry read:

> Mr. Will Melliar sent me a note this morning to desire me to be at the meeting of the Gentlemen etc., of this County, at Bridgwater tomorrow, to put in nomination two proper Persons to represent this County in Parliament . . . and it was so civil a note that I could not refuse him.

In the autumn he recorded:

> Very busy all day with my Barley, did not dine till near 5 in the afternoon, my Harvest Men dined here today, gave them some Beef and some plumb Pudding and as much liquor as they would drink. This evening finished my Harvest and all carried into the Barn—8 acres.

Priestly duties obtruded from time to time:

> My Squire called on me this morning to desire me to come over in the afternoon and privately name his new born son. I married one John Wont and Rose Branton this morning by License at Weston Church—a compelled marriage. N.B. am owed by Mr. Mann, the Church Warden, for marrying them, as I could not change a Guinea—0. 10. 6. . . . . Rec'd a printed Letter from the Bishop to send him an account of the Roman Catholics in my Parish—but I don't know of one in it.

On another day he wrote:

> I walked to Forsters this morning between 11 and 12 and read Prayers and administered the H. Sacrament to Mrs. Forster who is something better today—Her Mother was with her and received the Sacrament also. . . .

His servants were paid their year's wages in January, and the entries show that he kept two maids and a manservant in the house and a "farming man" and a boy to manage his glebe land. Occasionally, he enjoyed a modest day's sport:

> Soon after breakfast young Rose called here and desired me to lend him my Greyhounds, having found a Hare sitting. Mr. Walker and self took a Walk with the Greyhounds and saw the Hare coursed which gave great Sport indeed, but was killed at last. I never saw a better Course. I let Mr. Rose have the Hare for a Friend of his. After we had killed that Hare we went after another and found one in about an Hour, but we had very little Diversion with her. . . . Saw never another tho' we stayed out till 3 o'clock. Mr. Walker almost knocked up by walking so long, we were out from 11 till 3 in the Afternoon. . . . After Tea again this Evening we got to Whist, Partners the same. . . .

At Christmas he dispensed charity to the poor. After giving 6d. each to fifty-three persons, he commented: "The Poor today behaved extremely well indeed, tho' times were extremely hard for them—They all appeared very patient and submissive." Relations with the squire were excellent, and after noting that the squire had voluntarily paid for the innoculation of six children in the village, the parson exclaimed: "Pray God! they [the squire and his wife] may both long enjoy Health and Life, and blessings from above daily attend them."

Parson Woodforde's experiences may sound a trifle idyllic at times, but there is no reason to doubt that in the main he faithfully reflected the realities of life in the English countryside as they appeared to a person in authority. To the laboring poor, the rule of squires and parsons looked somewhat different; unfortunately, the poor left no diaries for posterity. But the contrast between the homes and daily lives of those who labored in the fields and those who lived in the hall and rectory is inescapable. The laboring man's cottage consisted of one or two rooms, with a bare brick, stone, or mud floor and unplastered walls. A few wooden or rush-bottomed chairs, a deal or old oak table, a bed in the corner, and a few pots and pans comprised his total possessions. A simple fireplace with an oven sometimes beside it provided the sole means of heating, cooking, and (frequently) lighting. To this home the laborer returned each evening, weary and often wet from his outdoor work, having eaten his dinner under a hedge or tree. After a simple meal and a few hours with his wife and children, he went to bed early and in winter was out again before daylight. The farmer's home was larger and more comfortable than the laborer's, and the household included servants who lived in. The daily routine of work in the fields, however, was equally hard and tedious. There was little leisure in such a life for the cultivation of the refinements of gentility.

The Age of Reason

One of the charms of English villages and small towns today is the frequency with which one finds graceful early Georgian houses tucked away behind the church or lining the main street. Their simple, classical lines, in mellowed red brick or golden stone, with finely proportioned doorways, remind us of the elegance (although perhaps it was only a veneer) of the Augustan age. These country rectories and comfortable tradesmen's homes, to say nothing of the more elaborate palaces of the aristocracy and halls of the gentry, were the fruits of an increasing prosperity and symbols of a determination to enjoy the humane blessings of a peaceful, ordered world. In brick and stone were reflected the ideological principles of Walpole's England. The intellectual and religious tone of the age favored a kind of worldly reasonableness and a pragmatic approach to the great problems of human life.

To a very considerable extent, the mold of scientific and philosophical thought was set by the ideas and methods of Sir Isaac Newton. He was president of the Royal Society until his death in 1727, although his main scientific work had been done many years earlier. Newton has gone down in history as the discoverer of the basic truths about the physical world. As Pope's eulogy put it:

Georgian elegance: Two doorways in Dublin. (B. T. Batsford, Ltd., London.)

> Nature and Nature's laws, lay hid in night.
> God said, "Let Newton be!" and all was light!

Contemporaries were dazzled by the immensity of Newton's achievement in the late seventeenth century; the implications of it challenged the very nature of the accepted view of the universe and opened up quite new intellectual possibilities. Similarly, the philosopher John Locke had explored the workings of the human mind, and his findings provided a new, psychological basis for explaining human behavior. This was all very exciting, but also frightening and unsettling. If the application of reason and experimental method could produce such profound results in some areas of knowledge, there was every encouragement to extend the enquiry to all fields. Old certainties began to be undermined, traditional faiths to crumble.

Naturally, the area most directly affected was religion. Newton himself believed in the validity of Biblical prophecy and saw no fundamental difficulty in reconciling the claims of Christianity and science. But the trend was away from the dogmatic theology of the seventeenth century and toward emphasis on the reasonableness of the Christian faith. Enthusiasm (and "fanaticks") was deprecated; miracles were played down; and disturbing problems of sin, guilt, and punishment were quietly avoided whenever possible. God was to a considerable extent depersonalized. Very few men were prepared to go as far as abandoning the idea of God altogether;

17

Georgian splendor: Lansdown Crescent, Bath, by John Palmer. (Keystone Press Agency, Inc.)

but the deity was frequently used as no more than a concept to explain the working of the universe. Conversely, the natural order itself afforded proof of the existence of a deity. Joseph Addison's hymn expresses this sentiment admirably:

> The spacious firmament on high,
> With all the blue Ethereal sky,
> And spangled Heavens, a shining frame
> Their great Original proclaim.
> Th' unwearied Sun, from day to day,
> Does his Creator's Power display
> And publishes to every land
> The work of an Almighty hand.

If God was required only as a "first cause" to account for the universe, it soon followed that one did not have to believe in his intervention in the daily affairs of men. The deists argued thus, and battle was therefore soon joined with orthodox clerics from the 1720s. Of greater import than the theological arguments, which as always were confined to a relatively small number of individuals, was the general tone of worldliness which deism encouraged and which reached far beyond the ranks of professed deists.

The Church of England was strongly affected by this worldliness. Institutionally part of the established order, the Church did virtually nothing to counteract the trend. Her leaders, the bishops, were Whig political appointees, and her parish clergy were stalwart supporters of the Tory squirearchy. Preferments in the Church were tightly integrated into the system of patronage. Only occasionally in a country rectory could be found a priest who kept alive something of the old seventeenth-century Anglican tradition of piety and rejection of the world and its values. In general, there was throughout the Church a complacent acceptance of the prevailing order of things and a broad, liberal theology, usually called latitudinarianism. The Church as an institution made her peace with the world, and her members learned to live at ease in Zion.

The reaction to latitudinarianism, however, came quickly. Such a limited form of Church life could not satisfy more spiritually minded Christians, and it was perhaps only a matter of time before some "enthusiast" challenged its whole basis. One such enthusiast was John Wesley. He was born in 1703, a son of the High Church, Tory rector of Epworth in Lincolnshire, and went to Oxford where he was ordained in the Church of England and elected a fellow of Lincoln College. In 1729 he and his brother Charles, together with George Whitefield and a small group of Oxford friends, formed a holy club, feeling the need for a deeper spiritual life and a more effective Christianity. They were nicknamed Methodists, because they had "agreed together to observe with strict formality the method of study and practice laid down in the statutes [of the Church]." After an unsuccessful mission to Georgia, Wesley was still seeking the way to salvation and had been much influenced by a group of Moravians, a German pietistic sect, whom he had met on the voyage. He later concluded that the lesson of Georgia was "that I, who went to America to convert others, was never myself converted." But in 1738, after his return from Georgia, he underwent the great experience of conversion, which he recorded in his *Journal*:

> Wednesday, May 24, 1738. . . . In the evening I went very unwillingly to a society in Aldersgate Street [London], where one was reading Luther's preface to the *Epistle to the Romans*. About a quarter before nine, while he was describing the change which God works in the heart through faith in Christ, I felt my heart strangely warmed. I felt I did trust in Christ, Christ alone for salvation; and an assurance was given me that He had taken away *my* sins, even *mine*, and saved *me* from the law of sin and death.

Wesley's account provided a classic model of conversion that became a central experience in the later Methodist movement. He himself was now convinced that he had heard the divine call and that his mission was to evangelize England, and ultimately the world. His task, he said, was "to promote as far as I am able vital, practical religion and by the grace of God to beget, preserve and increase the life of God in the souls of men." To that end he labored incessantly for the next fifty years, riding 250,000 miles on horseback and preaching thousands of sermons.

John Wesley: The founder of Methodism. (National Portrait Gallery, London.)

It was not Wesley's intention to found yet another Protestant sect. He was, and always remained, an ordained priest in the Anglican Church, and his hope was that through his work the Church of England would be reformed and revitalized. But, increasingly, his efforts were met with hostility, and he was driven to undertake activities outside the Church and to establish new and independent forms of organization. At first, Wesley was opposed to open-air preaching, but since churches were closed against him he was obliged to resort to the practice, and "field preaching" became one of the characteristics of early Methodism. He commissioned preachers from among his followers, and great crowds came to the meetings. Wesley's style of preaching was simple, earnest, and logical, and he cautioned against emotionalism ("Scream no more, at the peril of your soul," he admonished one of his preachers). But, as often with religious revivalism, manifestations of extreme religious fervor soon appeared: there were scenes of weeping, groaning, hysteria, and convulsions, public confessions of sins, and extravagant, emotional behavior.

The Methodists were organized for the cultivation of religious fellowship in small local societies, which were subdivided into smaller groups of bands and classes. They met weekly under a leader for prayer, exchange of religious experience, and mutual help. The class was the germ cell of early Methodism and a most efficient form of control. Societies were grouped together in circuits, round which a lay preacher rode, visiting each society in turn. Wesley spent his time directing the whole enterprise and visiting as many societies as he could. An annual conference was attended by delegates from the societies, and this became the supreme body in Methodism. At first, the societies were not separate from but auxiliary to the local Anglican churches, but they soon developed an independent existence. By 1784 some 356 Methodist chapels had been built, many of them in areas neglected by the Church.

Methodism was in many respects a paradoxical movement. Most of its members were humble people, without any advantages of education, wealth, or social position, although later in the century, their puritan virtues brought them worldly wealth, which Wesley feared would endanger their souls. Methodism was essentially a layman's religion, with a steadily growing number of lay preachers, trustees, stewards, class leaders, and Sunday school teachers. At times it was anti-intellectual and manifested some of the cruder characteristics of popular revivalism. Methodists were sharp critics of many aspects of contemporary society and won virtually no converts among "persons of quality," as Wesley put it. Yet doctrinally Methodism did not differ from Anglicanism. Wesley himself was highly educated, Tory, and autocratic. He had no time for radicalism and was conservative in his social views. In everyday life, Methodism tended to strengthen such puritan characteristics as hard work, self-help, honesty, and dedication. It also reinforced a certain amount of narrowness and bigotry. Later, in industrial England, Wesleyan Methodism became the religion of the middle classes, and other (more liberal) Connexions of Methodism provided chapels for the working classes. From its very beginning, Methodism challenged many of the values and assumptions of an aristocratic, rationalistic age. It was potentially a revolutionary force; and yet it frequently played a conservative role.

As long as Wesley was alive, there was no open breach with the Church of England. But after his death in 1791 the gap widened, and the schismatic inclinations already observable in Methodism led to successive breakaways from the parent (Wesleyan) body and the founding of new Connexions. Methodism began as an attack on the worldliness and complacency of early eighteenth-century Church and society. It flourished as the religion of individualism and early industrial capitalism. In the second half of the century, the size and influence of the Methodist body grew rapidly. By 1791 there were 80,000 members of the societies and nearly half a million adherents. Their England was not the England of squires and parsons, but the England of red brick chapels (the Zoars and Zions and Little Bethels) in Welsh valleys and northern industrial towns. In the Age of Reason, the Methodists were the people who talked of salvation.

CHAPTER TWO

Numerous and far-reaching as were all the multifarious changes in English history described so far, they are completely eclipsed by the magnitude of the changes that we have now to consider. Possibly the only time parallel to the events of 1760–1830 is to be found in the Neolithic Age, when man discovered how to become a settled agriculturist and herdsman instead of a hunter and nomad. Within the short span of one man's lifetime, England changed more fundamentally than it had for hundreds of years before. And the process then begun is continuing today, not only in England but in the rest of the world. To these momentous changes, historians have given the name Industrial Revolution.

Essentially, the Industrial Revolution created the kind of society with which we are familiar. There is for most of us an indescribable but inescapable feeling of remoteness about all preindustrial societies, be they ancient, medieval, or early modern. We are conscious of certain barriers to understanding, and these barriers are not primarily ignorance of the material facts of life in the past (for we can easily read books and look at pictures of our ancestors at work and play), but lack of sympathy for their fundamental ideas and attitudes. Only from the second half of the nineteenth century do we begin to recognize values and concerns that seem akin to our own. The Industrial Revolution was the great watershed in

The First
Industrial Society

recent history, dividing what we know as modern England from all previous types of society. This transformation was more than a series of technological innovations and economic changes. It offered to men, for the first time in human history, the way toward controlling their environment instead of being at its mercy. The possibility of material abundance for all was no longer an idle dream, although it took time before the full implications of this change were grasped by any large number of people. With the appearance of these new practical possibilities, men's ideas and assumptions also changed. The Industrial Revolution was a new way in which Englishmen looked at themselves, at society, and at the world at large. Ultimately, it offered a new dimension of freedom.

There can be no mistaking the main areas of change. Before about 1760 England was basically an agricultural country, with a small population, a low standard of living for the majority of the people, a hierarchical social system, and an aristocratic oligarchy in political control. As a result of the Industrial Revolution, she became a nation dependent on her manufacturing and extractive industries, with a large population, great urban centers, vastly increased wealth (some of which slowly percolated down to the lower classes), an increasing degree of social mobility, and political democracy. It can be said without exaggeration that virtually no English

institution or aspect of life was unaffected by these changes. The very face
of England that we see today, and which we imagine to be so "traditional,"
did not exist 200 years ago. A great majority of the buildings in English
towns and cities (including some of the most admired "medieval" Gothic)
were constructed in the nineteenth century or after. The neat patchwork
pattern of the fields, so beloved by visitors as evidence of Old England,
is largely the result of enclosures which accompanied the Industrial Revolution. Evidence of preindustrial England survives only in a few picturesque
villages and ancient towns like York or Norwich. To remind us of medieval
England, there is little beyond the churches and castles—the former usually
heavily "restored," the latter heavily decayed. So thickly lies the blanket
of the Industrial Revolution that the average Englishman today sees little
more of the visible past than does the American who lives in the eastern or
southern United States.

It is nowadays taken for granted that if a nation is to become prosperous and powerful it must have an industrial revolution. Following the
British lead, most Western and some Eastern societies industrialized in the
nineteenth and twentieth centuries, and the idea of an industrial revolution
is now accepted as a definite phase in the life of modern nations. Everywhere
the main characteristics of industrialization have been the same, although

Class structure, 1750–1961. (E. J. Hobsbawm: *Industry and Empire.* © E. J.
Hobsbawm, 1968, 1969, and Penguin Books, Ltd.)

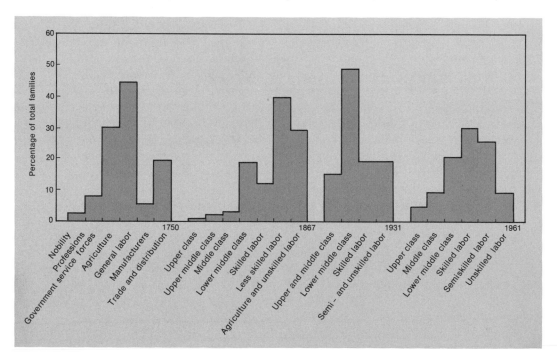

the details of the movement have varied according to the time and local context. The British Industrial Revolution, however, was unique in that it was the first. Unlike all succeeding industrial revolutions, it was endogenous; that is, it developed spontaneously and internally, without any significant stimulus from outside and without any model to copy. Once it had happened, it was irreversible. It was not deliberately planned, nor did its pioneers have any star to guide them. Just why the first industrial revolution should have occurred in England (rather than in, say, Holland or France) and at the particular time in the eighteenth century that it did continues to puzzle historians. But they are agreed that the Industrial Revolution was a complex and interlocking series of changes which defy any single-cause explanation. In this chapter, we shall elucidate the main factors that seem to account for the phenomenon.

Population of the United Kingdom, 1688–1950. (Census and U.K. Annual Abstract of Statistics.)

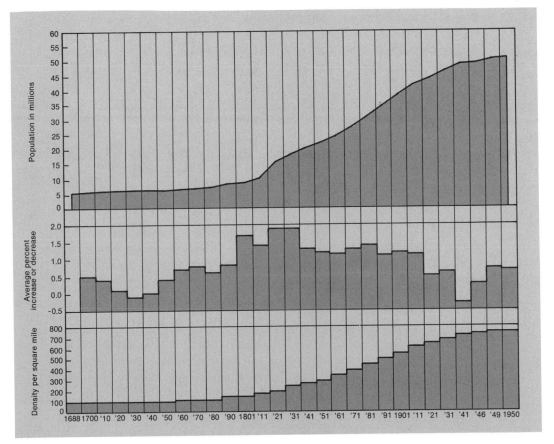

The Population Explosion

Our starting point will be population. There is a rough logic in considering demographic details first, for in a fundamental sense they determine all else. History is about people, both as individuals and in relation to each other, and the number of people in a country at a given time is one of the crucial factors in determining what sort of lives they are likely to be living. Leaving aside other variables, a Britain of two to three million people (as in the Middle Ages) will be a vastly different society from modern Britain with over fifty-five million, by sheer virtue of the difference in numbers; for the quantitative difference means also a difference in quality and sets the bounds for the potentialities and limits of human achievement. For many hundreds of years (indeed, throughout most of recorded history), the population had been small and had grown only slowly and intermittently: although the birth rate was high (35 or more live births per 1,000 of population per annum), the death rate was only slightly less, so that the rate of natural increase (the difference between birth and death rates) was low. By the early decades of the eighteenth century, the population of England and Wales was rather less than six million. We do not have precise population statistics before the first census that was taken in 1801, and the official registration of births and deaths was begun only in 1839. Population data has therefore to be compiled from other sources, notably the estimates of contemporaries (like Gregory King at the end of the seventeenth century), or from the parish registers which recorded baptisms, burials, and marriages. The figures we have before 1801 are estimates rather than hard data. Nevertheless, the general population trend (as distinct from details of short-term fluctuations) is quite clear. Beginning about 1740, the population began to grow, and it continued to do so throughout the nineteenth and twentieth centuries. Each decade there were, and are, more Englishmen than ever before; the same was true of the other nations of Western Europe. The 1801 census showed that the population of England and Wales had grown to nine million; by 1831 it was fourteen million. From 1750 the rate of growth accelerated each decade, until it reached a peak in the period 1811–21.

The massive facts of population growth are not in dispute. What is arguable among historians is the explanation of how and why this increase came about. Without entering into the niceties of this debate, it will be obvious that a rise in population can be caused by several factors: an increase in the birth rate, a decrease in mortality (death rate), and immigration. Any one of these, if on a sufficient scale, could affect the rate of population growth, and a combination of two or more would be decisive. The last factor (immigration) can be ruled out for the eighteenth century. In fact, the reverse was true: many Britons (perhaps as many as a million) left their country for other lands, either voluntarily as colonists or involuntarily as convicts. Not until the 1830s and 1840s did the Irish immigration into England attain significant proportions. As to the birth rate, it seems to have remained steady at the high level of thirty-six to thirty-seven, although some economic historians have speculated about whether a lowering of the age of marriage (thereby extending the fertile period during which a woman can bear children) might not have set off the increase in the 1740s.

The fall in the death rate seems at present to be the most likely explanation of the population explosion. Until 1740 mortality was high, especially in London. Thereafter, the death rate declined steadily, from about 33.5 to 21 in the 1820s. Contrary to older opinions, this decline in mortality is not to be attributed to progress in medical knowledge or techniques, but rather to a general improvement in standards of living, which strengthened people's resistance to disease and mitigated some of the worst harshness of life. In particular, there was some improvement in infant mortality, which was where the greatest waste of human life occurred. Deaths in childhood were far more common among all classes of society than today. Adam Smith, the famous economist, in his *Wealth of Nations* (1776), observed that in the Highlands of Scotland women sometimes bore as many as twenty children, but not even two lived to grow up. At the opposite end of the social scale, it is worth recalling that Queen Anne had seventeen children, but not one survived to succeed her on the throne. London was notorious for its high infant mortality: it has been estimated that three-quarters of the children born there before about 1760 died before they were ten. Even after there had been a considerable reduction in the infant death rate, it remained high by modern Western standards, which meant that all families in the eighteenth and nineteenth centuries were intimately acquainted with death in a way that is rare today. The infant deathbed scenes so beloved by the religious tract writers and the grief for the loss of a favorite child so often mentioned in biographies and novels were the results of these cold figures of mortality.

By the last decade of the eighteenth century, the growth of population was everywhere evident and becoming a matter of concern. The results of the first census in 1801 were greeted with incredulity in some quarters, since many Englishmen just could not believe that the population of England, Scotland, and Wales was as large as 10.6 million, with another 5.2 million in Ireland. William Cobbett, the radical journalist and self-appointed champion of rural England, for long denied that population was increasing: large village churches, he argued, were half empty on Sundays, which showed that the population must have been larger in past times, for our ancestors were not such fools as to build churches too big for their needs. But more temperate men were convinced that the statistics only confirmed the evidence of their senses that population growth was literally pressing hard on every side. And they were worried.

Among the most worried was a Church of England clergyman, the Reverend Thomas Malthus, who published *An Essay on the Principle of Population* in 1798. Before his death in 1834, six editions of his work had been published, and he had elaborated further upon his "principle of population," taken as a law of nature, and applied it to immediate social problems. The starting point of his theory was the capacity and constant tendency of population to grow faster than the means of subsistence. In practice, population was prevented from outstripping the means of feeding it by the operation of vice, misery, and moral restraint. These checks to population Malthus divided into two categories: positive and preventive. Positive checks included all causes of mortality outside the control of the individual, arising from what he called "vice and misery." Under this head, he argued, "may be enumerated all unwholesome occupations, severe labour and exposure to the seasons, extreme poverty, bad nursing of children, large towns, excesses of all kinds, the whole train of common diseases and epidemics, wars, plague, and famine." By preventive checks, Malthus meant limitation of births by means that are under the control of the individual and that relate to conscious and voluntary decisions. Some types of "vice," such as sexual perversity and artificial contraception within marriage, he included in this category. But the preventive check with which he was most concerned was moral restraint. This he defined as postponement of marriage until a man could afford to support a family, together with strict continence before marriage. Since mankind could not escape from the workings of the principle of population, the only way to avoid the evil and unhappiness caused by the positive checks was to embrace the alternative of moral restraint. In so doing, a man would rise to his full stature as a rational being.

Malthus was not the first or the only writer on population problems in the later eighteenth and early nineteenth centuries, but his brilliant *Essay* appeared at precisely the moment when those problems were beginning to cause consternation among thinking men. By simplifying the whole matter to a clash between numbers of population and means of subsistence, he dramatically presented his contemporaries with the need to make a choice. Not all of them accepted Malthus's theory in its entirety, but the *Essay* made a deep impression and defined the terms in which the population debate was carried on until late in the nineteenth century. The Malthusian theory was at bottom a very gloomy view of society. A note of pessimism is inescapable in nearly all Malthusian writing, for even Malthus himself, for all his encouragement of moral restraint, does not seem to have believed that mankind would in fact follow his advice. Perhaps this helps to account for Malthus's domination of the debate: he articulated the fears and pessimism of a great many people. Today, these fears still have the power to haunt people.

Without the advantage of hindsight, the men of the early nineteenth century can hardly be blamed for their concern (even panic) when they saw the quite unprecedented hordes of people everywhere arising around them. They could not know that industrial growth would ultimately dispel many of their fears—only to create new ones. They correctly perceived that this new population would result in a new society and that discussion of population problems was really discussion about the whole future of society. The fears of the Rev. Mr. Malthus were not just fears of numbers of people, but fears of radical social change, even of revolution. The great immediate value of Malthus's theory was that it focused on the relationship between population growth and economic development. Exactly how these two factors are related as cause and effect is a complex matter. How far an increasing population was responsible for an increase in economic output and how far economic growth encouraged a rise in population are hard to determine. What is clear is that the combination of unprecedented growth of both economic wealth and population was the basis of the Industrial Revolution.

Economic Growth: From Cottage to Factory Industry

The distinguishing characteristic of a preindustrial society is that by today's standards it is materially poor. Eighteenth-century England, although it was one of the three richest countries in the world (the other two being France and Holland), was, in comparison with modern society, a poor country. The total amount of wealth which it produced was relatively small. There was, as Professor Rostow puts it, "a ceiling . . . on the level of attainable output per head." In other words, productivity was low, and the possibilities of increasing output were limited. Why was this? In order to answer the question, it will be helpful to compare the main characteristics of production in a modern industrial society with the way in which industry was organized in England before the Industrial Revolution. We shall then be able to appreciate the achievement of the Industrial Revolution in providing a huge and sustained increase in economic growth.

Production in England today, as in other industrial countries, is a social enterprise; that is, it is carried on in large and complex units called "factories" or "plants." They are organized on a basis of mass (or flow) production, employing hundreds and sometimes thousands of workers.

Small firms continue to exist in many areas, but the pace is set by the large units which dominate vital areas of the economy. The worker is increasingly divorced from the means of production and from the end product. He does not own, or have responsibility for, the machinery he operates; nor is the product his own, for it is the result of collective, not individual effort. For instance, no one man produces an automobile or a pair of shoes. His interest is primarily in his job and its wage, rather than in the work and its product. There is also a divorce between the ownership and control of industry. Legal ownership is usually vested in the shareholders—an amorphous group whose only interest is in dividends. Control lies in the hands of the directors, a small body nominally elected by the shareholders but virtually self-coopting; while direction and the actual running of industry are in the hands of managers, who are technical and scientific experts. Lastly, industry is located in urban areas, with a concentration in London, the Midlands, and the North.

Before the Industrial Revolution almost the precise opposite of these characteristics was true. Production was on a small scale and carried on in the homes of the people, who used only simple tools and machinery. The whole family worked together as an economic unit, and the industry was organized by middlemen or entrepreneurs. This was called the "domestic" or "putting-out" system (because the raw material was "put out" by the middleman to be made into an article). The worker usually owned (although later he had to rent) his means of production, for which he was responsible, and the product was the direct result of his and his family's labor. Most industry was related to agriculture in one way or another and was rural rather than urban. To understand how the domestic system worked, it will be convenient to look rather more closely at one particular industry—textiles—although it should be emphasized that the same basic methods and organization were found in other trades, too.

The woolen industry had been the staple trade of the kingdom for centuries, symbolized by the woolsack on which the lord chancellor sits in the House of Lords. The industry was widely dispersed throughout all parts of the country, but by the eighteenth century three regions were preeminent: the West Riding of Yorkshire, East Anglia, and the West Country. Between different districts there were variations in organization, but the methods of production were basically the same. The loom—a noisy, clumsy machine made of wood—stood in the loomshop (a large room on the second floor of the more prosperous Yorkshire clothiers' houses) or in the living room of the humbler weavers' cottages. Here the weaver sat on his bench, monotonously throwing his shuttle from side to side for long hours each day, until he had completed his "piece" of cloth. The preparatory processes of carding and spinning the wool into yarn were performed by his wife and children, who used simple hand carders and a spinning wheel worked by a foot treadle. When the cloth was woven, it was taken to be

Domestic industry: Sketch of a handloom weaver at work in the eighteenth century. (B. T. Batsford, Ltd., London.)

"fulled" (that is, felted) at a fulling mill and was washed by the weaver and stretched on "tenters" (large hooks on a frame) out-of-doors to dry in the sun. He then took it to the nearest market town and sold it to a cloth merchant. The "finishing" of the cloth, which included processes such as dyeing and dressing, was supervised by the merchant.

Until the late eighteenth century, the weaver in some districts was still an independent producer, owning his tools and controlling the processes of manufacture from raw wool to cloth piece. Such was the pattern described in the *Report from the Select Committee appointed to consider the state of the Woollen Manufacture in England* (1806):

> In the domestic system, which is that of Yorkshire, the manufacture is conducted by a multitude of master manufacturers, generally possessing a very small and scarcely ever any large amount of capital. They buy the wool of the dealer and, in their own houses, assisted by their wives and children, and from two or three to six or seven journeymen, they dye it, when dyeing is necessary, and through all the different stages work it up into undressed cloth.

Daniel Defoe in his *Tour Through the Whole Island of Great Britain* (1724–26) was greatly impressed earlier in the century with the small master weavers, known as "clothiers," whom he observed in the West Riding. They lived in substantial stone houses (some of which can still be seen), surrounded by a few acres of enclosed land on which they grew vegetables and kept animals. The more prosperous of them had several looms, which they worked with the assistance of apprentices and journeymen. Spinning was often done for them by humbler cottagers, and Defoe noted how the women and children were "always busy carding, spinning, etc. . . .; hardly anything above four years old, but its hands are sufficient to itself." Each Saturday the clothier took his cloth to the Cloth Hall in Leeds or Halifax, sold it to a merchant, and returned laden with wool and foodstuffs. This picture of the Yorkshire clothier—independent, patriarchal, and prosperous—presents an almost classic view of the domestic system at its best. It was a memory that took long to fade and that haunted the hand-loom weavers later when they fell on evil times.

But this was not the only pattern of organization in the textile indus-try. In fact, such relatively simple and idyllic conditions were but rarely found. Since it took five or six spinners to supply one loom, the weaver had to go outside his family for an adequate supply of yarn. Again, once a clothier had several looms, he became an employer of wage labor, al-though he himself continued to work as an artisan. In nearby Bradford, the center of the worsted branch of the industry (in which the wool is combed instead of carded), the trade was controlled by wealthy manufac-turers. Similarly, in East Anglia, also a worsted center, the master combers of Norwich formed a dominant group of middlemen, who put out the raw wool to be combed and spun. It was not long before the once-independent weaver in many districts became virtually an employee of the merchant-manufacturer, who supplied the raw material, bought the woven cloth, and dictated the terms of the trade. Whenever the weaver was in need of money, as a result of poor trade or a bad harvest, he soon became indebted to the middleman, who thus became the real owner of the loom which he had originally taken as a pledge for an advance of money. In the hosiery branch of textiles, centered in Leicester and Nottingham, the stocking knitters paid a rent for the knitting frames which belonged wholly to the master stockingers.

However, it was not in wool or hosiery that the breakthrough in economic expansion that powered the Industrial Revolution came first, but in the newer and smaller branch of textiles: cotton. Localized mainly in Lancashire and parts of lowland Scotland, the cotton industry was organ-ized similarly to other textiles, with merchants and a putting-out system. Samuel Bamford, a weaver from Middleton, Lancashire, described the sys-tem as he remembered it around the turn of the century. The following account is from his autobiography, *Early Days* (1849):

> My uncle's domicile, like all the others, consisted of one principal room called "the house"; on the same floor with this was a loom-shop capable of containing four looms, and in the rear of the house on the same floor, were a small kitchen and a buttery. Over the house and loom-shop were chambers; and over the kitchen and buttery was another small apartment, and a flight of stairs. The whole of the rooms were lighted by windows of small square panes, framed in lead, in good condition; those in the front

being protected by shutters. The interior of this dwelling showed that cleanly and comfortable appearance which is always to be seen where a managing Englishwoman is present. There were a dozen good rush-bottomed chairs, the backs and rails bright with wax and rubbing; a handsome clock in mahogany case; a good chest of oaken drawers; a mahogany snap-table; a mahogany corner cupboard, all well polished; besides tables, weather-glass, cornice, and ornaments.

Bamford then describes how he accompanied his uncle to Manchester, carrying the woven cloth and returning with fresh material for the following week's work:

The family were, at that time, chiefly employed by Messrs. Samuel and James Broadbent, of Cannon Street, and as the work was for the most part "pollicat" and "romoll" handkerchiefs, with a finer reed, occasionally, of silk and cotton "garments," or handkerchiefs, the "bearing-home wallet" was often both bulky and heavy; and when it happened to be too much so for one person to carry, a neighbour's wallet would be borrowed, the burden divided into two, and I would go with one part over my shoulder, behind or before my uncle. He being, as already stated, rather heavy in person would walk deliberately, with a stick in his hand, his green woollen apron twisted around his waist, his clean shirt showing at the open breast of his waistcoat, his brown silk handkerchief wrapped round his neck, a quid of tobacco in his mouth, and a broad and rather slouched hat on his head. . . .

The warehouse of Messrs. Broadbent was nearly at the top of Cannon Street, on the right-hand side. We mounted some steps, went along a covered passage, and up a height or two of stairs, to a landing place, one side of which was railed off by the bannister, and the other furnished with a seat for weavers to rest upon when they arrived. Here we should probably find some half-dozen weavers and winders, waiting for their turn to deliver in their work and to receive fresh material; and the business betwixt workman and putter-out was generally done in an amicable, reasonable way. No captious fault-finding, no bullying, no arbitrary abatement, which have been too common since, were then practised. If the work were really faulty, the weaver was shown the fault, and if it were not a serious one he was only cautioned against repeating it; if the length or the weight was not what it should be, he was told of it, and would be expected to set it right, or account for it, at his next bearing-home, and if he were a frequent defaulter he was no longer employed. . . .

It would sometimes happen that warp or weft would not be ready until after dinner, and on such occasions, my uncle having left his wallet in care of the putter-out, would go downstairs and get paid at the counting-house, and from thence go to the public-house where we lunched on bread and cheese, or cold meat and bread, with ale, to which my uncle added his ever-favourite pipe of tobacco. This house, which was the "Hope and Anchor," in the old churchyard, was also frequented by other weavers; the putter-out at Broadbents generally dined there in the parlour, and when he had dined he would come and take a glass of ale, smoke his pipe, and chat with the weavers, after which, my uncle would again go to the warehouse, and getting what material he wanted, would buy a few groceries and tobacco in the town, or probably, as we returned through the apple market, to go down Long Mill Gate, he would purchase a peck of apples, and giving them to me to carry, we wended towards home.

By Bamford's time the domestic system had clearly been undermined, for his uncle was in effect simply an out-worker for a Manchester firm. This undermining came about through a series of inventions in the textile industry that enabled it greatly to increase its output, and thereby started a chain reaction that set in motion further changes in the rest of the economy. The first of these major inventions in textiles was John Kay's flying shuttle, perfected in 1733 and widely adopted in cotton by the 1760s. It enabled the weaver to produce both more and broader cloth, thus increasing still further the imbalance between the spinning and weaving sectors of the trade. Consequently, the next inventions were in spinning: James Hargreaves's spinning jenny of the 1760s, which could spin many threads at once—at first it had eight, later 120 spindles; Richard Arkwright's water-frame (patented in 1769), to produce stronger cotton yarn suitable for warp (hitherto linen had been used); and Samuel Crompton's mule (1779), which combined the jenny and the water-frame. The weavers were now assured of a plentiful supply of yarn, and the 1790s became the Golden Age of handloom weaving, when work was plentiful and wages high. This period of prosperity, however, did not last long, for in the 1780s the first power loom was developed, and although its adoption was slow for some years, by 1820 there were 14,000 power looms in Britain, and by 1833, 100,000.

Judged by today's standards, the early textile machines seem relatively simple. Yet it was not the new technology alone, but the new industrial system which it implied, that was revolutionary. The new machines required power to drive them, and so could not be housed in the homes of the people but only in what contemporaries called "manufactories." Water provided the motive power, and the early cotton factories or mills of the 1770s and 1780s were therefore located in remote areas of the Pennines and the Derbyshire hills where there was a plentiful supply of swift-flowing water. The new industry was initially based in country factories. This stage of the Industrial Revolution soon proved to be a false dawn, for in the 1780s the steam engine was perfected and immediately applied to driving textile machinery. Cotton spinners were thus freed from their dependence on water power, and further development of factories thence took place in urban areas where labor was more plentiful and coal supplies not far away. The basic elements in the pattern of modern British industrialism had begun to emerge: steam-powered machine production in urban factories. Manchester, which more than any other city was the symbol of the new industrial age, accurately reflected these changes. In 1773, with a

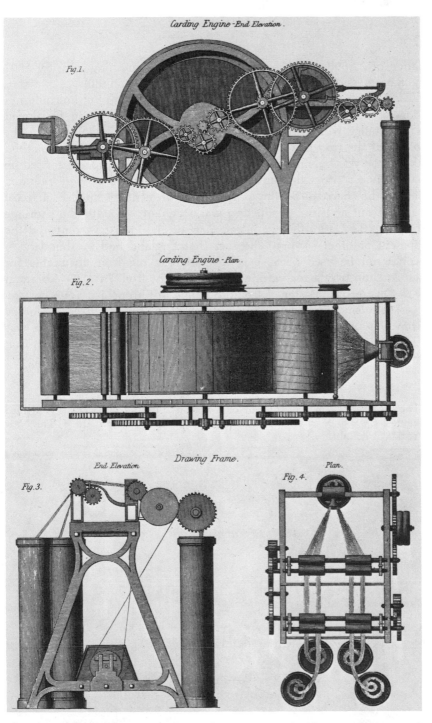

The new machines: Diagram of a carding engine and a drawing frame, used in the preparation of cotton for spinning, c. 1830. (Edward Baines, *History of the Cotton Manufacture in Great Britain, 1835*, The New York Public Library.)

population of 27,000, Manchester had not a single spinning mill; by 1802 the population was 95,000 and there were fifty-two cotton mills.

King Cotton powered the first Industrial Revolution, but he could not have done so without supportive changes in other industries, too. Of almost equal importance with the changes in textiles was the revolution in the technology of the iron and engineering industries. The traditional method of making iron was by smelting the ore with charcoal—a process carried on in small furnaces situated near the woods and forests that were required for making the charcoal. By the early eighteenth century English charcoal was running out and iron production was stagnant. As with the shortage of yarn in textiles, a bottleneck in one part of the industry hampered the development of other sectors. The fuel that England had in abundance—coal—could not be used because coke made the pig iron unsuitable for castings and too brittle for working into wrought iron. In 1709 Abraham Darby, a Quaker ironmaster of Coalbrookdale in Shropshire, found a way of successfully smelting iron with coke, and by the mid-eighteenth century such iron was used for castings. A similar invention in steel-making was made by Benjamin Huntsman of Sheffield in the 1740s. The wrought-iron branch of the industry was unaffected by these innovations, and it was not

The factory system: (1) Interior of a cotton-spinning mill, 1830s. (Edward Baines, *History of the Cotton Manufacture in Great Britain, 1835*, The New York Public Library.)

until 1783–84 when Henry Cort patented a process of "puddling" (that is, melting and stirring) and rolling that coal could be used for the production of bar iron. The iron and forge masters were now free of the restrictions imposed by the necessity of using only charcoal and high-grade imported (Swedish) ore. In 1760 the output of British pig iron was about 30,000 tons annually; fifty years later it was over a million tons.

This increase in iron output was dependent on the development of an efficient steam engine to provide the blast in the furnace and the power for heavy forging. Since Thomas Newcomen's invention in 1708, steam engines had been used for pumping water from mines. James Watt, a Scottish mathematical instrument-maker, worked for many years to improve the efficiency of the early atmospheric engine, and finally, in the 1780s, by means of a series of brilliant inventions, he perfected the first rotative steam engine. In conjunction with his Birmingham partner, Matthew Boulton, Watt built some 500 engines before 1800. This was the new form of power that underpinned the Industrial Revolution. It stimulated the demand for coal and dictated that the industrial centers of Britain should be adjacent to the coalfields. Wooden machinery was inadequate to the demands of steam, and so iron replaced it. A new industry of making machinery and a new race of men—the engineers—were called forth. England ceased to be a country of wood and water power and instead based her economy on coal and iron. Today we cannot imagine an industrialized society that is not built on a foundation of abundant and cheap iron, since this is basic to modern technology.

The great inventions in iron and textiles lay at the heart of the Industrial Revolution, but they were not by any means the whole of it. Inventions do not, in themselves, necessarily lead to change. It is only when they are adapted, that is, become innovations, that they are significant. The cluster of innovations which we have discussed in the period from about 1760 to 1800 resulted in cumulative changes that set in motion for the first time the process of industrialization. Other industries were affected and their output began to increase, even without any major inventions: for example, pottery and mining, building construction, and some sections of the worsted industry. In 1830 many industries were still unmechanized, such as the hardware trades of Birmingham and Sheffield, shoemaking, clothing, cabinet-making, and many artisan crafts. But everywhere there had been an enormous increase in total output. Continuous expansion had become built into the economy.

The industries considered so far were all directly productive of manufactured goods and raw materials. But a condition of their expansion was the provision of capital investment in enterprises that were not directly productive, such things as roads, harbors, canals, and bridges. These constituted "social overheads" and were mostly in transport. Without them the resources of a country remain largely undeveloped, as is obvious from the problems facing the underdeveloped countries of the world today. Because the amount of capital required for such undertakings is very large and the payoff is often delayed and of benefit to the whole community rather than to a few individuals, such investment has usually to be provided by the state or by foreign financiers from richer countries. In Britain, however, the capital came from within the country, through the initiative of private investors. As in other respects, this aspect of the Industrial Revolution in England was virtually unique.

Travelers in the first half of the eighteenth century complained that British roads were about the worst in Europe. Horrific stories of main roads strewn with boulders as big as a horse's head, ruts four feet deep, and regular seasonal flooding with several feet of water were common. The normal road was without any hard surface, so that in wet weather it became a muddy bog. Not since Roman times had roads been nationally surveyed and paved, and the remains of these great highways were still the best in Britain. Responsibility for the upkeep of roads was laid on the parish, which until 1835 could require each villager to labor a certain number of days each year on the roads. The result was not impressive, but as long as industry was essentially local and the pack horse sufficient for the needs of trade, it was adequate. When wagons began to increase in number and weight, however, the system became less satisfactory; and a series of Turnpike Acts was passed that granted to individuals the right to collect tolls from users in return for maintaining the roads in passable condition. In the eighteenth century the turnpikes, with their tollgates and tollhouses for the collectors, became a familiar sight, and were probably less inefficient than the old parish roads. Real improvement was dependent on better techniques of road-building, and here again a famous group of inventive engineers was responsible. John Metcalf used a technique similar to the Roman, building his roads on a stone foundation overlaid with chippings. Thomas Telford and John Loudon McAdam similarly used stone to provide roads with a hard surface that was passable in all weather. This type of road proved serviceable throughout the nineteenth century, and although confined to main routes was sufficent to ensure a considerable improvement in transport facilities. The era of the heavy wagon and the fast stagecoach had begun. In 1750 a journey from London to York took four days and one to Birmingham two days. By the 1780s these times had been halved, and by 1830 reduced to a third or a fifth of what they had been.

More important than the roads in the development of an early Industrial Revolution was cheap transportation by water. The cost and inconvenience of moving heavy goods by road was prohibitive in the eighteenth century, but fortunately Britain was blessed with a long seacoast (from which no part of the country was further than seventy miles) and rivers that could easily be made navigable. For many years a fleet of small ships had carried coal and grain and building materials from the ports along the east coast between Edinburgh and London. Until the 1750s this system was adequate to meet the fairly modest needs of the main towns, but thereafter the increased demand for coal in inland areas spurred the development of canals. Beginning with the Duke of Bridgewater's canal between Manchester and his coal mine at Worsley in 1759, which captured the imagination of the age with its impressive tunnel and aqueduct, a veritable canal mania seized the country. By the end of the century England was covered with a network of canals, linking up navigable sections of rivers, tunneling through hills, and defying the laws of gravity by means of long series of locks. Today these quiet waterways, meandering through lush fields and beneath hundreds of red-brick, humpbacked bridges, seem remote from any connection with industrialism. Yet in the heart of many an industrial town the stagnant canal basin and weed-grown wharfs remind us of this vanished era of the early Industrial Revolution. Without the canals, the coal and iron and bricks and a score of other bulky commodities could not have been moved, at a reasonable price, to where they were wanted. Essentially, the canals provided an enormous increase in transportation efficiency: a horse that could pull a load of two tons on a good road could drag fifty tons in a canal barge. When Benjamin Gott installed the first steam engine in his new Leeds woolen factory in 1793, the heavy parts had to be brought from Boulton and Watt's works in Birmingham via Gainsborough, using the canal and river network that was the only possible method of moving such machines. The canals were a means of breaking the bottleneck that threatened to develop when industrial progress demanded a cheap and practicable means of transporting coal and iron across the country. The canal age did not last long—only until the railways were built in the 1830s and 1840s. But by then the canals had effectively pioneered the first stage of the revolution in transport.

In our consideration of economic growth, we have dealt mainly with the two factors of natural resources (iron, coal, navigable rivers) and technical progress (inventions and new methods of organization). To complete the picture we have to include two further determinants of economic growth: capital and labor. These four factors are closely interlocked, but for purposes of analysis we have to separate them.

Capital is crucial in any industrial revolution. Without it, there cannot be the new machines and mines and canals, which in turn make possible an increase in the production of wealth and thereby raise the standard of living. Capital is simply accumulated wealth, in whatever form, which can be used to produce more. One of the great differences between an industrialized and a preindustrial society is that the latter has to consume almost all the wealth it produces; whereas the former has sufficient wealth to be able to set some of it aside to create additional means of production. The industrial nation puts back annually a certain percentage of the wealth it has produced, not only to replace worn-out equipment but to increase future output. This is called "investment," and at the beginning of an industrial revolution the rate of investment rises steeply.

There has been much discussion by economic historians about where the first capital for the Industrial Revolution came from—whether from the land or from overseas trade or from existing industries. But in the first instance it would seem that capital for new industries usually came from the families or friends of the innovators. Thus Arkwright got his first capital from a friend; Abraham Darby and John Wilkinson, the ironmasters, extended their family businesses; James Watt was financed at first by his friend, Dr. Black, and later went into partnership with Matthew Boulton, who had family means to back him; Robert Owen, who later made a fortune in cotton spinning, first borrowed £100 from his brother and entered into partnership with a machine maker to produce spinning-mules. Many of the early industrialists led a simple, puritan way of life, practicing the virtues of hard work, thrift, and sobriety. They plowed back much of their profits, so that expansion was financed by the industry itself. As industry throughout the country expanded and larger amounts of new capital were required, some additional source had to be found. Hence appeared new banks and banking houses, both in London and the provinces, which provided the necessary investment in industry. In this way, wealth from land and commerce could be transferred, via the banks, to industry. Investment ceased to be a matter of personal choice; it became institutionalized.

The role of labor in the Industrial Revolution was equally crucial with capital in making economic growth possible. Obviously, if the number of workers increases or if people work longer or more efficiently, then, other things being equal, more goods and services will be produced. We have already noted how the numbers of people grew rapidly in the second half of the eighteenth century. This increase provided the additional labor force that the new factories and the expanded older industries required. But the problems of labor in an industrial revolution are more complex than the provision of mere numbers. In Britain the building of an industrial labor force encountered three major hurdles which had to be surmounted. First, labor was in short supply during the early days of the Industrial Revolution. Second, it was relatively immobile. And, third, it was not adapted to the needs of factory industry.

It may seem strange to say that there was a labor shortage when we have just been describing a population explosion. But this is accounted for by the chronology of population growth. Until the 1780s the rate of growth was relatively modest, and it was only in the last two decades of the eighteenth century that it accelerated dramatically. In any case, the effects of demographic change are not immediate but delayed for a generation or more. The universal search for labor-saving devices, such as the spinning jenny, and the rise in real wages in the northern industrial areas suggest that at the beginning of the Industrial Revolution employers could not easily find all the labor they wanted. Moreover, the shortage was aggravated by the immobility of laboring men and women. In old centers of industry the restrictive practices of guilds and corporations (such as insistence on a seven-year apprenticeship in many crafts) prevented any great influx of newcomers. Even more effective in preventing people from moving to where there were new jobs were settlement laws, dating from 1602, under which a newcomer could be sent back within forty days to his last parish of settlement if he seemed likely to become a burden on the local poor relief system. The practice of granting poor relief to supplement inadequate wages, which spread in rural areas after 1795, was also felt to retard movement by removing any spur to self-help.

These factors, coupled with the need to locate the early water-driven

The factory system: (2) New Lanark cotton mills, Scotland, as they appeared c. 1825. Built by David Dale and Robert Owen. (Courtesy of The Gourock Ropework Co., Ltd., Scotland.)

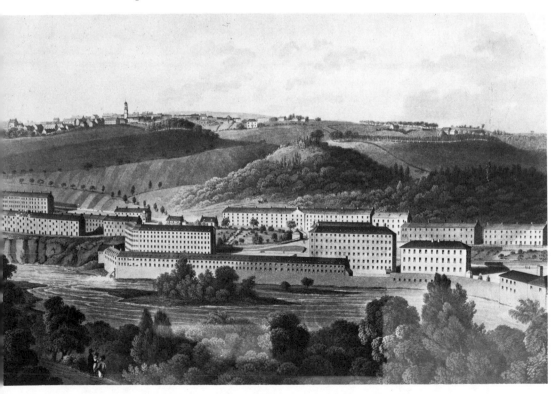

mills in isolated places where there was little local supply of labor, led to some of the worst practices of early industrialism, such as the employment of children. To overcome the labor shortage, pauper children from London workhouses were bound apprentice to northern mill owners who worked them long hours (5 A.M. to 8 P.M.) and boarded them in dormitories (apprentice houses). In one notorious case, reported to the House of Commons in 1815, a Lancashire mill owner agreed to take one idiot with every twenty normal children supplied by a London parish. The system of pauper apprenticeship in factories declined after legislation against it in 1816, but children continued to be employed as wage earners, and their working life differed little from the previous conditions. On the credit side of the balance, the need to attract workers stimulated some employers to provide housing and community facilities. The factory villages built at New Lanark, Scotland, by David Dale and in Derbyshire by Jedediah Strutt established patriarchal regimes with model housing, schools, sick clubs, and cooperative stores. In the next phase of factory building, when industry was no longer dependent on water power and so could develop in towns, this benevolent paternalism weakened or disappeared, and the employer cared little about the slums in which his workers spent their non-factory hours.

The third problem—the adaptation of labor to industry, or the creation of an industrial labor force—was the most intractable. We have grown up in a society in which regular work habits (8 A.M. to 4 P.M., with time out for lunch, Monday through Friday) are taken so much for granted that we never even question them. But preindustrial workers often had quite different rhythms of work, and their output varied from day to day and week to week. Weavers and cobblers would frequently work long hours from Tuesday to Saturday afternoon and then extend their weekend through Monday. In some places, the first day of the week was called St. Monday or Cobbler's Monday. Under the domestic system, each man could be his own master as far as working time was concerned. Such erratic habits of course were unsatisfactory in the new factories. There everyone had to begin work at the same time and observe the same rules of behavior. When the bell rang or the whistle blew and the great factory gates clanged open or shut, everyone had to respond in the same way. The creation of a docile race of operatives ("hands," as they were revealingly called in the northern textile towns), disciplined to the routine of the factory, was a major task in the early Industrial Revolution. It was soon found that young men past the age of puberty had difficulty in adjusting to the new discipline; this was one reason why children and women were preferred.

One of the earliest requirements of a system of industrial capitalism is the inculcation of the "economic motive." Without some degree of acquisitiveness, the worker will not become responsive to the demands of industry. For instance, in traditional society if a worker could earn enough to keep himself and his family for a week in four days, he did not see any necessity to work the other two simply to earn more money. This attitude had to be broken down before a capitalist economy could be built, for the worker was required to react in a predictable way to increases and decreases of wages. If he was not attracted by higher earnings and deterred by lower, the labor force would be immobile and the manufacturer would be unable to plan production rationally. The change from domestic to factory industry was not merely a change to higher wages and a larger work place, but a change in the whole way of thinking about life. The Industrial Revolution saw the birth of "economic man."

A shift of this magnitude, involving fundamental attitudes and values, could not be effected immediately or painlessly, and the process of the adaptation of labor to industry took two or three generations and involved many different methods. Some of these methods were direct and conscious. Punishment for lateness, deductions from wages for slowness, fines for bad work, and bonuses for good work were embodied in an elaborate system of factory codes. The adoption of piece-rates (that is, payment by output, not by the hour) spread widely in the first half of the nineteenth century. But the punitive aspect of factory life was deeply resented by laboring men and was a root cause of much of the early antagonism to the new industrial regime.

In the long run, the adaptation of labor by indirect means was much more effective. The discipline that a man applies to himself (that he "internalizes," as the sociologists say) is ever the most powerful. Once acquisitiveness began to spread, it soon gathered momentum and affected larger and larger sections of the community. The inner compulsion that drove a man to work hard and steadily, however, had to be based on something more than simple greed. And here the role of religion was vital. From the Puritan ethic of work, with its emphasis on frugality, "industry," and devotion to one's calling, came the elements necessary for the construction of a work discipline among laboring people. What had been a predominantly middle-class ethic in the seventeenth and early eighteenth centuries was transmitted to the working classes by means of popular religion, especially Methodism. Part of the social and economic role of the churches during the Industrial Revolution was to help create a sober, industrious, respectable working class. Likewise, much educational effort was directed toward "moral instruction," which was intended to strengthen acceptance of the new discipline of work and middle-class values. By 1830 the results of these pressures were apparent. The laboring poor of preindustrial England were being transformed into the working classes of an industrial society. For many thousands of people this was a very painful process, as we shall see later. It was part of the price of economic growth.

Change on the Land

The great changes in industrial growth did not develop in a vacuum, but within the framework of a traditional, agricultural economy and society. Agriculture—in some ways the most basic of man's activities, since its object is the production of food—was presented in the eighteenth century with challenges that, if they had not been successfully met, would have seriously retarded industrial progress. In the building of the first industrial society, British agriculture was vital in three respects. It provided the food for a growing population, especially the urban workers; it contributed substantially to the capital required for early industrialization; and it produced a surplus from the agricultural population that helped to swell the ranks of the industrial proletariat. In view of the essentially slow nature of agricultural change, it is perhaps misleading to speak of an agricultural revolution; but the actual achievements in increased agricultural output by the end of the eighteenth century were totally unprecedented.

In 1820 the population of England and Wales was more than double what it had been in 1750, but the proportion of families engaged in agriculture was less. Moreover, only a very small percentage of the food consumed was imported, and that happened usually in times of bad harvest. More food was produced by proportionately fewer workers; in other words, the efficiency of agriculture increased. Had this not come about, Britain would have had to import food for her growing population at the expense of the raw materials (cotton, iron ore, wool) required for the new industries, since she would not have been able to afford both. As it was, agriculture responded to the demands put on it and thus made possible the curious pattern of an industrial revolution in a country that had very few of the necessary raw materials (except coal) and that had therefore to rely on imports. The success of the agriculturists brought them increased incomes, which in turn stimulated the demand for the products of the new industry and also provided some surplus capital for investment in industry.

How was this great increase in agricultural productivity achieved, and what were its implications for the landlords, farmers, and laborers? Unlike industry, the agricultural revolution was not dependent to any significant extent on mechanical inventions. Jethro Tull's seed drill, which he publicized in the 1730s, was not widely used until the nineteenth century. Improved types of plow, which permitted the use of two horses instead of the traditional team of from four to eight oxen, were available after 1730; and the first threshing machines appeared in the 1780s. Nevertheless, most threshing was done with a flail until the 1830s, and hay and grain were mown and reaped by hand (with scythe and sickle) for many years after that. Although there was some reduction in manual labor, farming remained predominantly an occupation requiring a great amount of sheer, hard muscle power. The increase in agricultural output was the result of new techniques of production rather than technological innovation.

Traditional English farming—as inherited, with some modifications, from the Middle Ages—was handicapped by several weaknesses, some of which were technical and some of which were derived from the social structure of the village. The eighteenth century witnessed a clearing away of these obstacles to expansion, although the way had been prepared by piecemeal changes over the preceding two hundred years. Perhaps the most wasteful aspect of the old farming was the need to leave between a quarter and a third of the arable land fallow each year in order that the soil could recover its fertility after growing crops for two or three years. The numbers of livestock were insufficient to provide heavier manuring, and ignorance of soil and plant chemistry barred the way to alternative methods of putting back into the soil what had been taken out. This weakness was overcome in the eighteenth century by the discovery and adoption of new forms of crop rotation. Instead of the usual alternation of wheat, barley, and rye with fallow, fodder crops of grass and legumes such as clover and lucerne were introduced in some years. Turnips and potatoes were used as crops for clearing the ground of weeds. In this way, the fertility of the soil was maintained through the chemical action of the legumes and the increased amount of animal manure from the larger livestock population made possible by the new crops of fodder. The soil could thus be made to bear crops continuously, since the necessity of frequent fallowing had been removed; and more livestock could be kept because fodder was available for them throughout the winter.

Increased yields from the land could also be obtained by other improvements, such as marling, manuring, and draining. Sandy soils benefited greatly from the application of "marl," a type of clay that was dug from pits, and clay soils from a dressing of chalk and lime. The relative scarcity of animal manure encouraged the use of soot, bones, and seaweed, but until soil chemistry had advanced further, artificial fertilizers could not be developed. Draining of land, by means of ditches, or ridge and furrow (raising the land into ridges so that the water drained into lower ground through the furrows) also improved the yield. More and better fodder encouraged experiment in animal breeding, and new herds of cattle and types of sheep began to appear. The medieval sheep, for instance, was a thin, bony creature; by selective breeding Robert Bakewell produced his New Leicester sheep that had short legs, a small head, and a large barrel-shaped body and that was good both for its fat meat and its wool.

The combination of these new crops, rotations, and breeds of stock is sometimes referred to as the Norfolk system—not because it was confined to that county but because a number of "improving" landlords and farmers were concentrated there. Viscount ("Turnip") Townshend and Thomas Coke of Holkham are perhaps the best-known names, but they were typical of many more in other parts of the country. George III delighted in the title "Farmer George" and set the fashion for "improvement" and scientific experiment in agriculture. Publicists like William Marshall and Arthur Young advertised the new methods. A semiofficial Board of Agriculture (with Young as secretary) was founded in 1793; and local agricultural associations and exhibitions flourished. It is difficult to say how much of this "improvement" percolated down to the ordinary farmers. Regional differences in soils and methods of husbandry meant that what was successful in one county was not necessarily so in the next. Nevertheless, the overall increase in agricultural output during the eighteenth century was in the region of 40 to 50 percent, which suggests that by 1800 the new farming had begun to produce significant results.

Before the new techniques of production could be fully employed, however, another basic weakness in the traditional agricultural system had to be eliminated. At the beginning of the eighteenth century about half the arable land was still cultivated, as it had been in the Middle Ages, on the open-field system. That is to say, the land around each village, instead of being divided up and fenced into fairly small fields as it is today, lay open in great areas of hundreds of acres. Each farmer's holding was made up of a number of scattered strips of land. In addition, a share in the meadows, commons, or "wastes" was allotted to each farmer, and this provided him with hay and pasturage for his animals and wood for fuel or building materials. By 1820 there were only a few counties in which the open-field system remained, and by the 1830s it had virtually disappeared. This dramatic transformation of the face of the country was effected by the enclosure movement.

Enclosure became a slogan of the period from 1760 to 1820; but, originally, it meant simply rearranging the open fields and commons into smaller, consolidated, individual units. Three separate types of enclosure can be distinguished: the enclosure of arable land in order to convert it to pasture for sheep; the consolidation of scattered arable strips into one compact holding; and the enclosure of common land (sometimes called "waste") that had previously been uncultivated. The first type of enclosure had been carried out mainly in the sixteenth century. The second had proceeded spasmodically and slowly for many generations, as individuals made private arrangements to reorganize or enlarge their holdings; and there had also been incorporation of new land from the waste that was usually enclosed. Until about 1760 these developments had been slow and fairly steady. Thereafter, the pressure of increasing population and urbanization, with the consequent rise in food prices, greatly accelerated the rate of change.

The reasons for enclosure arose, in one form or another, from frustration with the conservatism and rigidities of the open-field system. An "improving" farmer or landlord found it extremely difficult to institute new crops and rotations or a new drainage system if his neighbors refused to cooperate, since cultivation (and indeed the whole life of the village) was governed by the rule of custom. In a communal system there is little scope for individual deviation or experiment. A compact, enclosed farm was easier to work and enabled an enterprising farmer to try out the new farming techniques. The enclosure of commons and wastes made them available for commercially profitable use and increased the total amount of land under cultivation. In general, enclosure strengthened a trend toward larger units and a more capitalist-minded approach to agriculture.

Before 1760 most enclosure was by private agreement among the owners of the land concerned. Where the number of owners was small or where they were prepared to sell out their rights, no problem was presented. But where there was opposition, the only way to overcome it was by a special act of Parliament ordering the enclosure of that particular parish or manor. In the sixty years before 1760 slightly more than 200 such enclosure acts were passed; between 1781 and 1801 there were about 2,000; and another 2,000 were enacted between 1802 and 1844. The total area of land affected by these enclosures was over six million acres, or about a quarter of all the land in cultivation.

Contemporaries, like historians later, were divided in their views of the effects and desirability of enclosures. On the whole, the landlords and larger farmers fared best, and the poorer villagers fared worst. The enclosure commissioners, who were responsible for dividing up the land after an Enclosure Act had been passed, respected the rights of all who had a legal title to land, but usually disregarded claims based on custom or tenancy. This meant that small farmers and cottagers, who had customarily used the commons for grazing a cow and for cutting fuel, received no share of the land when it was divided and were thus deprived of their former rights. Previously, they had been able to eke out a living from their combined resources of wage-labor, a small holding, and common rights. Enclosure took away a vital element in this economy and reduced some of them to simple wage laborers. The same fate was even more likely for the "squatters," a class of laborers who lived in hovels on the edge of the commons and who had no legal claim to land or common rights; on enclosure their homes were simply pulled down. Even when small farmers and cottagers had enforceable claims, they were faced with the problem of how to pay for their share of the legal costs of enclosure (which were heavy) and the cost of fencing. At such times the temptation to sell out to a richer neighbor was great.

It is unlikely that enclosures were responsible for all the social evils that were once ascribed to them, although the loss of the commons was an important step toward the pauperization of the rural poor in the early nineteenth century. For two famous writers on agricultural conditions, Arthur Young and William Cobbett, enclosure was a slogan denoting a complex of social problems arising out of the changes in the agricultural community. Basically, these changes were a response to a growing population, the demand for more food, and, after 1760, the first stages of an industrial revolution. Agriculture was made more efficient and its output was raised. But the social price of this was a weakening of traditional community values in the villages, a hardening of class divisions, and the degradation arising from rural poverty. In the new industrial society agriculture had ultimately to conform to the same pattern of capitalist development as manufacturing and commerce.

Why First in Britain?

The greatest historical problem of the Industrial Revolution remains to be answered. Why did it occur first in Britain, and why at the particular time that it did? There was, of course, no one cause which can be singled out as the prime factor of the Industrial Revolution. All the elements described above interacted to form a complex of causes which resulted in the emergence after 1760 of the world's first industrial civilization. If one piece of the jigsaw puzzle had been missing, the Industrial Revolution would not have taken place as and when it did. In fact, England was the only country in which all the pieces could be fitted together to make a complete picture. We have now to see briefly how the various pieces of this jigsaw puzzle interlocked and in what order.

If we start with the great increase in economic productivity, the immediate cause was the series of inventions in industry which led to Britain's becoming the "workshop of the world." These technological changes, however, were dependent on other factors. Adequate natural resources, such as ample supplies of coal and water and navigable rivers and estuaries, facilitated the solution of the technological problems which faced the early industrialists. Innovation in industry and agriculture also required sufficient supplies of capital and labor, and these were to be found only in a certain type of society. Moreover, for output to be stimulated there had to be a demand for the products, and this implied a community that was rich enough to purchase them. By the standards of a modern Western society early eighteenth-century Britain was poor; but, in comparison with today's underdeveloped countries, it was not (with the exception of the Celtic fringe) underdeveloped. For the previous 200 years there had been steady if unspectacular economic development, so that by the mid-eighteenth century consumer demand was strong enough to support an expansion in output.

Visitors to Britain in the eighteenth century were usually impressed by its apparent wealth, especially the preeminence accorded to trade. The country was already well on the way to becoming that "nation of shopkeepers" which Napoleon later derided. Outwardly British society was aristocratic, with effective political power in the hands of a small landed oligarchy. But it was an aristocracy very different from the French or German nobilities. The great Whig peers in England, far from being opposed or indifferent to commercial development, were only too ready to make money. The general climate of English society was favorable to essentially "bourgeois" pursuits and enterprise.

Similarly, the role of government in Britain contributed to the genesis of an industrial revolution. In an age when most European governments sought to control economic development and regulate trade, Britain was notable for the absence of government interference in large areas of internal trade and industry. The state was prepared to follow a policy of laissez-faire and was content to do no more than provide favorable conditions in which private enterprise could flourish. Later industrial revolutions in other countries often required the active support of the state in supplying social overhead capital, such as railways, roads, and harbors. But the comparatively negative role of the British state in internal economic affairs seems to have been an encouragement to spontaneous and individual initiative. When government did act more positively, as in foreign relations, economic interests were put first. Britain was engaged in five great wars in the eighteenth century and in all of them her aims were primarily to secure commercial, industrial, and naval advantages. Whereas her chief rival, France, was predominantly a military power, Britain put her main efforts into building a superior navy, as a means of protecting and extending her overseas trade and colonies.

A commercially minded society and government thus provided a fertile seeding ground for an industrial revolution. If we probe further we can uncover ancillary factors. The stability of English society since 1660, the tradition of personal liberty and security of property, the partial tolerance of dissenting religious views—all helped to strengthen conditions favorable to enterprise and innovation. The sociologist Max Weber developed a famous theory to show the correlation between capitalism and the religion of Protestantism. Complex as are the ramifications of this theory, the basic facts are clear, namely, that the kind of behavior and attitudes of mind encouraged by the Protestant churches were precisely those most conducive to success in capitalist trade and industry. The number of leaders in the Industrial Revolution who were Dissenters (Quakers, Presbyterians, Congregationalists, Unitarians) was disproportionately large. This may have been because their practice of the puritan virtues brought success in their "calling," but equally it may have been because they were simply the most serious-minded and better-educated members of the middle class. The same considerations probably also account for the large numbers of Scots who pioneered British industrialism. Scottish primary education was far ahead of the English system, and the Scottish universities of Glasgow and Edinburgh were superior to Oxford and Cambridge as centers of learning. Whatever the reason for it, the main point is that British society in the eighteenth century was fortunate in being able to draw on the skill and enterprise of these minority groups.

The factors that we have so far considered attempt to explain why an industrial revolution was possible in England (although not in Ireland, Wales, and the Highlands of Scotland) some time between the late seventeenth and mid-nineteenth centuries. But we have not shown why it happened just when it did. To account for the timing of the Industrial Revolution in the late eighteenth century, it is necessary to examine two more factors: population and foreign trade.

The sudden and unprecedented growth of population after 1750 need not necessarily have been the spark that set off the train of causes resulting in an industrial revolution. Other European countries experienced similar population growth without its producing any such result. To produce an industrial revolution, the population had to expand rapidly enough to create a demand for more food and more consumer goods and also to provide an increase in the labor force. Yet, if population grew too rapidly, it would outstrip food supplies, cheapen the cost of labor, and dampen the incentive to find labor-saving machines. This delicate balance of not too much and not too little increase in population was achieved for the first time only in the second half of the eighteenth century. Even then, the spark might not have produced more than a small explosion had it not been for the possibilities for expansion offered by foreign trade. Until about 1780 the international trade of the main European nations had been growing steadily, and Britain had already acquired a large share. A temporary interruption of British overseas trade resulted from the American War of Independence, but it was immediately succeeded by a boom in the 1780s, and this was soon reinforced by the monopoly of international trade which came to Britain through the elimination of all competitors in the long drawn-out wars against France. Foreign demands thus grew rapidly, providing a base for the great new cotton industry, which in turn powered the first phase of the Industrial Revolution. By 1780 Britain had acquired all the prerequisites for rapid industrial growth. The pressure of an increase in population coupled with new export markets was sufficient to set in motion the self-sustaining process of industrialization.

Returning to our original metaphor of the jigsaw puzzle, we can now see that the Industrial Revolution occurred first in Britain because she alone had all the pieces of the picture: natural resources, technology, economic advance, favorable psychological and religious attitudes, population growth, foreign trade, a noninterfering government, and a society whose structure was sufficiently flexible to take advantage of opportunities when they appeared. The only other country with comparable advantages in the eighteenth century was Holland, and she lacked natural resources. It therefore fell to Britain to pioneer the world's first industrial civilization.

CHAPTER THREE

The Industrial Revolution was the greatest, but by no means the only, series of momentous happenings in the long reign of George III (1760–1820). George III was a mentally dull and exceedingly obstinate man, whose policies proved disastrous. To Americans, he was the most notorious of all British monarchs. He was the son of the Prince of Wales who died in 1751, leaving the heir apparent to be brought up by his mother and his tutor, the Earl of Bute. Unlike his grandfather, George II, the new king had no love for Hanover and announced at the very beginning of his reign that he gloried in the name of Briton. Indeed, his most attractive quality was a certain "John Bullishness." He enjoyed being a gentleman farmer ("Farmer George") and his love of simple domestic pleasures endeared him to his humbler subjects. In early middle age he suffered from attacks of insanity, and when these later became more severe and prolonged his son, the Prince of Wales (who succeeded as George IV in 1820), became prince regent.

The monarch, as we saw earlier, still possessed considerable political power, although under George I and George II much of it had been delegated to the great Whig leaders: the Pelhams (Dukes of Newcastle), the Russells (Dukes of Bedford), the Cavendishes (Dukes of Devonshire), and the Townshends. George III determined that he would resume personal

Empire, War, and Revolution

control of this power and patronage and assert his constitutional position as executive head of the government. "Be King, George," his mother is supposed to have reiterated during his adolescence, and he doggedly followed this advice for the rest of his life. At first, he was inexperienced and relied on the advice of his old tutor, Lord Bute, but in time he became as adept at playing the political game as "those proud dukes" (Newcastle and Devonshire) whom he denounced. The "king's friends" consisted of politicians who held office in return for their loyalty to the monarch's wishes. He forced the resignation of the greatest statesman of the age, William Pitt (later, Earl of Chatham), and got rid of Newcastle, the master of the Whig patronage system. But for the first ten years of his reign George III was not strong enough to impose his own ministry, and the 1760s was a period of government by successive Whig coalitions. Finally, in 1770, the king was able to appoint Lord North as head of the administration, and for twelve years achieved the stability of government that was his main aim.

The issue on which Pitt resigned in 1761 was, significantly, the continuation of the Seven Years War, for overseas wars provided an almost continuous backdrop to internal politics throughout the eighteenth century. France was the main enemy—so much so that it seemed as if Britain were conducting a second Hundred Years War, culminating in the victory of Waterloo in 1815. Following William III's war against France to defend the Revolution Settlement and the Protestant succession at the end of the seventeenth century had come the War of the Spanish Succession (1702–13) to prevent Louis XIV from uniting France and Spain. Fought mainly in the Netherlands, the war redounded to the credit of John Churchill, who was rewarded for his military victories with the dukedom of Marlborough and Blenheim Palace in Oxfordshire. During Walpole's ascendancy peace was maintained, but in 1739 he was unable to prevent a war with Spain (the War of Jenkins's Ear), which was soon extended to France and which dragged on until 1748. The struggle against France was renewed on a worldwide scale in the Seven Years War (1756–63) under the leadership of William Pitt, and resulted in prestigious military and naval victories, particularly in 1759. But the assertion of British naval, commercial, and colonial power provoked further rivalries and ambitions. In 1775 the American War of Independence unleashed more fighting which lasted until the British army surrendered in 1781. The American colonists were supported by France and Spain. A decade later Britain went to war with revolutionary France, and the resulting struggle dragged on for twenty-two years (1793–1815), with only a short break in 1802–03. None of this fighting took place in Britain itself, with the exception of the French-supported Jacobite rebellions of 1715 and 1745 and the Irish rebellion of 1798. In this respect, the British were singularly fortunate in escaping the horrors of war while benefiting from the gains that accrued from victory. The rationale for British participation in most of her wars in the eighteenth century was the protection and advancement of trade, which in turn involved her deeply in imperial problems. The age of George III was also a period of revolutions—political in America and France, industrial in Lancashire. Yet, ironically, the great themes of empire, war, and revolution were almost totally beyond the comprehension of the king for whom the age was named.

An Empire Lost

In view of later theories of imperialism, it has to be emphasized that the eighteenth-century view of empire was primarily commercial. Colonies existed for the benefit of the trade of the mother country. They were also useful as dumping grounds for undesirable elements at home—thieves and prostitutes, surplus population, social and religious dissenters. Since other European nations had similar views, competition for control of the most lucrative areas of colonization developed. William Pitt decided early in his political career that France was the greatest rival to Britain's overseas trade, and he therefore devoted his great talents as a war leader to destroying

French colonial power and substituting British control. This was largely achieved by the victories in the Seven Years War, which was fought on land and sea in the four main areas of trade: North America, the West Indies, India, and Africa. The interests of the colonial population, whether native or immigrant, were always presumed to be secondary to British interests. In areas of white settlement, where the colonials claimed their rights as "free-born Englishmen," such an attitude inevitably caused friction, and a very sympathetic and flexible policy by the home government was possibly the only way in which ultimate separation could have been avoided. But such a policy was not forthcoming from George III's government. At the end of the Seven Years War in 1763, the first British empire reached its climax, and British maritime and colonial power was preeminent among European nations. Twenty years later this empire had collapsed. Britain had been defeated militarily by rebellious colonials, and her prestige had sunk accordingly. The stage for this remarkable denouement was North America.

In 1763, with the territories gained during the Seven Years War, the British empire in the New World was potentially vast. It consisted of eighteen colonies on the North American mainland, twelve in the West Indies, and two in South America, together with part of the Virgin Islands and the huge, unknown area of Hudson Bay. Most highly regarded were the West Indies because of their prosperous economy based on sugar and slaves. But the true center of colonial power was the string of thirteen colonies on the mainland, stretching from New Hampshire to Georgia. They had been settled steadily during successive periods from the early seventeenth century along the sea coast, extending inland for no more than fifty miles. The population increased rapidly in the eighteenth century, and by 1775 there were about 2.5 million people in the thirteen colonies. As the coastal areas filled up, settlement expanded into the "back country." The valleys in the Appalachian Mountains were settled, and by 1763 the Alleghenies had been crossed and the Ohio Valley was beginning to be opened up. Most Americans were farmers; only 10 percent of the population was engaged in nonagricultural pursuits. Nevertheless, towns grew rapidly in the eighteenth century: New York, Boston, and Charleston were comparable in size with English provincial cities. Philadelphia, with 30,000 inhabitants in 1775, was probably as large as any English city except London and Bristol. The original immigration in the seventeenth century had been mainly English. After 1713 other nationals joined them, especially Germans, Scots-Irish, and Negro slaves. Diversity of religious beliefs enjoined practical toleration, and an overall unity of life was maintained within a framework of basically English institutions. For the great majority of immigrants (apart from the slaves), America was a land of opportunity. Wages were higher, social mobility was easier, and the chances of owning land were far greater than in the Old World. Over a period of 150 years, the attitudes and assumptions of the colonists became more and more distinct from those in the Old Country. A new man—the American—began to emerge.

The economic life of the American colonies was based on the production and export of agricultural surpluses. Wheat, rice, corn (maize), indigo, tobacco, dried and pickled fish, timber, pitch, and turpentine were the main products exported, and imports consisted of manufactured goods from Britain, sugar, molasses, and rum. This extensive trade was in the hands of wealthy American merchants, whose ships traded to Britain, Spain, Portugal, and the West Indies and whose economic power dominated the main colonial cities. British policy was to control this economic activity for the benefit of the home country, and to this end the Navigation Acts, dating from 1660, established a monopoly position. Some commodities, including sugar, tobacco, rice, and naval stores, could be exported only to England or another colonial country, and only in English or colonial ships. Manufactured goods from foreign countries had to be imported via English ports. In practice, this mercantilist policy was not as oppressive as it sounds. The Acts of Trade were laxly administered for a long time, and smuggling was a highly profitable business. Colonial producers were also assured the benefits of protected markets in Britain and the empire.

Government in the colonies was in theory similarly centralized to ensure control from London, but in practice it allowed a large measure of local control of internal affairs. Each colony was headed by a governor, appointed by the Crown in the case of royal colonies (which were the majority), by the proprietor in Pennsylvania, Delaware, and Maryland, and by election in the two corporation colonies, Connecticut and Rhode Island. The governor was assisted by an appointed council, which also served as an upper house of the legislature. The lower house of the legislative body was elected. Local government was in the hands of the townships in New England and in the counties elsewhere. Although property ownership and the right to vote were more widespread than in the Old World, colonial society was far from democratic. Effective power was firmly in the hands of the wealthy merchants and planters, and their representatives occupied most of the governmental and legislative offices. Between individual colonies there were significant differences in economic interest and political and social ideology; and within each colony there were tensions and conflicts between farmers and merchants, slave holders and slaves, backcountry settlers and government in older areas. So great were the differences between the colonies that one of the founding fathers, John Adams, long afterward thought the union in 1776 was unique in the history of mankind: "Thirteen clocks were made to strike together—a perfection of mechanism which no artist had ever before effected."

The immediate cause of this rare unanimity among the thirteen colonies was British policy, although the roots of the American Revolution went much deeper. Until 1763 French power in North America, extending along the St. Lawrence River and down through the Mississippi Valley to Louisiana and New Orleans, was a constant threat to the English colonies and a check to their ambitions of westward expansion. British military protection against the French and also against the Indians was welcome. The Seven Years War, however, removed this menace, although the British government felt that it was still necessary to maintain an army of 10,000 men in North America against a possible French revival and the ever-present Indian raids on the frontier. Financially, the war had been very costly; the British national debt had risen from £70 million to £130 million in 1763. Beset with financial problems and desperate for new sources of income, it was hardly surprising that the British government, under the leadership of George Grenville, should have decided to make the Americans increase their share of taxation. It seemed not unreasonable that the colonists should contribute toward the cost of their own protection, and any policy that offered an alternative to increasing taxes at home was certain to be popular. Grenville therefore ordered that the laws of trade (long unenforced) should be tightened, the Navigation Acts enforced, and smuggling suppressed. At the same time, the colonists' westward expansion beyond the Alleghenies into Indian territory was prohibited, and Indian affairs were put under the direct control of British officials. All this was not so much a new policy as a more rigorous observance of traditional colonial and mercantilist attitudes. But the decision to tax the colonies directly by Parliament was an innovation and led ultimately to catastrophe.

The Stamp Act of 1765 extended to the colonies the English tax on legal documents, the money raised being for colonial defense. It was a direct tax, which seemed moderate and harmless enough to Grenville but which to the colonists was an act of tyranny—"taxation without representation." So great was the outcry in America that the government backed down; Grenville was replaced by another Whig prime minister, the Marquis of Rockingham, and the Stamp Act was repealed. Parliament, however, asserted its right to tax the colonies by passing a Declaratory Act, which exacerbated both the Americans and English liberals who sympathized with them. Then in 1767 the chancellor of the Exchequer, Charles Townshend, imposed a new series of revenue duties, emphasizing the need to be firm with the Americans on this issue. Opposition in the colonies burst out again, and the British government (under the leadership from 1770 of the king's protégé, Lord North) once more withdrew the offending duties—with the exception of a tax on tea which was retained to assert the principle of the Declaratory Act of 1766. By now a large number of Americans were deeply resentful and suspicious of any move by the British government; it was argued, for instance, that the withdrawal of the Townshend duties was a diabolical plan to ruin American manufacturers by flooding the market with cheap goods. The basic grievances of the colonists remained, and the fear of fresh attacks on what they had come to define as their liberties was ever present. More and more Americans were prepared to listen to the popular leaders who were vigilant for the least infringement of American rights by British officials and by the British government. Within each colony a different pattern of tension and opposition between American and British interests developed, but everywhere the direction was toward a showdown in the not very distant future.

The crisis came in 1773. It was precipitated by the decision to let the East India Company sell tea cheaply in America through its own agents instead of as usual through middlemen who bought it at public auction. This was to help the company out of its financial difficulties, for in the previous year it had been almost bankrupt. The colonists were hopeful that the tea duty would soon be repealed and were highly incensed when this was not the case. Upon hearing that the East India Company's tea was on its way, the four main ports—Boston, New York, Philadelphia, and Charleston—agreed to resist its importation. At Boston a party of extremists dressed as Indians boarded the ships and dumped the tea in the harbor. The Boston Tea Party was interpreted in Britain as a challenge that could not be ignored, and Parliament replied with punitive legislation. These "Intolerable Acts," as the colonists called them, closed the port of Boston, revised the Massachusetts charter by strengthening the governor's powers and substituting an appointed for an elected council, and made possible the quartering of troops in the town. To the surprise of many Britons, these measures did not bring the colonists to heel. Instead, the people of America drew closer together and turned their thoughts seriously toward the idea of an American union. At Philadelphia in September 1774 the delegates of the First Continental Congress met for the first time. The American Revolution (which John Adams always held was essentially "in the minds of the people") was under way.

So far there had been no fighting. But in April 1775 war broke out. General Gage, commanding the British troops in Boston, ordered the seizure of illegal military stores in Concord, and during the march the British troops were engaged in a skirmish with colonials at Lexington and then seriously harassed by them on the return journey. The "shot heard round the world" had been fired, and the American War of Independence had begun. It was not a war in which either side showed military competence of a very high order. Despite the difficulty of operating some 3,000 miles from their bases, the British army of professional soldiers (including Hessian mercenaries), small as it was, should have been more than a match for the Americans, who at first were without adequate artillery or military experience and who had to create an army from scratch. But poor generalship, niggardly support from home, and determined, skillful opposition from George Washington's patriot army nullified the initial advantages of the British forces. Lord North was totally incompetent as a war leader, with the result that the British were soon in trouble. For many months, even after fighting had begun, there was reluctance on both sides to admit the possibility of a final and irrevocable break between the colonies and the home country. English ministers hoped that loyalists would be sufficiently strong to restrain the radical leadership in at least some colonies, and time appeared to be on the side of the government: if there was no

The American colonies and the War of Independence. (J. S. Watson, *Reign of George III*, The Clarendon Press, Oxford.)

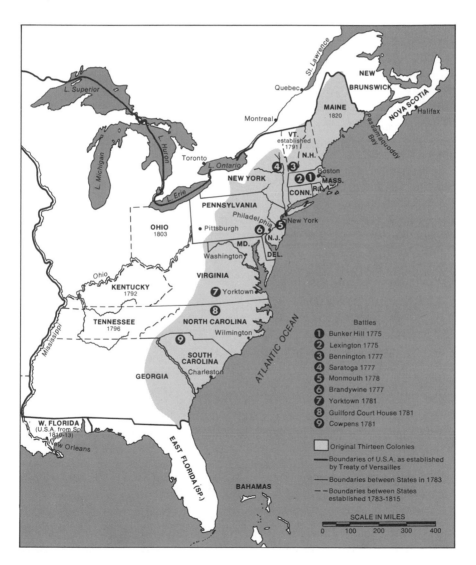

undue provocation the rebellion would perhaps peter out. The American Congress, even after it had decided to create a continental army, still dreamed of reconciliation. By the spring of 1776, however, the advocates of independence in Congress gradually got the upper hand, and public opinion was stirred by Thomas Paine's arguments in favor of separation in his pamphlet *Common Sense.* In Britain there was a hardening of attitudes, and Parliament passed a Prohibitory Act treating the Americans as enemies and outlaws. All hope of reconciliation was now gone. On July 4, 1776, Congress adopted the Declaration of Independence.

The British plan for defeating the colonists was to divide New England from the rest of the country and thus subdue each region in turn. General Burgoyne was to advance from Canada and link up with the New York army under General Howe at Albany. But communication between the two armies broke down, and as a result Burgoyne was defeated at Saratoga in October 1777 and forced to surrender with his whole army. This victory convinced the French that the Americans were in earnest about their struggle with Britain, and in the spring of 1778 the two nations signed a treaty of alliance. Before long Spain and the Netherlands also came out in support of the Americans, and the war assumed the usual eighteenth-century pattern of European rivalries. Neither at sea nor on land were the British able to make any decisive headway, and finally, in October 1781, another British army, commanded by General Cornwallis, was forced to surrender at Yorktown. This was virtually the end of the war. It was clear that no early British victory was possible, and few politicians were prepared for an indefinitely protracted struggle. Lord North was discredited and resigned in 1782, and peace was concluded with the United States. The young republic was bounded to the north by the Great Lakes and westward by the Mississippi, and shared the continent with three other powers: Britain (in Canada and Nova Scotia), France (Louisiana), and Spain (Florida and Mexico).

The loss of the American colonies was a severe jolt to British ideas of empire. Under mercantilist doctrine, the sole object of colonies was the benefit (mainly economic and commercial) that they would be to the home country. Too late came the realization that a whole new nation, and not merely a series of trading posts and plantations, had come into existence. By the time of the War of Independence the Americans were already de facto an independent people. As John Adams insisted, the American Revolution was accomplished before the Revolutionary War. To win the war, the British would have had to reconquer America and impose a strong, even tyrannous, government. And for this the Whigs did not have the stomach. Better was it to let the Americans have their own way, like children in whose maturity we cannot believe but must acknowledge. So philosophized many Englishmen in the later eighteenth century. A few, like the Earl of Shelburne, who succeeded North and concluded the peace negotiations at the Treaty of Paris in 1783, dared to believe that a free America, exploiting the resources of the interior of the continent, would be more valuable as an economic partner than as a colonial dependency; let the Americans assume the responsibility for governing the western lands while Britain exported to them her manufactures. But public opinion generally was not so forward-looking, and could not see beyond the stark facts of defeat and national humiliation—which the sooner forgotten, the better. For the time being, the idea of an empire of settlement was distinctly passé. Yet the logic of the Industrial Revolution was soon to provide the imperative for a new kind of imperialism.

An Empire Gained

Before the collapse of the first British empire in America the roots of a second had already been put down in a different part of the world. Commercial contact with the Far East had been developed by European nations, including Britain, in the seventeenth century. Discovery of new territories also opened up possibilities of trading outlets. James Cook, in a series of exploratory voyages between 1768 and 1779, discovered hitherto unknown islands in the South Seas and charted the coasts of New Zealand and eastern Australia. Later these became colonies of settlement, but in the eighteenth and early nineteenth centuries they were regarded strictly as mercantile and convict colonies. British interest in the Pacific and Indian oceans was geared primarily to support of her main asset, India.

The British involvement with India, extending over a period of two hundred years, was one of the most remarkable episodes of modern history. How a small, remote island off the coast of Europe, some four or five months distant by sailing ship, came to dominate a subcontinent of over a hundred million people of diverse races and ancient cultures is a story that invites reflection and research. The story is usually told in terms of military conquest, but of greater significance are the complex economic, social, and cultural relationships between an immensely old civilization and a Western, industrial-capitalist society. The discovery of Indian civilization (along with that of China) was part of a general appreciation of Oriental culture that revolutionized European taste in the eighteenth century. In Brighton today, the prince regent's fabulous seaside palace, the Pavilion, reminds us of this attraction to Asian architecture and decor. India presented a deadly fascination and temptation to Englishmen. They were greatly impressed by the legendary splendor of the Moghul emperors who lived in a dazzling palace at Delhi. The throne of the last of the great Moghuls, Aurangzeb, who died in 1707, was said to be "encrusted with diamonds, decorated with vine-branches made of pure gold, their leaves enamelled in natural colors, the grapes being of emerald, ruby and garnet." But thereafter Moghul power disintegrated, and one Indian vassal after another took the opportunity to assert his independence. Into this world of crumbling central authority came the Europeans, and through their greed and mutual rivalries were soon sucked into the complex of Indian affairs. The first Englishmen had gone to India to trade, but in the pursuit of this deceptively simple end their successors were tempted into politics and war with Indian princes and European rivals.

The British, unlike earlier conquerors, penetrated India from the sea. In the east they entered through the Ganges, established themselves in Bengal, and built their headquarters in the steaming swamps of Calcutta. Bombay, presented to Charles II on his marriage to a Portuguese princess, was made into a powerful center of operations in the west. Along the Coromandel Coast, Madras was founded in a key position to dominate the ancient maritime trade of the area and also to provide a base for expansion into the hinterland of the Carnatic. Challenging these positions were similar posts established by the Portuguese in Goa and by the French in Pondicherry and Chandernagore. In the 1740s the pace was set by Dupleix, the governor of Pondicherry, who sought to extend French influence in the interior by intrigues and alliances with Indian rulers. This soon led to a clash with the British, who pursued similar policies with rival local princes. India became a main theater of Anglo-French hostilities in the Seven Years War, and after Robert Clive's great victory at Plassey in 1757 French influence dwindled rapidly. By 1763 Britain was without any serious European rival in India and was in virtual control of Bengal.

The British position, however, was somewhat anomalous. In accordance with mercantilist doctrine, all trade between India and Britain was monopolized by the East India Company, and until the Mutiny of 1857 "John Company" represented the British presence in India. It was apparent by the mid-eighteenth century that the original idea of a purely trading company was inadequate. Clive had gone to India to make his fortune (which he successfully did) and became the builder of an empire. His work was continued, with greater awareness and calculation, by Warren Hastings, whose governor-generalship from 1773 to 1785 committed Britain to a thoroughgoing policy of administration, expansion, and war in India. Contemporaries were very much divided over the wisdom of such a policy, and Hastings's enemies were able to impeach him before the House of Lords, although he was acquitted after the trial had lasted for seven years. Criticism of the company was that its profits were inadequate, its officials were corrupt, and it had allowed itself to be drawn into political activities, which were no concern of a trading company. To take account of the altered role of the company, North passed a Regulating Act in 1773 and Pitt an India Act in 1784. The company was not superseded by direct government rule, but its powers were modified by a public board of control which could give orders to the directors. Appointment to offices

in India and the great perquisites of patronage remained with the company.

The original and essential nature of the British relationship with India was thus preserved, although it was increasingly curbed to some degree by reforming pressures at home. In the long run this was unfortunate, for it injected a fatal poison into Europe's contact with Asia. Despite later talk of Britain's civilizing mission and the genuine belief of Britons in India

India in 1856. (From *Modern England* by Robert K. Webb. © 1968 by Dodd, Mead & Company, Inc.)

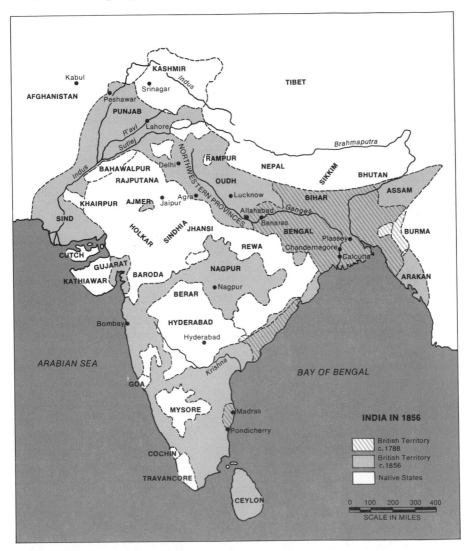

that without the British Raj the whole subcontinent would fall into a state of anarchy, the prime object of the East India Company was to make a profit for Englishmen. That India later benefited from westernization and the investment of British capital was incidental. Stripped of euphemisms and qualifications, the British encounter with India in the eighteenth century was at first an adventurous plundering and later a methodical exploitation. India had suffered and survived earlier invasions by foreigners and was to do likewise with the British conquerors. For Britain, the Indian experience was crucial in that relations with the peoples of India formed the pattern of imperial relationships with other "natives" in different parts of the world in the nineteenth century. India became the true heart of the second British empire.

Individual Englishmen who returned home, having made a fortune in India, were dubbed "nabobs." The opportunities for gaining wealth quickly were immense, although not everyone survived to enjoy his riches. Actual trading was often less lucrative than the spoils of office. The administration of justice and collection of taxes provided rich pickings. Service in the army or dabbling in local politics brought handsome rewards from Indian potentates who were thereby enabled to triumph over their rivals. Clive acquired a fortune of £234,000. Hastings on his retirement brought home £100,000, and during his service in India received £300,000 in presents from Indian rulers, which he used for company affairs. The combination of eighteenth-century English notions of spoils and patronage with Indian traditions of rewards and present-giving and methods of tax collection provided a system of self-enrichment seldom equaled before or since. It was comparatively easy to acquire, in the space of a few years, sufficient wealth to purchase an estate at home and to lead the life of a country gentleman or enter Parliament by buying a rotten borough. Such new wealth inevitably excited envy and invited questions about what was going on in India. Critics of the government questioned the morality of exploiting India and demanded searching investigations of the company and its officers. But self-interest and the new imperialism were more than a match for such doubts.

The company itself never flourished as heartily as its servants. While the administrators and soldiers feathered their own nests, caring little for the institution that employed them, the company was barely solvent and had to rely on successive loans from the government. Trade with India presented certain difficulties. Her exports to Europe were larger than her imports, which created a balance-of-payments problem. The Indian tea, cotton, and muslins could not be balanced by equivalent cargoes from England, since the main British export of woolen cloth was not wanted in a hot climate, and the Indian demand for other manufactured goods was insufficient to close the gap. Moreover, the company's trade with China encountered similar difficulties, which were partly met by exporting opium from India. This further aggravated the imbalance with India. Throughout

the eighteenth century, therefore, the imports from the Far East had to be balanced by the export of bullion, that is, gold and silver which had been earned in other parts of the world, mainly in Europe. In addition, there were "invisible" balances in the form of profits made in India by the nabobs and others, but these did not help the company's position since they were private gains of individuals. A way out of these difficulties, however, was soon forthcoming. The development of the Lancashire cotton industry radically changed the whole basis of trade with India. Manufactured cotton goods provided a new British export that undercut Indian textiles, and after 1815 a new pattern of capitalist-imperial relationships developed. The new empire became an integral part of industrial Britain.

By the early nineteenth century Anglo-Indian relationships had changed considerably from what they had been fifty years earlier. In the mid-eighteenth century the habits of the ordinary Englishman in India were tempered by respect for and curiosity about an inscrutable and ancient civilization. Feelings of moral superiority were usually absent, and Indian society was accepted as it was and in its own right. When the number of company's servants was small, they were assimilated into the population, adopting Indian dress and styles of living. Some Englishmen, in the true spirit of the Enlightenment, studied Sanskrit and admired the Brahmins as an intellectual elite. But in the later eighteenth century this attitude changed. As the number of Britons in India increased, they withdrew from social intercourse with Indians and isolated themselves in their own cantonments. Worse still, they began to despise the "natives" and to regard anything Indian as inferior. British experience in India had begun in Bengal, among a people who were fairly dark-skinned and of a mild and inoffensive nature, and this encouraged feelings of racial superiority. The African slave trade was also at its height in this period, and the British were deeply involved. It was scarcely to be expected that Englishmen in India would be free from racism. By the early nineteenth century, strengthened by evangelical morality and utilitarian reforming zeal, the ideology of imperialism was well established. The stereotypes of Indians as lazy, fraudulent, and prey to gross superstitution were created, and a new master class settled down to rule (for the natives' own good, to be sure) the "millions of Hindoostan." The cheerful, plundering greed of the early British traders in India had gone; in its place was the conviction that it was Britain's duty to bring the benefits of Western civilization to this part of the world.

The French Revolution

Western societies in the nineteenth century lived beneath the shadow of two great revolutions: the British Industrial Revolution and the French (political) Revolution. The former provided the model for revolutionizing the economy and social structure; the latter was the inspiration for political change and the ideology of liberalism, democracy, and socialism. So great was the impact of these changes in the later eighteenth and early nineteenth centuries that recent historians have referred to the period as the "age of democratic revolution" or the age of the "dual revolution." We have already noted the profound effects of the early Industrial Revolution in Britain. Somewhat less spectacular (because muted and disguised), but of far-reaching significance in Britain, were the ideas and immediate political consequences of the French Revolution.

The first response in Britain to the events of 1789 in France was generally approval. Coming so soon after the centenary celebrations of the Glorious Revolution of 1688, it was tempting for Englishmen to flatter themselves that their old rival had at last come around to imitating the institutions of British constitutionalism. The storming of the Bastille was rightly interpreted as a symbol of the end of despotism and the release of the forces of liberalism. In some circles of British society, enthusiasm for the Revolution went much further. Among intellectuals, artists, and some aristocrats and working men, the principles of the Rights of Man and the overthrow of the Bourbons were hailed as the dawn of a new age, in which a new freedom would be found. "Bliss was it in that dawn to be alive," sang the romantic poet William Wordsworth, "but to be young was very Heaven." For two years the moderate reformers in France, through the Constituent Assembly, strove to liberalize the basic economic and political institutions of the country. But the king, the nobility, and the Church were not prepared to accept drastic changes in their situation, and began to intrigue for foreign invasion to restore the old regime. This led to war, the overthrow of the monarchy, and the establishment of the Republic in 1792. The Revolution now entered a new and more extreme phase: under the pressure of war and counterrevolution the king was executed, and the Jacobins took over the Republic and established the revolutionary dictatorship of the Terror (1793–94). For another five years the regime retained its revolutionary form, but increasingly the army emerged as the single most powerful force in France, and the ablest of its leaders soon found himself at the head of the nation. Napoleon Bonaparte had little difficulty in supplanting the relatively feeble regime of the Directory (1795–99), becoming consecutively first consul, consul for life, and, finally, emperor. To many Englishmen, the French Revolution seemed more analogous to the events of 1641–59 than to 1688–89; and for such memories there was little enthusiasm. Moreover, in 1793 the French declared war on Britain, so that support for the French Revolution or its principles incurred the penalties of lack of patriotism. During the twenty-two long years of war traditional anti-French sentiment obscured the fundamental and ecumenical nature of the Revolution and diminished the strength of the Jacobin and Napoleonic myths which gripped the rest of Europe.

Nevertheless, British insularity was far from complete: both the ferment of ideas and the logic of revolutionary events made their impact in many different quarters.

Open support for the French Revolution in Britain came mainly from three groups. First, Charles James Fox led a small band of Whig followers who were prepared to defend the basic liberalism of the Revolution and to oppose the war. They were mostly young aristocrats who believed in the need for parliamentary reform and who stood to gain from an attack on Pitt, the prime minister, and his increasingly conservative administration. Older radicals, like Major John Cartwright, who had defended the American colonists, took a similar stance. Second, the British intelligentsia, like their European counterparts, sympathized with the Revolution because it marked a sharp break with tradition and seemed to embody the best elements of the Enlightenment. Poets (William Wordsworth, Samuel Taylor Coleridge, William Blake, Robert Burns), scientists (Joseph Priestley), engineers (Thomas Telford), and Unitarians (Richard Price) welcomed the events of 1789. Leading sympathizers like Jeremy Bentham and James Mackintosh (who wrote a book in defense of the Revolution) were made honorary French citizens. Not until the rallying of intellectuals to the cause of the Spanish Republic in 1936–39 was there a comparable response to this widespread support for the principles of revolution among young, educated, and talented people in Britain.

The third group of supporters of the French Revolution was found among radical working men. Throughout the kingdom small radical clubs of artisans and petty tradesmen were formed to spread Jacobin principles and agitate for parliamentary reform. The London Corresponding Society, started by Thomas Hardy, a shoemaker, in 1792, acted as a center of the movement. Although the societies attracted only a tiny minority of laboring men, they are significant as the first independent political organization of that class. Certainly the government took them very seriously. In 1793 Scottish reformers who had attended a British convention of the Delegates of the People were punished with harsh sentences of transportation, and the following year Hardy and the London leaders were prosecuted for high treason, but acquitted. Repressive legislation against the radicals was passed (habeas corpus was suspended in 1790 and again in 1794), and Jacobinism was crushed or driven underground.

The members of the Corresponding Societies found a powerful propaganda instrument in Thomas Paine's *Rights of Man*. This was the text most studied in their meetings, and it remained (in innumerable cheap editions) the staple intellectual diet of working-men radicals for the next fifty years. It was published in 1791–92 as a reply to Edmund Burke's *Reflections on the Revolution in France* (1790), which brilliantly denounced revolutionary change. These two works neatly portray the polarization of ideas about the French Revolution: each was enormously successful and provided an intellectual foundation for an important strand in the British political tradition. But at the time their fates seemed grossly unequal. The *Rights of Man* was condemned as seditious libel, and its author had to flee to France. Burke's *Reflections* was approved in the highest circles ("a good book, a very good book; every gentleman ought to read it," said the king), and Burke himself joined the younger Pitt's administration, which became the ancestor of the nineteenth-century Tory party. Burke's insistence that society was essentially "organic" (growing and living like a plant, rooted in time and place) provided the basis for a modern conservative political philosophy. From Paine came basic notions of equality and social rights that inspired democratic reformers throughout the nineteenth century.

Disenchantment with the French Revolution set in early among some of its British supporters and became more widespread after the execution of the king and the beginning of the Terror. But its wider effects, notably in the arts and in the tone of intellectual life, remained. Quite simply, the Revolution was an enormous repudiation of the aristocratic, ordered, classical world of the eighteenth century, and for all who lived through it life could never be quite the same as it was before 1789. In this respect, the Revolution reinforced that complex of changes in sensibility known as the romantic movement—although, paradoxically, romanticism worked on both sides of the great debate and is equally present in Burke's hostility and Wordsworth's early enthusiasm. Romanticism was a quest for the inner nature of man himself. It sought to get below the classical, rationalistic conventions of the time and to uncover man's true, "natural" self. Such a repudiation of the supremacy of reason led to a new approach in politics (witness Burke) and in the arts and literature. A taste for medievalism, and especially for gothic architecture, developed. Gentlemen carefully constructed ruins to improve the landscape of their estates, and a new appreciation of wild and mountainous scenery (the Lake District and Scotland) was cultivated. At a popular level, the novels, tales, and poems of Sir Walter Scott enthralled two generations of readers with descriptions of medieval barbarism and Scottish lore. The emphasis in literature and painting was on feeling and imagination and away from the artificial forms and conventions of the eighteenth century. In their *Lyrical Ballads* (1798), Wordsworth and Coleridge proclaimed the new doctrines, exemplified in poems written in everyday language and about everyday themes:

> One impulse from a vernal wood
> May teach you more of man,
> Of moral evil and of good,
> Than all the sages can.

> Sweet is the lore which nature brings;
> Our meddling intellect
> Misshapes the beauteous forms of things;
> —We murder to dissect.

Enough of Science and of Art;
Close up these barren leaves;
Come forth, and bring with you a heart
That watches and receives.

From *The Tables Turned,* William Wordsworth

From 1793 the ideological and long-term effects of the Revolution were complicated by war with France. William Pitt (son of the Earl of Chatham) and his administration had no more love for the Revolution than had other established governments in Europe. Yet the extended, bitter, and total nature of the conflict cannot be explained solely, or even primarily, by British dislike of revolutionary principles. At the root of the struggle was the continuing Anglo-French commercial rivalry. Britain was prepared to go to almost any lengths to defeat her chief competitor and to secure worldwide dominance of markets and indisputable control of imperial trading routes. In Europe this policy meant preventing the dominance of the Continent by any one power. When France moved into the Netherlands, Pitt reacted in the traditional British way by sending troops and supplies to Holland. For the next twenty-two years Britain sought to organize the "Allies"—Prussia, Russia, Austria, Holland, Spain, and any other country that could be persuaded to join—in coalitions against France. It was the British hope that with the aid of monetary subsidies the Allies would be able to contain France, while England took care of the naval side of the war and acquired additional colonies. But since each of these states had separate interests in relation to France and to each other, the coalitions were unstable and easily upset by French military victories. The old-style, professional armies of the Allies were no match for the mobile, courageous French conscripts, especially after 1796 under the superb leadership of Napoleon. With only minor exceptions, the war on land was until 1812 a series of great French victories.

At sea, however, the record was very different. The British navy, which had been allowed to decline in strength after the ending of the American War of Independence, was rapidly built up again. The qualities that made the French armies so formidable were less decisive in naval warfare, where qualified officers and trained seamen could not be quickly produced, with the result that the French navy was inferior in size and quality to the British. Destruction of the French fleet—and also of the Spanish and Dutch when they deserted the Allied cause—was accomplished by successive naval battles, culminating in the battle of Trafalgar in 1805. The war at this stage had reached a stalemate, with the French victorious on land and the British at sea. It was (as has often been remarked) rather like a struggle between an elephant and a whale. To try to break the deadlock, Napoleon turned to large-scale economic warfare, using the weapon of the blockade. His "Continental System" closed the ports of

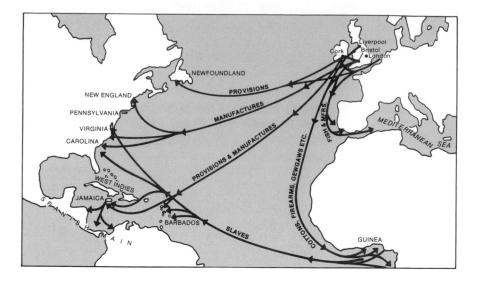

Trade patterns in the first half of the eighteenth century: (1) Exports from Great Britain. (M. W. Flinn, *An Economic & Social History of Britain Since 1700*, St. Martin's Press, Inc., Macmillan & Co., Ltd.)

Europe to all ships trading with Britain or her colonies. The British retaliated with "orders in council," which banned all sea-borne trade between France and other enemy countries and required neutrals to ship their goods to the enemy only via British ports. Although these measures caused considerable economic distress in Britain, they were in no sense decisive, and to make the Continental System more effective Napoleon invaded Portugal and Spain. England then sent an army under the Duke of Wellington to fight in the Iberian Peninsula—where it remained until the end of the war. More serious from Napoleon's point of view was his disastrous invasion of Russia—also to enforce his Continental System—in 1812, which resulted in defeat and the loss of most of his Grand Army. Heartened by French reverses, the Allies rallied in their fourth and final coalition. Wellington advanced from Spain into southwest France and the other Allies invaded from the east. In March 1814 Paris was captured, and Napoleon was sent into exile. A year later he escaped from the island of Elba, rallied an army around himself, and for a hundred days was once more Emperor of France. But he was defeated at Waterloo in June 1815 by the combined armies of Prussia (under General Blücher) and Britain (led by Wellington), and thereafter he was banished to the remote island of St. Helena in the southern Atlantic. At the Congress of Vienna, where the Allies decided on the terms of peace, Britain secured her main objectives: a balance of power in Europe, security and independence for the Netherlands, and colonial gains in Malta, the West Indies, the Cape of Good Hope (South Africa), Mauritius, and Ceylon.

Although victory was finally achieved in 1815, it had been a long time coming. And at times defeat had seemed very near. Even the battle of Waterloo was described by Wellington as "the nearest run thing you ever

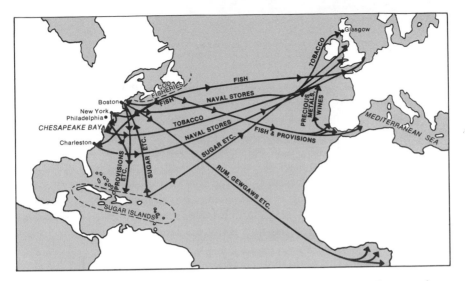

Trade patterns in the first half of the eighteenth century: (2) Imports from the British colonies. M. W. Flinn, *An Economic & Social History of Britain Since 1700*, St. Martin's Press, Inc., Macmillan & Co., Ltd.)

saw in your life." The war had cost Britain many privations, and it raised patriotic feeling to new heights. For a "nation of shopkeepers," as Napoleon had dubbed England, it was an unprecedented military experience. The army had grown to 350,000 men—small by French standards, but huge to a noncontinental power. The navy in 1801 had over 130,000 men, with 202 ships of the line and 277 frigates. To this day, the heroes of the Napoleonic Wars are household names in Britain. Nelson, killed at Trafalgar in 1805 and commemorated in the central square of London, is the popular symbol of British naval power. The Duke of Wellington, the victor of Waterloo, was revered for the rest of his life as the savior of the nation and finally given a huge and splendid state funeral in 1852. Contrary to the national mythology, however, it was not the prowess of British arms that had enabled the nation to survive and ultimately triumph but her great economic strength and her mastery of the seas. British naval supremacy was not based on technical superiority nor on the high morale of the ordinary seamen (who mutinied at the Nore and Spithead in 1797), but rather on the great numbers of ships and well-qualified officers, backed up by a tradition that accorded the admiralty priority in the national counsels. With this protection, British overseas trade continued to expand, although the Continental System and the orders in council caused serious interruption. Supplying the Allies with clothing, armaments, and money both stimulated and strained the British economy. The cost of the war was paid partly by taxes and partly by borrowing. As a result, the national debt rose from £228 million in 1793 to £876 million in 1815. Underlying the sustained war effort was the massive economic growth of the Industrial Revolution.

In order to defeat England, it seems probable that France would have had to invade her. Napoleon made plans for such an invasion in 1804–05, but the strength of the British navy (and particularly the battle of Trafalgar) frustrated his designs. An earlier attempt, however, in 1798 might well have been successful had the weaknesses of the British position been skillfully exploited. Ireland was Britain's Achilles' heel, and pro-French sentiment among sections of the Irish people guaranteed sympathetic support for a French revolutionary army that promised to liberate Ireland from the English yoke. In 1797–98, when the first coalition of Allies had fallen apart and England was standing alone against France, this danger seemed very real. Not for the first time, England's difficulty was Ireland's opportunity.

Throughout the eighteenth century, Ireland's relationship to Britain was basically colonial. Mercantilist principles were applied to the Irish just as they were to the American coloni .s, thus prohibiting the development of native industry and restricting Irish trade. The land was largely owned by Englishmen or Anglo-Irish Protestants, and rents were paid to absentee landlords. Wool and beef were exported, while the peasantry lived increasingly on potatoes which they grew on their small holdings. Although the majority of the people were Roman Catholics, the established church was Anglican; and, as in Britain, Catholics were excluded from all part in government. Ireland was dominated economically and politically by a small Protestant elite, known as the "Ascendancy." From the time of the Reformation, the British viewed Ireland with suspicion, and repeated Irish rebellions had been put down harshly. There was, therefore, a backlog of grievances on the one side, and the fear of Catholic revolt on the other. The "problem" of Ireland was unresolved—as it had been for many generations. But the successful revolt of the Americans was a lesson that the Irish were quick to learn, and they used it to extract concessions from Britain. While troops were withdrawn from Ireland to fight in America, the Irish organized a volunteer army, ostensibly to repel any attack by the French, but also very useful in backing demands for self-government. The British government relaxed the commercial restrictions, and in 1783 the Irish Parliament became independent. Concessions were made to the Catholics, who from 1793 were enfranchised if they were forty-shilling freeholders (those who owned land assessed for taxation purposes at an annual value of at least forty shillings) and allowed to hold minor offices, but they could not sit in Parliament or hold major offices. Within the framework of British eighteenth-century politics, these concessions were fairly liberal. They did not, however, go far enough to satisfy Irish demands for full independence from the subordinating policies of Whitehall and the Ascendancy.

The French Revolution provided a second opportunity for Ireland to make a bid for freedom. Beginning in Protestant Ulster in 1791, the Society of United Irishmen soon spread to the Catholic South and also made contact with radicals in England. A scheme for an Irish Republic on the French model was concocted, and under the leadership of young middle-class and aristocratic patriots an insurrection was planned. The rising was to be concerted with a French invasion, and mass support was expected from the peasantry. The ideological pedigree of the United Irishmen was made plain in their catechism:

Question: What have you got in your hand?
Answer: A green bough.
Question: Where did it first grow?
Answer: In America.
Question: Where did it bud?
Answer: In France.
Question: Where are you going to plant it?
Answer: In the Crown of Great Britain.

Unfortunately for the revolutionaries, their ranks were infiltrated by government agents, with the result that the Dublin leaders were all arrested before the rising. The country leaders nevertheless went ahead with their plans, and in May 1798 a hundred thousand peasants rose in revolt. By the time they had been crushed four months later, 25,000 were dead, villages and towns were in ruins, and the struggle for revolutionary independence had become a ferocious war between Catholics and Protestants. The promised French aid arrived too late, and the small expeditionary force, after proclaiming the Republic of Connaught, surrendered to the British forces in September. Reprisals followed: the leaders were hanged, prisoners were transported as convicts to Botany Bay (Australia) or forced to join the British army and navy, and in the villages old scores were paid in blood. The rebellion convinced Pitt and the British government that the existing arrangements in Ireland should not be allowed to continue. In 1800 the Irish Parliament was therefore abolished, and on the model of the successful union with Scotland in 1707 the Irish members were incorporated into the central Parliament at Westminster. From January 1, 1801, they were part of the United Kingdom of Great Britain and Ireland.

CHAPTER FOUR

Englishmen in the first half of the nineteenth century were conscious above all else of living in a time of unprecedented change. The combined impact of the Industrial Revolution, the French Revolution, and the Napoleonic Wars had shaken British society profoundly. In the following years (1815–48) the pace of change quickened still further. All reflective commentators of the time agreed that in many areas of the national life the tight grip of tradition had been largely broken and that "ancient wisdom" in matters of belief, values, and social relationships was being increasingly questioned. Progress, improvement, reform—these were the slogans of the age. They all implied change; and change meant that the equilibrium of society was to a greater or lesser extent upset. Today most advanced Western societies have developed approved patterns of change and innovation, although they have not been able to eliminate strains and conflicts entirely. In Regency and early Victorian Britain the strains and tensions of adjustment were very great, and the fear of a complete breakdown resulting in revolution haunted contemporaries. We shall examine four main aspects of this process of change in more detail.

The Forces of Change:
1815-1848

Reform

To an older generation of historians, the years 1815–48 were the Age of Reform, meaning basically political reform, centering on the Great Reform Bill of 1832. During these years the framework of English government was altered to accord with the shifting bases of economic and social power. Slowly, and after long delay, the political institutions of the country reacted to social change. Pressure to bring this about was mobilized under the banner of reform.

Today the need for political reform before 1832 seems to us so obvious that we have difficulty in understanding why it was not effected earlier. We have come to accept the assumptions and attitudes of modern Western representative democracy so completely that we unconsciously think of it as the norm—although, in fact, only a tiny fraction of the world's population has ever lived under this type of government. In many ways, the oligarchic system, or the earlier Tudor and Stuart monarchy, is closer to the governmental experience of a majority of the people in the world today. Most Englishmen in 1832 did not share our political expectations, nor did they think of democracy as their descendants were to do later in the century. The Reform Act of 1832 was not passed because the British people and their leaders had become convinced that democracy was a "good thing," but because of the practical need to modify the old system in several ways if government was to be even moderately efficient and acceptable to important sections of the nation.

The reformers concentrated their efforts in the first instance on one part only of the constitution, the House of Commons. This, they argued, was in need of reform on three main counts: the unrepresentative nature of the constituencies, the defective franchise, and the corrupt electoral methods. The defects and abuses of the system stemmed mainly from the retention of institutions and practices that were completely out-of-date. "England," observed the great French historian, Elie Halévy, "was a museum of constitutional archaeology where the relics of past ages accumulated."[1]

The rationale behind this illogical and archaic political system was that Parliament should represent the various "interests" of the country: landed property, trade and industry, banking, the Church, the professions, the colonies. This representation was secured, in a rough-and-ready manner, by the variety of franchises and "pocket" (nomination) boroughs. Until the end of the eighteenth century there was perhaps some plausibility in this argument; but it became increasingly unacceptable as new and powerful "interests" appeared that were either not represented at all or not represented as strongly as they felt they should be. The new middle classes, the working classes, and the whole world of northern and Midlands industry were by 1830 impatient with their virtual exclusion from political power under the old system. They were prepared to press hard for their demands.

The demand for political reform, far from being new, had begun fifty years earlier. In the 1780s, under the stimulus of the American Revolution, radical reformers had put forward a program calling for equalization of constituencies, annual elections, universal male suffrage, registration of electors, secret ballot, payment of M.P.s, and abolition of the property qualification for membership of the Commons. Extraparliamentary pressure for reform was organized through John Wilkes's Society for the Defense of the Bill of Rights (founded in 1769), the Society for Constitutional Information (led by Major John Cartwright and John Horne Tooke), and the Rev. Christopher Wyvill's Yorkshire Association. In the House of Commons Pitt proposed a measure of reform in 1783 and again in 1785 but was defeated. Very soon, however, the political climate in which reform could be considered was drastically altered by the impact of the French

---

[1] For details of the parliamentary system, see pp. 8–10.

Revolution. The first reaction was to encourage radical and reforming hopes. A Society of the Friends of the People was formed in 1792 by a group of Whig reformers, and Corresponding Societies were established by radical artisans in London and the provinces. Throughout 1792 and 1793 the radical ferment grew. Then, following the execution of Louis XVI and the declaration of war against France, the reform movement lost way. The government, already alarmed by the specter of English Jacobinism, clamped down on the radicals; and by 1800 this repressive policy had driven reform underground. The first phase of the movement for parliamentary reform had come to an end; but the combination of forces which would ultimately carry the day—Whig aristocrats, middle-class radicals, and working-class reformers—was already identifiable.

The second phase of reform agitation, from 1816 to 1822, was closely associated with the economic distress that followed the ending of the war with France. Working-class radicalism during these years was extraordinarily complex and was not confined to peaceful demands for political reform. Luddism, a machine-breaking movement that had appeared in the northern and Midlands textile areas in 1811–13, broke out again in 1816–17. At the end of 1816 a mass meeting at Spa Fields in London turned into a riot, and the following month an attempt was made on the life of the prince regent. The year 1817 also saw the march of the Blanketeers—unemployed weavers who set out from Manchester for London; and in Derbyshire at Pentridge there was an attempt at armed insurrection. The response of the Tory government was repression: suspension of habeas corpus (1817), trials for blasphemy and sedition, imprisonment and execution of the leaders. Spies and agents provocateurs infiltrated the radical movement, and a general air of panic spread throughout the God-fearing and propertied classes. The campaign for parliamentary reform was carried on through Hampden clubs (initiated by the veteran radical, Major Cartwright), mass demonstrations addressed by Henry (Orator) Hunt and other popular heroes, and a flourishing radical press inspired by the success of Cobbett's *Political Register*. Throughout the country this activity accelerated, reaching a climax at Peterloo in 1819.

The massacre at what was derisively dubbed "Peterloo" took place in St. Peter's Fields, Manchester, on August 16. It had been intended as a massive culmination of the northern reform campaign and as a follow-up to similar meetings at Birmingham and elsewhere. When some 60,000 men and women had peaceably assembled and were about to listen to Orator Hunt, the magistrates ordered the yeomanry (local, part-time cavalry) to arrest the speaker, and in their efforts to do so the yeomanry set about the crowd with their swords. In the panic that ensued 11 people were killed and some 400 wounded. The outcry from liberals and reformers of every shade was immediate; the government equally promptly congratulated the magistrates and within a matter of weeks rushed through the notorious

Six Acts, aimed at curbing radical journals and meetings as well as the danger of armed insurrection. Sentiment on the reform issue was now sharply polarized. The Tory government, the local upholders of law and order and men of property in general, became fearful of any mass action by the "lower orders" and were in no mood to contemplate liberal changes in the political system. The radical reformers on their part felt that they were living through the blackest and most reactionary period of English history. In his sonnet *England in 1819*, the young radical poet Percy Bysshe Shelley captured their mood of shock and outrage:

> An old, mad, blind, despised, and dying king, —
> Princes, the dregs of their dull race, who flow
> Through public scorn —mud from a muddy spring, —
> Rulers who neither see, nor feel, nor know,
> But leech-like to their fainting country cling,
> Till they drop, blind in blood, without a blow, —
> A people starved and stabbed in the untilled field, —
> An army, which liberticide and prey
> Makes as a two-edged sword to all who wield, —
> Golden and sanguine laws which tempt and slay;
> Religion Christless, Godless—a book sealed;
> A Senate, —Time's worst statute unrepealed, —
> Are graves, from which a glorious Phantom may
> Burst, to illumine our tempestuous day.

With an improvement in economic conditions in 1820, the ferment for reform declined. A plot to murder the members of the cabinet (the Cato Street Conspiracy) was exposed in 1820; it was perhaps a last fling of the insurrectionary Jacobinism of the 1790s. But although the momentum of the political reform movement slowed down in the 1820s, the memories of recent struggles, especially Peterloo, remained. When the movement entered its third and final phase, it did so with renewed determination born of past organizational experience and with a consciousness of belonging to a great radical tradition.

The dynamics of the third phase, from 1830 to 1832, were different from earlier stages of the reform struggle in important respects. Essentially, the Reform Bill of 1832 was a party measure, carried by one section of the ruling elite, the Whigs, against the other, the Tories, amid a great popular agitation throughout the country. The extraparliamentary agitation was fierce and more widespread than ever before, but in addition battle was now joined in earnest in Parliament. Reform was made the central issue between the contending political parties once the long period of Tory dominance was ended. For almost fifty years before 1830 the Tories had formed the government, and their home policy—at best conservative and at the worst repressive—was opposed to any significant parliamentary reform. The prime minister from 1812 to 1827 was Lord Liverpool, a man of long political experience (he had held office since 1793) but modest intellectual endowment. He was largely overshadowed by his colleagues, three of whom became notorious for their ultraconservatism and implacable opposition to liberal measures: Lord Eldon, the lord chancellor; Viscount Castlereagh, the foreign secretary; and Viscount Sidmouth, the home secretary. In the 1820s Liverpool "liberalized" his government somewhat by bringing in able and more moderate men, notably Robert Peel (son of a rich cotton manufacturer from Lancashire) as home secretary, George Canning at the foreign office, and William Huskisson as president of the Board of Trade. They began to modify the tone of the old Toryism by demonstrating that the administration was not averse to moderate change or judicious "improvement." Canning's foreign policy pleased liberals: he disengaged Britain from any involvement with the reactionary rulers of Russia, Prussia, and Austria and skillfully promoted British interests by a liberal policy of supporting the independence of Portugal, Greece, and the Spanish colonies in South America. Peel carried out a major reorganization of the criminal law (including the abolition of the death penalty for nearly 300 offenses), and in 1829 went on to establish the Metropolitan Police Force—thereby giving London, and later the rest of the country, the first modern, professional police force, whose members were promptly nicknamed "peelers," "bobbies," and (somewhat less affectionately) "blue bottles." Huskisson, like his predecessor at the Board of Trade, Frederick Robinson, moved the government in the general direction of free trade, in accordance with the teachings of contemporary political economists and to the alarm of the agricultural interest and the die-hard members of his party.

These liberalizing tendencies weakened the unity of the Tories, but the issue on which they finally split was Catholic emancipation. Although in practice Roman Catholics were allowed to worship as they pleased and in their everyday doings were treated more or less like anyone else, they were legally barred from holding office, including membership in Parliament. Ever since Pitt had resigned in 1801 because the king refused to grant Catholic emancipation as part of the implementation of the Act of Union with Ireland, the Catholic question had been a major political issue. It raised the thorny question of the relation between the Church of England and the state; it aroused ancient Protestant fears and prejudices; and it involved a complex of problems in Ireland, which was the only part of the British Isles where the majority of the population belonged to the Roman Catholic faith. Emancipationist agitation in Ireland and successive motions in the Commons kept the question continually to the fore in the 1820s. Liverpool tried to avoid taking any action on the matter—and he succeeded up to the time when he suffered a stroke and had to resign in 1827. Had he continued in office he would almost certainly have had to abandon his neutrality. As it was, his successor was faced immediately with the need to persuade the king that emancipation could no longer be put off.

After Liverpool's resignation, the king invited first Canning (who died in August 1827) and then Robinson (now Viscount Goderich) to form a government. But the Tories were so divided that Goderich could not continue. And so the Duke of Wellington agreed to become prime minister. The duke was not a great politician (he thought too much in military terms), but he enjoyed immense prestige as the victor of Waterloo and the savior of his country. He was completely and solidly Tory in an old-fashioned way, and his cabinet reflected a similar determination to defend the old order. Ironically, they soon found themselves the unwilling instruments of a constitutional revolution. In February 1828 Lord John Russell, a leading Whig, introduced a motion in the Commons for the repeal of the Test and Corporation Acts which had been passed in Charles II's reign to prevent Dissenters and Catholics from holding office. The motion was carried, and although it made little difference in practice, since Dissenters had been able to circumvent most of their legal disabilities, it was an ominous precedent. Two months later Sir Francis Burdett, a radical, once again proposed Catholic emancipation, and this time it was carried in the Commons, although the Lords rejected it. Wellington opposed emancipation and tried to delay the matter. But the threatening state of Ireland forced him and his henchman, Peel, to give up their opposition. After several months of negotiation Wellington persuaded the king and a sufficient number of the Tories that emancipation was inevitable; in April 1829 the measure was enacted. But the ultra-Tories voted against it, and the Tory party was now deeply divided.

Once Catholic emancipation was out of the way, political reform became the burning issue of the day. Wellington and most of the Tories hated reform even more than emancipation and were emotionally incapable of responding to the mood of the country, which from 1830 was strongly in favor of a change. The Whigs, as the traditional party of reform, would at last have their chance. They were nearly as divided as the Tories, however, and were not agreed on the details of any scheme for reform. Moreover, the central core of Whiggery was impeccably aristocratic and was based on the power of great landed magnates. Their supporters were the commercial interests of the City of London, the Dissenters, and many of the new industrial middle classes from the North. This was hardly a revolutionary mixture, but the Whigs as a whole were prepared for a moderate degree of change—which was sufficient to mark them off from the Tories.

The return of the Whigs to power was precipitated by two events in the summer of 1830: the death of George IV on June 26 and the July revolution in France. The king's death necessitated an election, as Parliament was automatically dissolved, and reform was made the central issue in the contest. The fall of Charles X of France and his replacement by the "bourgeois king," Louis Philippe, served to strengthen the conviction of British liberals that reactionary governments could be defeated, if only "the people" were sufficiently determined. Far from responding to the national mood with a moderate reform proposal, Wellington declared in November 1830 that he did not believe the representative system could be improved, and that in fact the present arrangements were well nigh perfect. A storm of protest burst from the country at this provocative speech, and the government was defeated in the Commons. Wellington then resigned, and the king invited Lord Grey, the leader of the Whigs, to form a ministry.

The new government was pledged to parliamentary reform and included some Tories who had voted against Wellington, as well as the dominant Whig groups. Grey's cabinet was extremely aristocratic: ten of its fourteen members sat in the House of Lords and all but one owned large estates. They favored reform as the wisest policy to maintain their own political and social leadership. Democracy appealed to them no more than it did to the Tories, and they were firmly convinced that property should remain the basis of political power. But unlike the Tories, the Whigs saw the need to bring the middle classes within the political system, to attach them to the constitution, lest they should be forced into an alliance with the working classes. Thomas Babington Macaulay, the Whig historian and politician, urged the House of Commons, "Reform, that you may preserve." Grey intended reform to be a practical remedy for felt grievances, especially those of the wealthy, respectable middle classes. Some Whigs, such as Lord Durham and Henry Brougham, were prepared to go further than Grey in the extent of reform, and a small group of radicals pressed for the full slate of popular, democratic demands.

In the country at large the demand for reform swelled mightily after 1830 and provided a continuous background to the debates and maneuverings of the politicians at Westminster. The reformers in the provinces were more radical than the basically conservative Whigs in Parliament, and the effect of the extraparliamentary agitation was to apply pressure that encouraged or alarmed the various groups in the Commons. Middle-class radical reformers were organized in a series of political unions, modeled on the successful Birmingham Political Union established by Thomas Attwood late in 1829. Working-class radical organizations were revived in the North, but were suspicious of the middle-class reformers whom they distrusted as mere "Whigs." In London the National Union of the Working Classes was founded in the midst of the struggle (April 1831) to demand universal suffrage and much more thoroughgoing reform than the Whigs promised. Throughout the country meetings, demonstrations, marches, and petitions became the order of the day. Memories of Peterloo and past struggles for reform were revived. William Cobbett thundered away every week in his *Political Register*; and his acquittal on a charge of inciting the agricultural laborers to riot in the fall of 1830 was interpreted as a triumph for the radical reformers.

It was, therefore, amidst great excitement that Lord John Russell introduced the Whigs' reform bill in the House of Commons on March 1, 1831. The bill, although modest by radical standards, was more drastic than the house had expected. After passing on the second reading by one vote, it was defeated by the Tories in committee, and Grey persuaded the king to dissolve Parliament and let the question of reform go to the country at a general election. The Whigs were again returned to office, and Russell introduced a new reform bill in June, which was passed by the Commons but defeated in the House of Lords. Immediately a great outcry came from all over the country at this defiance by the Lords. Riots broke out in Nottingham (where the castle was burned down), Derby, Worcester, Bath, and (most severely) Bristol. In December Russell tried again, and the Whigs' third reform bill was defeated on a minor point in the Lords. Grey then asked the king to create fifty new peers to overcome the Tory opposition in the Lords, and when this was refused Grey and his ministers resigned. Wellington tried to form an antireform government but failed, and within a week Grey was back in office, with an assurance that enough new peers would be created to pass the bill. In June 1832 the Whigs' final reform bill passed both houses and received the royal assent. The reformers had won what they said was their minimum demand: "the bill, the whole bill, and nothing but the bill." The great news of its passing was celebrated with banquets, bonfires, and the ringing of church bells: Grey and the Whigs were the heroes of the hour.

When the excitement had subsided, however, it was apparent that something less than a revolution had been achieved. The Whigs had steered a course between the Tory opposition to any changes and the radical program of thoroughgoing democratic reform. The result was seen in the new electoral system. As regards the franchise, the old distinction between counties and boroughs was retained. In the counties the forty-shilling freeholders continued to vote, but to them were added tenants who paid at least £50 per annum in rent. This provision (the Chandos Clause) was an amendment carried by the Tories and designed to strengthen landlord influence in the counties, since the new voters would be tenant farmers dependent on (mostly Tory) landlords. In the boroughs a new basic qualification for voting was introduced: occupation of premises of an annual value of £10. The enfranchisement of the £10 householders was the Whigs' solution to a dilemma: how to extend the voting qualification to include sufficient numbers of the middle classes to ensure adequate support for the Whig cause, without at the same time widening the suffrage until it introduced the dangers of democracy. In practice, the £10 qualification worked unevenly in different parts of the country. Where rents were low, as in

Leeds, few working men had the vote; but where rents were higher, as in Manchester and London, some respectable working-class householders were enfranchised. "Ancient right" voters (that is, those who had the vote before 1832) were allowed to continue to vote provided they remained resident in their old borough. In general, the new dispensation brought into the electoral system the tenant farmers in the counties, and held the line at the level of the lower middle and some respectable working classes in the towns.

The most fiercely contested part of the Whigs' reform bill was not the extension of the franchise but the redistribution of seats. To the Tories, the disenfranchisement of the close boroughs was an intolerable interference with property rights; it was, they argued, simply robbery. But the bill as passed swept away these old Tory strongholds and gave the franchise to new towns which became centers of Whig-liberal power. In all, fifty-six boroughs lost their representation in Parliament completely, and a further thirty were reduced to returning one member instead of two. Most of these boroughs were in agricultural areas and in the South and West. In their place twenty-two towns were newly enfranchised to return two members: these were large urban areas like Manchester, Leeds, and Birmingham. And another twenty boroughs were given one member each.

The overall effect of the Reform Bill was to increase the number of voters by about 50 percent: it added some 217,000 to an electorate of 435,000 in England and Wales. But 650,000 electors in a population of 14 million were a small minority. Most Englishmen, and all English women, were still without the vote, and were to remain so until very much later. A complex system of registration, the continuance of open (that is, non-secret) voting, the survival of some "pocket" boroughs in which family influence was dominant, and the strengthening of aristocratic control in the counties—all served to mitigate the impact of the changes. The Reform Bill proved to be, in many respects, a symbol rather than a substantive change. Not until the later years of the century were the bases of political power significantly altered. But reform as an idea had triumphed. Its opponents (the Duke of Wellington and the Tories) were discredited, and the initiative was now with the moderate reformers. It strengthened the belief in the possibility and desirability of change. If Old Corruption (as Cobbett called the political power structure) could be successfully attacked, there was hope that other traditional institutions could be abolished or greatly modified. The Tories warned that reform would open the floodgates to many other forms of change. They were right, although not in the catastrophic sense they feared.

Indeed, the first Parliament elected under the new franchises looked little different from its predecessors. When it met in 1833 the landed interest was strongly represented, and 217 M.P.s were sons of peers or baronets. The House of Commons was certainly not flooded with tradesmen and

Dissenters, as the Tories had prognosticated. Nevertheless, the Whigs were firmly entrenched and remained so until 1841. The impetus to reform was by no means spent, and the 1830s were occupied with a backlog of legislative amendments and innovations from the pre-1830 period. A drastic New Poor Law in 1834 (of which we shall hear more later) was followed in 1835 by the Municipal Corporations Act, which extended to local government the principles of the 1832 Reform Bill. Lord Melbourne, the Whig prime minister who succeeded Grey in 1834, was not an enthusiast for reform. But he was propelled forward by more convinced reformers among the Whigs, like Lord John Russell, and by the small but vocal group of Radicals who espoused the gospel of "improvement."

However, the most impressive politician of the 1830s and 1840s was not a Whig but a Tory, Sir Robert Peel. First in opposition, and then after 1841 as prime minister, Peel tried to guide the various refractory Tory groups to an acceptance of the realities of political life in an industrial age. A deeply conservative and cautious man, he strove to move the old Toryism a few steps along the road that ultimately led to modern Conservatism. After 1841 he continued the policy of piecemeal reform that the Whigs had begun; but in 1846 his increasing difficulties in persuading the aristocratic members of his party to support him came to a head. The issue was the Corn Laws. In 1815 a law was passed forbidding the import of foreign corn (meaning wheat) until the price on the home market reached the high figure of 80s. a quarter; the system was modified in 1822 and 1828 by a sliding scale that varied the duty on imported corn according to the home price. The object of the Corn Laws was to protect the agricultural interest against foreign competition, but at the expense of the consumer who had to pay higher prices. From 1815 to 1846 the Corn Laws were a major political issue, with the Tories supporting the protectionist agricultural interest and the Whigs and radicals arguing for free trade in the interests of industry and cheaper food. The abolition of the Corn Laws became the objective of a powerful middle-class organization, the Anti-Corn Law League, founded in 1838. Peel, as a good Tory, had originally favored the Corn Laws, but between 1842 and 1845 he gradually changed his opinion and became more and more a free trader. Then in 1845, after a particularly wet summer, the potato crop failed in Ireland and the Irish were faced with famine. To ease the situation, Peel brought in a bill to repeal the Corn Laws in 1846. He was successful, but only at the cost of splitting his party. The protectionist Tories regarded Peel as a traitor, and so they voted with the Whigs to defeat him on the issue of an Irish coercion bill. In June 1846 he therefore resigned, and Russell and the Whigs took office.

The repeal of the Corn Laws was a middle-class victory and a logical working-out of the principles of reform, although Peel saw it not as a class or party measure but simply as his "public duty." Throughout his career Peel repeatedly found himself in the position of a reluctant agent of changes that he had previously feared and opposed. The Tory party as a whole refused to follow him, and his supporters (the Peelites) lost their unity after his death in 1850. English politics then entered a confused era of coalitions and regroupings until the emergence of something like the modern two-party system under Gladstone and Disraeli.

The Workshop of the World

In 1847 George Richardson Porter, a statistician at the Board of Trade, brought out a new edition of his *Progress of the Nation, in its various Social and Economical Relations, from the Beginning of the Nineteenth Century*. The book professed "to mark the progress of this United Kingdom, in which all the elements of improvement are working with incessant and increasing energy." The figures which Porter produced certainly looked impressive. Not one of his innumerable tables, covering everything from emigration and manufactures to taxes and food, failed to show a substantial increase during the previous forty years. In 1847 Britain just had more of everything: more raw cotton imported, more tons of coal dug out, more miles of railway built—also more crime—than ever before. Even the increase in population was taken as evidence of prosperity, and the dark fears of the Malthusians were dispelled by the growth in food production. The early Victorians were the last people to claim that worldly wealth was the sole end of man's existence. Nevertheless, the material achievement was so dazzling that at times they were quite carried away and wrote of it in lyrical, even transcendental, language. They admitted that of course there were other constituents of progress, but none was so conveniently measurable nor so dear to the heart of a generation that, like Mr. Gradgrind in Dickens's novel *Hard Times*, had a veritable passion for "facts." Porter had difficulty, because of insufficiency of data, in measuring the growth of total national wealth. But modern economists have calculated that the total gross national income of Great Britain rose from £340 million in 1831 to £523.3 million in 1851. There could hardly be much doubt, in this sense, about the progress of the nation.

The developments which Porter was outlining constituted the second phase of the Industrial Revolution. By 1832 the first stage had been completed, with the successful application of steampower to new machines in the textile mills, the expansion of production in the coal, iron, and engineering industries, and the concentration of production in the North and Midlands. The 1830s and 1840s saw an intensification of the trend toward factory production and a ruthless exploitation of economic resources. At this stage (which would be completed by 1840) the economy made sustained, if fluctuating, progress as it moved beyond the narrow range of industries (textiles, coal, and iron) that had powered the original take-off.

A high proportion of the national income went into investment (thus ensuring that production kept ahead of population increase), and full use was made of the most advanced technology of the day. As yet, however, the main thrust of the economy was in the basic industries sector and the shift to consumers' goods and services was still in the future.

There are two aspects of this phase of the Industrial Revolution that have briefly to be considered. First is the pattern of industrial development. Porter's statistics, supplemented by the census of 1851, make it clear that the largest industry was still agriculture. Over 1.75 million people were directly engaged in it, and when harvests were reasonably good Britain was virtually self-supporting in food supplies. With only a small increase in the labor force, agricultural production during the 1830s and 1840s was almost able to keep pace with the expanding demands of the town population. In the nonagricultural sector of the economy, the textile industry dominated the life of the nation, as it had done for the previous sixty years. The numbers employed in the main branches of the trade were large (probably about 1.1 million, excluding hosiery and lace), but even more important was the role of textiles, especially cotton, as a pace-setter for the whole of industry in matters of economic organization, industrial relations, and technological innovation. In conjunction with coal, iron, and engineering, textiles provided the basis of British achievement. "It is to the spinning-jenny and the steam-engine," observed Porter, "that we must look as having been the true moving powers of our fleets and armies, and the chief support also of a long-continued agricultural prosperity." Mechanical engineering had by the 1840s developed most of the machine tools necessary for precision work: James Nasmyth's steam hammer could forge a huge casting or gently crack an egg in a wineglass, while Joseph Whitworth produced gauges that were accurate to one ten-thousandth of an inch. No such technical progress was observable in the coal industry, which increased output simply by sinking deeper shafts and employing more men. In 1836 the mines produced thirty million tons of coal, and ten years later this figure had increased to forty-four million. Closely geared to coal as a main consumer was the iron industry. Continuous innovation in the iron-making processes greatly improved efficiency, and total output rose spectacularly from about 700,000 tons per year in 1830 to 1 million tons in 1835 and 2 million in 1847. The basic sector of the economy (sometimes called the Great Industry) comprising manufacturing and mining probably did not employ more than 1.7 million workers. This was less than a quarter of the occupied persons listed in 1851, and only a fraction of the total population. Yet it provided the motive force for "the workshop of the world," as Britain proudly described herself in the mid-nineteenth century.

The second aspect to be noted is the fluctuation of the economy. After the ending of the Napoleonic Wars there was acute economic distress. An improvement came in the early 1820s, but after a trade boom in 1825 depression returned. In the years following the Reform Bill of 1832 harvests were good and the price of wheat (always taken as an index of food prices) fell drastically. Investment in home industries was stimulated and there was a boom in railway construction after the success of the Liverpool and Manchester line (begun in 1826) became apparent. The prosperity, however, was short-lived: in 1836 the good harvests and the trade boom came to an end, and by 1837 the country was plunged into a prolonged depression lasting until 1842. These six years were the grimmest period in the history of the nineteenth century. Industry came to a standstill, unemployment reached hitherto unknown proportions, and with high food prices and inadequate relief the manufacturing population faced hunger and destitution. At no time did the whole system seem nearer to complete breakdown. Revival began in 1843 and continued into the 1850s, although broken by another recession in 1847–48. A second railway boom in the mid-forties contributed largely to the recovery (between 1843 and 1848 the length of line in the United Kingdom was extended from 2,000 to 5,000 miles), and by 1851 the Great Exhibition was able, with some plausibility, to suggest that the "Hungry Forties" were no more than a temporary interruption in the rapid progress of the nation toward prosperity for all.

From an economic point of view, the prime characteristic of industrialism is economic growth. This is the main evidence on which Porter relied to establish the progress of the nation—but he was well aware that this was not the whole of the story. Associated with economic growth are certain forms of social organization and also (as was very evident in the 1830s and 1840s) social disorganization, without which the expansion cannot take place. Industrialism therefore implies social change, and the context in which this change takes place is indicated by the "problems" which the participants identify: overpopulation, poor laws, great cities, the factory system.

The census of 1851 showed that for the first time slightly more than half the population was urban. The period of fastest urban growth had been the decade 1821–31, but the increase was not much less during the succeeding twenty years. Most of what are now the principal cities of modern Britain continued to grow rapidly between 1831 and 1851: Manchester from 182,000 to 303,000; Leeds, 123,000 to 172,000; Birmingham, 144,000 to 233,000; Glasgow, 202,000 to 345,000. Bradford, the fastest growing town in this period of the Industrial Revolution, had 13,000 inhabitants in 1801, 26,000 in 1821, and 104,000 by 1851. At the beginning of the century London (with nearly a million) was the only city with more than 100,000 population; by 1851 there were nine. This massive growth had come from both natural increase and immigration, the proportion differing considerably from town to town. In 1851 a half or more of the adult inhabitants of Leeds, Sheffield, and Norwich had been born in the town; in Manchester, Bradford, and Glasgow just over a quarter were natives; and in Liverpool the proportion was even less.

The facts of demography provided a foundation for the Victorians' great debate about cities, but the debate focused on "problems" rather than numbers. Harking back to a much older tradition of rural-urban dichotomy, in which country life was assumed to be the norm and cities an "unnatural" development which required special explanation, conservative critics of the new towns concentrated their attention on what was wrong. Cobbett's denunciation of London as "the great Wen" is a picturesque and well-known example of this view. Reformers of a different stamp also joined the chorus of disapproval; and even prourbanites like the Rev. Robert Vaughan, who saw cities as centers of civilization, adopted a problems approach. Vaughan's book *The Age of Great Cities; or modern society viewed in its relation to intelligence, morals and religion* (1843), was indicative of the interest in the subject from the 1840s.

One of the more unfortunate impressions left by an older generation of historians and sociologists is that all large towns in the nineteenth century were more or less the same—that is, equally smoky, soulless, and horrible to live in. The tendency to lump them all together, ignoring any modifying differences, was in part derived from contemporary caricatures like Dickens's Coketown and encouraged by references in the 1840s to "Cottonopolis" and "Worstedopolis." This is very misleading. Quite apart from obvious regional differences in traditional culture and economic and social relationships, the impact of population increase was very uneven. Not all towns were in the position of a Bradford or a Liverpool. Virtually all towns did increase in the first half of the nineteenth century, but in some instances the expansion was relatively modest. Cambridge, Chester, Exeter, and Norwich were of this order. Too often our impressions of urban growth have been derived from an overconcentration on the northern textile towns, although even among them the problems were by no means identical. London, again, stood by itself. In 1851 it was still by far the largest British city, although its position relative to the rest of the population had changed. The contrast with all other cities remained. "London," wrote Friedrich Engels, the young businessman and future collaborator of Karl Marx, "is unique, because it is a city in which one can roam for hours without leaving the built-up area and without seeing the slightest sign of the approach of open country. This enormous agglomeration of population on a single spot has multiplied a hundredfold the economic strength of the two and a half million inhabitants concentrated there." Here the process of urbanization had begun earliest, had gone farthest, and was more easily distinguishable as such than in the northern towns of the classic Industrial Revolution.

Closely associated, indeed often taken as synonymous with industrialism and urban growth, was the factory system. Objectively, this was simply a system of concentrated large-scale production, using power machinery and large numbers of operatives, together with the correspondingly necessary social institutions. Until 1850 the factory system was still mainly confined to the textile industries. The Factory Acts were designed to regulate working conditions in cotton and woolen mills, and the home of the factory system was assumed to be Lancashire, the West Riding of Yorkshire, and parts of Scotland. To establish the unique characteristics of the factory system it was, and still is, customary to contrast it with the previous mode of production, the domestic system. In textiles, relics of this domestic form of organization of industry continued into the 1840s, side by side with the factory system. The handloom weaver remained as a sad reminder of an earlier and once-prosperous type of economy; and in times of distress the older hands could look back nostalgically to this alternative order.

The factory operatives represented for most observers the heart of the new industrial civilization, about whose benefits or iniquities there was so much argument. As always, investigators tended to find what they were looking for: the lot of the factory operative was presented both as a state of continual misery and as a life of modest comfort and respectability. Here are two contrasting examples. The first is a rosy description of the homes of the operatives near Messrs. Ashworth's model cotton mill at Turton, near Bolton, Lancashire. It was written by William Cooke Taylor in his *Notes of a Tour in the Manufacturing Districts* (1842):

> The situation [of Banktop, the operatives' village], though open and airy, is not unsheltered; the cottages are built of stone, and contain from four to six rooms each; back-premises with suitable conveniences are attached to them all. . . . I visited the interior of nearly every cottage; I found all well, and very many respectably, furnished: there were generally a mahogany table and chest of drawers. Daughters from most of the houses, but wives, as far as I could learn, from none, worked in the factory. Many of the women were not a little proud of their housewifery, and exhibited the Sunday wardrobes of their husbands, the stock of neatly folded shirts, etc; . . . I found that there were some processes connected with the cotton manufacture which the women were permitted to execute in their own houses. "The pay," said one of the women, "is not much, but it helps to boil the pot." . . . I was informed by the operatives that permission to rent one of the cottages was regarded as a privilege and favour, that it was in fact a reward reserved for honesty, industry and sobriety. . . . All were not merely contented with their situation, but proud of it. . . . It is not easy to fix upon a statistical test for measuring the intelligence of the adult operatives. I found clocks and small collections of books in all their dwellings; several had wheel-barometers. . . . I have more than once gone down in the evening to Turton Mills, to see the operatives coming from work. . . . The boys were as merry as crickets: there was not one of the girls who looked as if she would refuse an invitation to a dance.

A very different impression is left by William Dodd's account in his *Factory System Illustrated* (1842) of a young girl factory worker in Manchester in 1841. After the watchman has knocked on the window at 4:30 in the morning, the girl's mother

> rouses the unwilling girl to another day of toil. At length you hear her on the floor; the clock is striking five. Then, for the first time, the girl becomes conscious of the necessity for haste; and having slipped on her clothes,

and (if she thinks there is time) washed herself, she takes a drink of cold coffee, which has been left standing in the fireplace, a mouthful of bread (if she can eat it), and having packed up her breakfast in her handkerchief, hastens to the factory. The bell rings as she leaves the threshold of her home. Five minutes more, and she is in the factory, stripped and ready for work. The clock strikes half-past five; the engine starts, and her day's work commences.

At half-past seven . . . the engine slacks its pace (seldom stopping) for a short time till the hands have cleaned the machinery and swallowed a little food. It then goes on again, and continues at full speed till twelve o'clock when it stops for dinner. Previously to leaving the factory, and in her dinner-hour, she has her machines to clean. The distance of the factory is about five minutes' walk from her home. I noticed every day that she came in at half-past twelve, or within a minute or two, and once she was over the half hour; the first thing she did was to wash herself, then get her dinner (which she was seldom able to eat), and pack up her drinking for the afternoon. This done, it was time to be on her way to work again, where she remains, without one minute's relaxation, till seven o'clock. She then comes home, and throws herself into a chair exhausted. This [is] repeated six days in the week (save that on Saturdays she may get back a little earlier, say, an hour or two). . . . This young woman looks very pale and delicate, and has every appearance of an approaching decline. I was asked to guess her age; I said, perhaps fifteen. . . . Her mother . . . told me she was going nineteen. . . . She is a fair specimen of a great proportion of factory girls in Manchester.

By the 1840s the term "factory system" had ceased to be an objective description of a certain type of economic and social organization and had become a slogan or a convenient label for a complex of social attitudes and assumptions. This is not hard to appreciate, for the changes demanded by the new order were terrifyingly fundamental and aroused men's deepest responses. The factory integrated men and machines in a way that had never before been attempted. "Whilst the engine runs, the people must work—men, women and children are yoked together with iron and steam. The animal machine . . . is chained fast to the iron machine, which knows no suffering and no weariness," wrote James Kay Shuttleworth in 1832. Reactions to this phenomenon varied according to a man's position in life and his social and temperamental attitudes. To some the factory system was the practical application of Adam Smith's principle of the division of labor; others saw it as a system of gross immorality in which sexual appetite and precociousness were fostered by the overheated atmosphere of mills; working men complained that too often it meant the introduction of machines that put them out of work; and reformers denounced it as a system of child slavery. The factory system was all of these things, but was not bounded by any one of them. It was more than simply an aggregate of individual factories; it was a new order, a completely new way of life.

"A feeling very generally exists," wrote the prophet of the early

Victorian age, Thomas Carlyle, in 1839, "that the condition and disposition of the Working Classes is a rather ominous matter at present; that something ought to be said, something ought to be done, in regard to it." Carlyle was reacting to the "bitter discontent grown fierce and mad," and he voiced the widespread concern about the economic and social plight of the laboring poor. This concern was both a cause and a result of many investigations into living and working conditions in the 1830s and 1840s. No previous age had been so much enquired into by select committees, royal commissions, statistical societies, and local bodies, nor had there been such a spate of bluebooks (government publications) and reports by amateur investigators. Documentation of "the condition-of-England question" was very thorough.

But contemporaries were divided in their interpretations of these facts, and consequently also in their views as to what "ought to be done." Historians also have differed among themselves for many years on this issue. The debate has been between those who took an optimistic view of the new industrial civilization and those whose verdict was pessimistic. Dr. Andrew Ure in his *Philosophy of Manufactures* (1835) and G. R. Porter, quoted earlier, regarded the industrial changes as a blessing; Carlyle and Engels saw them as a curse. More recently, the issues have been narrowed down by historians to an argument as to whether the standard of living of the working classes improved or deteriorated between 1780 and 1850. No very clear conclusion has so far emerged, perhaps because of failure to agree on standards of measurement. Statistics of earnings and prices, unemployment, patterns of consumption (including food), and population growth have all been introduced as variables in assessing changes in working-class living standards. Even more difficult to ascertain is firm information about the qualitative aspects of life of the laboring poor; for here there is almost no escape from personal judgments, whether by contemporaries or historians. If a general statement about the material condition of the working classes during the Industrial Revolution were to be hazarded, it would be that the real income of skilled artisans increased, the lot of the domestic workers deteriorated, and the living standards of the majority of the laboring poor remained stationary or at best improved slightly. During the crucial second quarter of the nineteenth century even this cautious evaluation may be disputed. So fluctuating was the economy in booms and slumps, so widespread the incidence of unemployment, and so low the living standards of the eight million inhabitants of Ireland that generalization becomes meaningless. It is clear that large numbers, possibly a majority, of the laboring poor suffered an absolute decline in living standards during the 1830s and 1840s, and that the working class as a whole declined relative to other groups in their share of the national income. From the late forties improvement began, and continued until late in the century.

As an illustration of living conditions, we may look more closely at working-class housing. In general, most urban and some rural workers lived in cottages of three or four rooms and a kitchen. Such homes were two-storeyed and (in the towns) were built in terraces or round courts. Unlike the laboring poor on the Continent, very few British workers lived in tenements: only in the old town of Edinburgh were there to be found tenement buildings up to ten storeys high. British towns expanded outward rather than upward. Long rows of terrace houses in red brick, or sometimes of stone in the northern towns, sprawled outward from the older city centers. Having first filled up all available space within the existing town, they snaked across the surrounding hills or clustered near the factories in the valley bottoms. In the medieval town (the relics of which had survived into the eighteenth century) rich and poor, merchants and laborers, had been more or less intermingled, but in the nineteenth century the laboring poor became segregated in exclusively working-class districts.

In Leeds, for instance, the statistical committee of the town council in 1839 estimated that of the total population of 82,120 in the township, 61,212 belonged to the working classes, and the majority of these lived in certain well-defined areas of the town. The North, North East, and Kirkgate wards, together with the rapidly growing out-townships of Holbeck and Hunslet, formed a densely populated working-class area; while the middle classes occupied the healthier and more pleasantly situated areas in the Mill Hill, West, and North West wards. The sorting out of the population into different areas on a basis of social status was thus far advanced, and the social distinctions between the working classes and their more affluent neighbors, already apparent in differences of dress, speech, and mental attitudes, were reinforced by physical isolation. The gulf between classes inevitably widened, and to many social reformers the bridging of this gulf seemed the most urgent and yet most difficult task of all.

Within this warren of working-class housing in Leeds there was a big variation between the best and the worst. The homes of respectable working men usually rented for 2s.6d. to 7s.6d. a week. In 1839, 8,331 houses rented at between £5 and £10 per year, and a further 2,640 at between £10 and £20. The cheapest of these houses consisted of two rooms and a cellar, built back to back, and sharing an outside privy. Describing such cottages in the 1850s, Edward Hall, the Unitarian domestic missionary in Holbeck, emphasized the details of daily life in such accommodation:

> They are built back to back, with no possibility of good ventilation, and contain a cellar for coals and food, the coal department being frequently tenanted with fowls, pigeons, or rabbits, and in some cases with two or all three of these—a room from 9 to 14 feet by from 10 to 12 or 14 feet, to do all the cooking, washing, and the necessary work of a family, and another of the same size for all to sleep in. Think for a moment what must be the inconvenience, the danger both in a moral and physical sense, when parents

and children, young men and women, married and single, are crowded together in this way, with three beds in a room, and barely a couple of yards in the middle for the whole family to undress and dress in.

Taking further Hall's invitation to consider the implications of such housing, it is not difficult to imagine some of the rawer aspects of working-class life in the home: the lack of indoor sanitation and consequent use of chamber pots; the absence of a water tap in the house and the difficulties of keeping personally clean; the aggravation of these problems by an aged and incontinent relative or by a sick person; the difficulty of ever airing the house because through ventilation was made impossible by the back-to-back construction. Even in the better cottages with two bedrooms ("two up and two down"), these problems were mitigated but not removed. And while there was little enough room for the family indoors, there was even less outside in the way of a garden or a yard. The houses opened directly onto the street, with the result that, "the intersection of the street with clothes-lines is an anomaly in street regulations. In the township of Leeds, out of the total number of 586 streets, 276, or nearly one-half are weekly

The new industrial towns: A view of Leeds, 1846. (J. F. C. Harrison, *Learning and Living*, Routledge & Kegan Paul, Ltd.)

so full of lines and linen as to be impassable for horses and carriages, and almost for foot-passengers."

Skilled artisans enjoyed considerably more comfort at home. Their cottages were larger, in more salubrious areas of the town, and usually had a small yard at the back. The windows were often well-proportioned, and the doorways showed traces of simple Regency elegance. Today such terraces of artisans' and lower middle-class houses can still be found in most towns, and in the Chelsea and Islington boroughs of London are much sought-after for fashionable "doing up." Inside, the furnishings were usually described as comfortable, meaning something beyond the basic necessities of bed, table, and chairs. Such things as clocks, pictures, books, ornaments, floor coverings, oak or mahogany chests of drawers were taken as signs of decency and prosperity. And if a parlor, separate from the everyday living room, could be maintained, then respectability was assured. Standards of housewifery were high, with much emphasis on scrubbing and scouring and polishing (the custom of whitening doorsteps and window sills in northern towns persists to this day). Nowhere did the great Victorian virtues of frugality, cleanliness, and sobriety appear more attractively and to greater purpose than in the "cottage homes of England." They provided the inspiration for dozens of building societies, model cottage societies, and improved dwellings associations: for, it was argued, what some members of the working class had achieved, all should be encouraged to strive for.

Both the need and the difficulties of such improvement were amply demonstrated at the other extreme. The worst housing conditions were the slums of the big towns, and in particular the cellar dwellings and common lodging houses. Engels, in his *Condition of the Working Class in England in 1844*, described in vivid detail the squalor of the cellar dwellings in Manchester, of which there were 20,000 in 1832. The same story was repeated in Glasgow, London, Liverpool, and other industrial towns where there were immigrant Irish and handloom weavers. Robert Baker, a surgeon and factory inspector of Leeds, described local Irish cellar dwellings he had visited:

> I have been in one of these damp cellars, without the slightest drainage, every drop of wet and every morsel of dirt and filth having to be carried up into the street; two corded frames for beds, overlaid with sacks for five persons; scarcely anything in the room else to sit on but a stool, or a few bricks; the floor, in many places, absolutely wet; a pig in the corner also; and in a street where filth of all kinds had accumulated for years. In another house, where no rent had been paid for years by reason of apparent inability to do it, I found a father and mother and their two boys, both under the age of 16 years, the parents sleeping on similar corded frames, and the two boys upon straw, on the floor upstairs; never changing their clothes from week's end to week's end, working in the dusty department of a flax mill, and existing upon coffee and bread.

There is all too much evidence from the 1830s to make it clear that this report was neither exaggerated nor untypical. In the area of Greater Manchester a total of 40–50,000 people lived in cellars, in Liverpool more than 45,000. The evil arose from the subdivision of what had been intended as a home for a single family into a series of tenements with each room occupied by one or even more families, the cheapest and most undesirable room being the cellar, which was below street level and lighted only by a grating.

Equally sordid conditions were found in many of the dwellings in courts and alleys that were above ground. In some cases, older and larger houses had been broken down into single-room dwellings. But more frequently cottages were built around a court entered by a narrow alley from the street. In London the districts of Seven Dials and Bethnal Green, in Glasgow the wynds, in Manchester the old town, in Leeds the Kirkgate ward—all contained examples of this type of housing. Sites in the central areas of towns were at a premium and there was every encouragement to build as many houses as possible per acre. In York and Leeds the courts were built in what had been the gardens of older and more spacious homes: in Nottingham and Coventry overcrowded "rookeries" were created by the shortage of building land consequent on the refusal to enclose the common lands that hemmed the town in. Lodging houses were usually found in these areas and were particularly noisome and notorious as the haunts of beggars, tramps, thieves, and prostitutes. A report on lodging houses in Leeds was prepared by the police in 1851 after an outbreak of typhus fever had been traced to some of the lodgers. Within a half-circle drawn at a radius of a quarter of a mile from the parish church were found 222 lodging houses, 53 of them being in Wellington Yard alone. Nearly 2,500 people lived in these lodgings, averaging 2½ persons to each bed and 4½ persons to each room. In one house there were 10 persons per bed. Men and women slept indiscriminately together in the same room in 220 of the 222 houses The charge for lodging was 2d.–3d. per night. Only 40 of the 220 houses were even moderately clean, and 6 were cellar dwellings in a filthy condition.

The inadequacy of private dwellings was matched by the paucity of social provision of utilities and amenities. Edwin Chadwick, more than any other single person, aroused his countrymen to an awareness of the "sanitary condition" of England, but it was only gradually and reluctantly that municipalities accepted the duty of providing a minimum of basic services. The early Victorian town was still largely unpaved, unsewered, poorly lit, and inadequately supplied with clean water. Working-class housing areas were nearly always in the low-lying parts of the town, in what had previously been meadows and marshes along the banks of a river—precisely those areas in which efficient sewerage and drainage was at once the most necessary and yet the most difficult to construct. In 1839 in the North East ward of Leeds, containing a working-class population of over 15,000, only three streets were wholly and twelve partly sewered out of a total of ninety-three. It was a common habit in the poorest areas to empty chamber pots in the street. Even when privies were provided, if they could not be flushed into a sewer the contents had to be periodically dug out and carted away. Investigators commented frequently on the disgusting smells and "excrementitious matter" lying about in all directions. An equally small number of streets was paved; the rest were simply beaten earth. In Leeds ashes were sometimes laid down to form a pavement, which in dry weather produced an irritating black dust and on wet days a spongy black puddle. Only in the superior type of artisan's cottage was water laid on. In the normal back-to-back terrace house water had to be drawn from a common tap in the yard or on the privy wall.

The health hazard from such conditions was only tardily admitted. There was a strange reluctance to accept the idea of a causal relationship between the incidence of disease and the effectiveness of the sanitation system. But typhus fever, cholera, and smallpox were no respecters of persons. Although the diseases usually originated among and ravaged most severely the very poorest of the laboring classes, they inevitably took their toll of all sections of the people living in the congested areas of the town. It was Robert Baker who, from the time of his first report on the Leeds cholera epidemic of 1832, showed repeatedly how epidemic disease and high mortality rates clung to the working-class areas. Chadwick's *Report on the Sanitary Conditions of the Labouring Population of Great Britain* (1842) put the matter succinctly:

> By the inspection of a map of Leeds, which Mr. Baker has prepared at my request, to show the localities of epidemic diseases, it will be perceived that they similarly fall on the uncleansed and close streets and wards occupied by the labouring classes; and that the track of the cholera is nearly identical with the track of fever. It will also be observed that in the badly cleansed and badly drained wards to the right of the map, the proportional mortality is nearly double that which prevails in the better conditioned districts to the left.

Despite such convincing reports it was long before municipal authorities could bring themselves to incur the cost of adequate sewerage for the whole of their towns.

In rural areas the living conditions of the laboring poor were not essentially different from those of comparable groups in the towns. Although lodging houses and cellar dwellings were absent from the villages, there were rural slums which were as squalid as anything in Manchester. The cottages of most farm laborers were no larger than those of town workers, although the general rural environment was perhaps less depressing than the smoky pall that hung over the low-lying centers of industrial towns. William Blades, an East Riding agricultural worker, was born in 1839 at Nafferton, a large village on the eastern side of the Wolds in the heart of a rich corn-growing district, and his account of his life there in the forties and fifties was set down many years later by a sympathetic country rector:

> The house of the Blades family was, like all the houses of the agricultural labourers, small, consisting of two rooms on the ground floor called the "house," or living room, and the parlour, with two bedrooms above. In many of the cottages at that time there was over one or other of the sleeping chambers a space or area, it could not be dignified with the title of room, which was frequently used as a sleeping-place for some of the children; it was just possible to get a small bed or two into it; and there they slept in their beds in the manner shortly to be described. So contracted was the space, that in getting out of bed the youngsters had to exercise great caution so as not to knock their heads against the rafters of the roof. This upper area always went by the name of "cockloft." . . . In addition to these rooms there was what was called a "backer-end," which was a kind of lean-to shanty at one end of the house.

The Bladeses' home may be taken as a fairly standard English rural cottage: a few (approaching small farmhouses) were better, but many were much worse. Regional variations accounted for some of the differences; thus in

Rural life: (1) A village in Dorsetshire, 1846. (*Illustrated London News*, Vol. IX, 1846, The New York Public Library.)

the Cotswolds and the West Riding the building was of stone, in Lancashire and the Midlands, of brick. Older cottages were made of wattle and daub, and in some areas a half-timbered construction was used. Turf houses were still common in parts of Scotland, and of course were practically universal in Ireland. The amount of accommodation seldom exceeded the Bladeses' house, and in northern England and the Lowlands of Scotland there were one-roomed cottages, sometimes with animals living under the same roof and divided from the dwelling room by only a nominal partition wall. Floors were usually of brick, pebble, or earth; furnishings were utilitarian; and privies were sometimes completely absent. Idyllic as many English cottages looked in summer, when they were embowered in honeysuckle and hollyhocks and roses, and superior as they undoubtedly were to rural homes in Ireland and on the Continent, life in such conditions did not leave much margin for comfort. The cottage afforded little more than the basic requirements of shelter, warmth, and a place to eat.

Inadequate as such conditions seem to us today, they were made even worse by unemployment, or, as the Victorians preferred to call it, "overpopulation." This problem was handled through the Poor Laws. Superficially, the Poor Laws were simply a matter of relief, but in fact they raised fundamental questions of social policy. The various aspects of the condition-of-England question were not for the most part regarded as appropriate for governmental action, but in the extreme case of destitution it had long been recognized that the state had an obligation to see that provision was made to relieve the distress. In a rural society, where the poor were taken for granted, the periodic need to help them beyond the extent of normal Christian charity was acknowledged. From Elizabethan times the responsibility for looking after its own poor was laid squarely upon each parish, under the direction of the justices of the peace. The Poor Law Act of 1601 provided overseers of the poor who were to levy a poor rate for the relief of the sick, aged, and unemployed. With the spread of enclosures after 1760 and the rise in food prices during the French wars, the number of poor to be relieved increased rapidly, and the poor rates jumped accordingly. In 1775 they had amounted to less than £2 million, by 1801 they had doubled, and in 1831 they were nearly £7 million—provoking loud protestations from the rate-payers. In many districts the practice of granting outdoor relief to employed as well as unemployed laborers had grown up, and in 1795 this became semiregularized as the "Speenhamland system." It was the intention of the Berkshire justices, meeting at the village of Speenhamland, to help the poor by ensuring that each family had a minimum income calculated according to the price of bread and number of dependants, but the effect was to subsidize low wages out of poor rates. The system was adopted widely in the southern counties and was held by orthodox political economists to be largely responsible for rural pauperization. For over forty years the problem of how to reduce the growing burden of poor rates (which fell mainly on the farmers in the countryside and the middle classes in the towns) had been debated, without any conclusive result. But by the early 1830s the pressure to do away with the Old Poor Law and to create a free labor market in accordance with the principles of political economy was sufficiently strong to overcome working-class radical and Tory opposition. In the autumn of 1830 the "swing" riots of agricultural laborers throughout the southern and eastern counties had been savagely put down (19 men hung, 644 imprisoned, 481 transported), and the new Whig government decided that drastic action was required. A royal commission on the poor laws was appointed, and its *Report* provided the basis for a New Poor Law, enacted in 1834.

The new law, like the old, accepted the principle that every necessitous person had a claim to relief; but the relief was to be given only under new and stricter conditions. First, outdoor relief was to be abolished and all recipients made to enter the workhouse. Second, conditions in the workhouse were made "less eligible" (that is, more miserable) than the condition of the lowest paid worker outside. A rigorous workhouse test was thus applied to all applicants for relief, the intention being to deter all but the really "deserving" (that is, desperate) cases. To carry out this sweeping reform of the Old Poor Law system, a centralized administration was established, consisting of a board of three commissioners, who in turn appointed

Rural life: (2) Agricultural laborers, 1846. (*Illustrated London News*, Vol. IX, 1846, The New York Public Library.)

regional assistant commissioners. The old parish workhouses were abolished and the parishes grouped together in "unions," each with one large central workhouse. Boards of guardians were elected by the rate-payers in each Poor Law Union and were responsible for carrying out the regulations imposed by the commissioners.

The rationale of the New Poor Law lay in the doctrines of orthodox political economy. Anything that interfered with the working of the "natural" laws of supply and demand was felt to be undesirable. By this test trade unions, factory regulations, and poor relief stood alike condemned. The widespread acceptance among the educated classes of a laissez-faire philosophy, coupled with the desire to reduce the poor rates, ensured a sympathetic response to the Poor Law *Report* and support for the government's act of 1834. Edwin Chadwick, the first secretary of the central board and drafter of the *Report*, was a disciple of Jeremy Bentham, the philosopher who questioned the value of all institutions and customs by the test of whether they contributed to "the greatest happiness of the greatest number." Benthamism led to positive action by the state in the furtherance of administrative reform—which conflicted to some extent with the doctrines of the classical political economists, who advocated strictly limiting the role of government in social and economic affairs. Nassau Senior, Chadwick's colleague and professor of political economy at Oxford, favored doing away with the poor laws altogether. Between them they concocted a drastic revision of English social policy. Ramshackle and inefficient as the Old Poor Law had been, it nevertheless provided the rudiments of a system of social welfare: income maintenance for the poorest workers, unemployment compensation, and family endowment. This was now to be swept away, on the grounds that public charity was incompatible with the principles of the economists.

Critics, however, saw the matter differently. To Thomas Carlyle, it was not the application of natural, scientific, or immutable laws of political economy but the application of a very simple and brutal axiom: "If paupers are made miserable, paupers will needs decline in multitude. It is a secret known to all rat-catchers." And he sarcastically suggested that poisoning paupers, like rats, with arsenic would be even more efficient. The "social principle" of the New Poor Law was no principle at all, he argued, but simply an attempt to sweep the problems of the poor and luckless out of sight. In one sense Carlyle was right: the New Poor Law was an attempt to deal not with the fundamental causes of destitution but only with its symptoms as expressed in the demand for relief. In other respects, however, the 1834 act was a basic measure, for it defined the social policy of the state, as it affected a majority of the population, in a new way. The issue was more than the replacement of a lenient by a severe administration of the laws governing relief; it was the announcement that henceforth the laboring poor must abandon many of their traditional attitudes and expectations and conform to new standards of social and economic rectitude.

The new measures were greeted with bitter opposition from working people. Inevitably, the poor laws affected the life of a laboring man at its most tender spots. In times of distress caused by unemployment, sickness, old age, and death, he and his family were under strain and most in need of sympathetic help and consideration. Yet this was the last thing to be expected under the new regime. As they watched the building of the great, grim new workhouses and heard the rumors of the prisonlike discipline enforced behind the high walls, the working classes were seized with a great and sudden fear. On the outskirts of every medium-sized town and at remote crossroads in country districts, the new, raw red-brick buildings appeared. They looked like prisons and were called the "bastilles." Inside them, life was made as dreary and comfortless as was possible without actually endangering health. When a pauper family presented itself for relief at the gates of the workhouse it was immediately broken up, men, women, and children being housed in separate parts of the building and forbidden to reunite as long as they remained. Able-bodied men were set to work at breaking stone, grinding corn, or picking oakum. Food was plain and monotonous: mainly bread and gruel, with a small allowance of meat and cheese. Until 1842 all meals were eaten in silence, and smoking was forbidden. A special workhouse dress was worn, and the master of the workhouse was enjoined "to enforce industry, order, punctuality, and cleanliness" at all times. Visitors were allowed infrequently and only in the presence of the master or matron. The commissioners (and usually also the guardians) were especially keen that the greatest economy should be exercised; any little comfort that might be considered a luxury was carefully excluded: an occasional cup of tea for the old folks or a few extra delicacies for Christmas dinner (although paid for by a private benefactor) were considered exceedingly dubious relaxations of the regulations.

Such a system would have been sufficiently terrifying had all the masters and matrons, overseers and guardians been humane and honest. But given the normal incidence of sadism, greed, and petty-mindedness among mankind, and the credulity with which reports of abuses are received, it was inevitable that the horror of the new workhouses would be magnified further. There were in any event sufficient bad cases to nourish the worst of contemporary fears and rumors. Most notorious was the scandal in the Andover workhouse, where the paupers were so hungry that they fought among themselves for bits of gristle and marrow among the old bones they were set to crush. Typical of the insensitivity of the commissioners was the attempt in 1836 to save the cost of tolling the bell at pauper funerals. The desire for a respectable burial was (and long remained) deeply ingrained in the English poor, and Chadwick's circular was an outrage upon their feelings of common decency. The New Poor Law was by its very nature a piece of class legislation, in that decisions affecting one class (the poor) were made by another. Even so, it was unusually blatant in the way it trampled on so much that the laboring poor held dear.

Insofar as the New Poor Law was an attempt to deal with pauperism rather than poverty, its results could be judged fairly satisfactory. Applied first to the southern counties, where rural pauperism was worst, and helped by two good harvests and the demand for labor to build railways, the abuses of the allowance (or Speenhamland) system were speedily removed, and the old evil of underemployment in agriculture largely disappeared. To this extent the New Poor Law succeeded in its aim of restoring the laborer to something like a condition of formal independence. The social disease of pauperism, it was argued, had been cured by the drastic but necessary surgery of cutting off outdoor relief. In fact, the guardians in rural areas had to continue outdoor relief for the able-bodied in cases of urgency as well as for some of the aged and infirm. When the commissioners turned their attention to the industrial districts in 1837, they found even less possibility of a blanket application of the new regulations to all

Manual labor: *(1)* Ballast-heavers in the London docks, 1850s. (Henry Mayhew, *London Labour and the London Poor*, Vol. III, 1861, The Emmet Collection, The New York Public Library.)

and sundry. The needs of industrial workers were not the same as for agricultural laborers, and moreover they were on the brink of the worst economic depression of the nineteenth century. Factory operatives and handworkers were not suffering the effects of an allowance system that artificially depressed wages; they required short-term relief to tide them over periods of temporary unemployment until good times returned. They regarded the idea of having to enter the workhouse in order to get relief as monstrous and totally irrelevant to their real needs. The resistance to the New Poor Law in the northern towns delayed its introduction for many months, but by 1840 poor law unions were established throughout the country. It proved impossible to implement all the principles of the "harsh but salutary Act": outdoor relief simply could not be completely abolished, nor did the mixed workhouse (catering to all types of indigent poor from orphans to old people, able-bodied, and sick), which had been condemned in the 1834 *Report*, disappear. The principle of less eligibility, however, was sufficiently enforced to make the workhouse a terror and shame to

Manual labor: *(2)* Coal-porters filling wagons at a London wharf, 1850s. (Henry Mayhew, *London Labour and the London Poor*, Vol. III, 1861, The Emmet Collection, The New York Public Library.)

ordinary people. Its shadow fell across the lives of laboring men, reminding them always of the price of indigency.

The attack on out-relief owed much to the influence of Malthus, and the New Poor Law as a whole reflected accurately the dominant social philosophy of the middle classes. Carlyle interpreted the New Poor Law as "an announcement, sufficiently distinct, that whosover will not work ought not to live." To the problem of the man who was willing to work but for whom no work was available, no satisfactory answer was forthcoming. It was an assumption of the New Poor Law that pauperism was in most cases culpable, that indigency was due largely to personal weakness. From this it followed that improvement could be effected by individual effort, given the necessary will and determination. The condition-of-England question was to be solved by the great Victorian panacea, self-help.

Protest and Revolt

No period in British history has been richer in movements for radical and social reform than the years between 1815 and 1848. The list of only the major movements which flourished in these years is an indication of the variety and extent of the efforts to bring about far-reaching changes in British society: political reform, Chartism, trade unionism, factory reform, Owenite socialism, cooperation, anti-poor law agitation, secularism, the struggle for an unstamped press, friendly benefit societies, workers' and adult education, temperance, phrenology, vegetarianism, universal peace, the Anti-Corn Law League, anti-state church campaign, millenarianism, machine-breaking, and agricultural riots. The very existence of this plethora of movements suggests a general discontent on the part of many people with their lot under the new conditions of industrialism and a determination to try to change things.

It is not easy to see a pattern in this ferment of reform. Contemporary reformers were confused by the legion of causes, which intermingled and faded into one another. The new cause with the more urgent dynamic absorbed the energies that had previously gone into an earlier movement, which had either achieved its object, or, more usually, come up against opposition which it could not overcome. Thus the radical political unions of 1816–23 took the place of the Corresponding Societies of the 1790s, and were themselves overshadowed by trade union activities, which were in turn caught up in the factory reform movement from 1831 to 1833. From the fall of 1833 the Owenite socialists took the lead in working-class organization; but their Grand National Consolidated Trades Union collapsed in 1834, and when working-class hopes revived in 1837 they were embodied in a new movement, Chartism. Nevertheless, the nature of this protest and revolt becomes somewhat clearer when we select particular movements, especially of the 1830s and 1840s, for consideration.

A combination of disillusionment with the Reform Act of 1832 and a continuing belief in the possibility and efficacy of reform provided the immediate enthusiasm for the greatest of all the popular movements, Chartism. For nearly twenty years after 1837, Chartism was a name to evoke the wildest hopes and the worst fears, like Bolshevism in a later age. No other movement before the rise of modern labor and socialism at the end of the century had anything like the mass following of Chartism. It was the first attempt to build an independent political party representing the interests of the laboring and unprivileged sections of the nation. Contemporaries noted that for many of its followers Chartism was basically "a knife and fork question." Yet its program was a series of political demands. This has puzzled historians, who have concluded that one of the main reasons for Chartism's lack of success was its contradiction in seeking political remedies for economic grievances. In fact, the Chartists' tactics made a good deal of sense at that time, and their analysis of what we should now call the power structure was evidently shrewder than that of the historians. The link between economic ills and political representation was constantly elaborated in Chartist pamphlets and oratory; how, it was asked, could a "rotten House of Commons," representing the interests of landholders, speculators, manufacturers, and capitalists, be expected to do anything but uphold an economic system in which the poor were ground down and oppressed? Given the options open to them in the 1830s, and the experience of alternative paths which they had pursued and found blocked, the Chartists' program for social advance through political power was perfectly sound. It was also the method adopted, though with more success, by the middle classes; and this lesson was by no means lost upon the Chartists. If Chartism did not gain its objectives, the reasons have to be sought elsewhere than in the apparent paradox of economic ends through political means. It is also salutary to remember that movements which "failed" did not necessarily have to fail. History is not simply a record of success stories.

The Chartists were so named because they formulated their demands in a six-point charter: universal (manhood) suffrage, annual Parliaments, vote by (secret) ballot, abolition of the property qualification for M.P.s, payment of M.P.s, and equal electoral districts. The object was to make the charter the law of the land, by legal, constitutional means if possible, or by force if necessary—or by a mixture of both. Most Chartist leaders were reluctant to be labeled as "moral force" or "physical force" men. "We will have the charter," they declared, "peaceably if we can, forcibly if we must." Great efforts were made to collect support for a petition to the House of Commons on behalf of the charter; but on each occasion that it was presented the House rejected its demands. Alternative methods were therefore bound to be advocated. There were plans for making the central body of Chartist delegates, the national convention, a people's parliament to bypass Westminster; a general strike ("national holiday") was attempted in August 1839; and local riots, and perhaps an abortive insurrection (in November 1839), showed that physical force might not be ruled out. But the Chartists were unable to repeat the tactics of 1830–32, when the Reform Bill was carried by a combination of support in Parliament and the threat of force outside.

There was little that was new in the six points of the charter. They were drawn up by William Lovett and his friends in the London Working Men's Association in 1837, though the People's Charter was not officially published until the following year. Politically, Chartism was in the central tradition of British radicalism, stretching back to the Corresponding Societies of 1792–93, and the Chartists were proud of their heritage. It was a tradition of mass meetings, imprisonments, and conflicts with authority. In the provinces working men's associations were formed on the London model in 1837, in each case building on the remains of earlier radical reform organizations, such as the political unions that had carried on the popular struggle for the Reform Bill. The earlier martyrs of the radical cause were constantly remembered in Chartist speeches, and no rally was complete without a banner commemorating the "Massacre of Peterloo" at Manchester in 1819.

The origins of Chartism, however, were more complex than a simple development from the London Working Men's Association. In Birmingham, the movement at first was closely allied with middle-class radical and currency reformers. In Leeds, Owenite socialists combined with middle-class radicals and physical-force militants to launch the Leeds Working Men's Association. And in other towns of the West Riding and the industrial North and Northeast, local movements and grievances provided a basis for Chartism. Thus, right from the start, Chartism was not a national movement with its central headquarters in London, but a series of local and regional movements loosely federated. This posed a problem of concerted action which was never solved. Attempts to build a national organization repeatedly fell apart; and the most effective link among Chartists was not their system of delegates to a national convention but the widely read Chartist newspaper, *The Northern Star*. The geography of Chartism points up a characteristic which is found in other contemporary movements, such as the Anti-Corn Law League, namely, the strength of provincial roots and the relative isolation of London. A clue to the reasons for this can be found in the economic and social patterns described earlier.

The point was made that the British economy in the period 1830–50 was only partly industrialized and that machinery and factory organization had been introduced unevenly between different industries and between different sectors of the same industry. Levels of wages, employment opportunities, social relationships, and general working conditions varied between industries and localities, creating different types and intensities of grievance. Within the laboring population, divisions were created by differences of skill and earnings. Chartism was directly related to these varieties within the labor force, and faithfully reflected them in its regional peculiarities. Wherever there was a substantial number of skilled artisans, especially shoemakers, printers, tailors, and cabinet-makers, a Chartist organization on the lines of the working men's associations was to be expected, with an emphasis on self-help, independence, and propaganda for universal suffrage. Such was the movement in London or Birmingham. But in areas where there were substantial numbers of distressed handloom weavers, as in Lancashire and the West Riding, Chartism assumed an altogether fiercer visage and adopted a more strident tone. The idol of the northern Chartists was not the reasoned, respectable artisan, William Lovett, with his appeal to "the most intelligent and influential portion of the working classes," but the flamboyant Irish orator, Feargus O'Connor, who claimed to be the champion of the "unshorn chins, blistered hands, and fustian jackets." In Leicestershire and the East Midlands the backbone of the Chartist movement was the framework knitters—another group of domestic workers laboring, like the handloom weavers, in an overstocked trade. Leeds and Sheffield in the 1840s produced another type of Chartism, based on lower middle-class radicalism and artisan support. The Chartists in these towns elected their own candidates to the town council and concerned themselves with local issues of importance to shopkeepers and tradesmen.

Just as the local variations of Chartism were related to the structure of the economy, so the chronology of the movement reflected the cycle of booms and slumps between 1836 and 1851. The first climax of Chartism came in the winter of 1839, at the height of the trade depression. In 1842 a second peak of Chartist activity was reached with the Plug riots, arising out of mass unemployment in the northern towns. And the last great flare-up of Chartism came in 1848, following a winter of economic recession and inspired by revolutions on the Continent. In periods of relative prosperity (1843–47 and after 1848), Chartism lost its mass support. It then became a movement promoting education, temperance, municipal reforms, and settlement on the land—while never losing faith that universal suffrage would some day, somehow, be won. After 1848, as a tantalizing sort of epilogue, a group of Chartists tried to steer the movement toward socialism and the international working-class movement of Marx and Engels.

If, as has been stressed, Chartism was in many ways a logical development within the tradition of radical reform, in what sense was it a distinctive movement, and in what lay its significance as a vehicle for social change in the 1830s and 1840s? Two characteristics seem to stand out from the Chartist record, especially in its early phase: first, its class-conscious tone and temper; second, its mass size. There are not many points in modern British history at which the historian can profitably speculate whether a revolutionary situation might have developed but did not. Among the dates for consideration, however, would have to be included the winter of 1839 and the spring and summer of 1848. At both these times Chartism seemed, to many contemporaries, to pose the threat of the barricades.

Chartists of many shades of opinion emphasized that their movement was concerned to promote the interests of working men as a class. The artisans of the working men's associations, no less than the distressed handworkers of the North, assumed the need for class solidarity, and their leaders talked the language of class struggle. They denounced the Reform Act of 1832 as a middle-class measure, complained that the working classes had been deliberately duped, and argued that Whigs and Tories alike were enemies of the people. So strong was the feeling of working-class identification in Chartism that it defeated all attempts to form an alliance with middle-class reformers in the Anti-Corn Law League or the Complete Suffrage Union. Even in Birmingham, where such an alliance had the greatest hope of success, the proposal to drop the name Charter in favor of some new organization was sufficient to unite in opposition the mutually antagonistic Chartist leaders, Lovett and O'Connor. When this working-class consciousness was matched by an even stronger middle-class consciousness, as it was in the 1830s and 1840s, the possibility of social conflict was enhanced.

The fear of Chartism by the opulent classes was inspired by the very large number of followers who appeared to be sympathetic to its militant tactics. Membership of popular movements in the nineteenth century is difficult to assess, and accounts of numbers at meetings are notoriously divergent between one newspaper and another. Contemporaries, however, were agreed that attendances at Chartist meetings were greater than anything they could remember previously. Something of the tone of these rallies is conveyed by R. G. Gammage, the only Chartist to attempt a history of the movement. He is describing the torchlight meetings held on the Lancashire moors in the autumn of 1838:

> For a short period the factory districts presented a series of such imposing popular demonstrations, as were perhaps never witnessed in any previous agitation. Bolton, Stockport, Ashton, Hyde, Staleybridge, Leigh, and various other places, large and small, were the scenes of these magnificent gatherings. At the whole of them the working people met in their thousands and tens of thousands to swear devotion to the common cause. It is almost impossible to imagine the excitement caused by these manifestations. . . . The people did not go singly to the place of meeting, but met in a body at a starting point, from whence, at a given time, they issued in huge numbers,

formed into procession, traversing the principal streets, making the heavens echo with the thunder of their cheers on recognizing the idols of their worship in the men who were to address them, and sending forth volleys of the most hideous groans on passing the office of some hostile newspaper, or the house of some obnoxious magistrate or employer. The banners containing the more formidable devices, viewed by the red light of the glaring torches, presented a scene of awful grandeur. The death's heads represented on some of them grinned like ghostly spectres, and served to remind many a mammon-worshipper of his expected doom. The uncouth appearance of thousands of artisans who had not time from leaving the factory to go home and attend to the ordinary duties of cleanliness, and whose faces were therefore begrimed with sweat and dirt, added to the strange aspect of the scene. The processions were frequently of immense length, sometimes containing as many as fifty thousand people; and along the whole line there blazed a stream of light, illuminating the lofty sky, like the reflection from a large city in a general conflagration. The meetings themselves were of a still more terrific character. The very appearance of such a vast number of blazing torches only seemed more effectually to inflame the minds alike of speaker and hearers.

Another, and less inflammatory, type of Chartist meeting was the great open-air rally held on a public holiday. Contingents would march, with bands and banners, from surrounding towns and villages to a central meeting place, where they would listen to speeches from local and national leaders. Booths and stalls were set up, and the marchers were accompanied by their sweethearts, wives, and children, so that the whole gathering had some of the atmosphere of a fair. In the West Riding of Yorkshire, for example, such Chartist rallies were held at Peep Green, a natural amphitheater in the hills and equally accessible from all the main industrial towns of the region. Ben Wilson, the Halifax Chartist, estimated that 200,000 people were present at the meeting there on Whit Monday 1839.

In its most vigorous years (1837–42) Chartism seemed to swallow up lesser popular movements and to incorporate their demands with its own. The agitation against the New Poor Law in the North, which was extremely militant in 1837, was absorbed into the new Chartist movement —just as the Anti-Poor Law opposition had been led and supported by the stalwarts of the Short Time Committees, established in 1830–31 to work for factory reform. Contemporary with these movements was the struggle against the newspaper stamp duties, the "taxes on knowledge." Unstamped papers were published by radicals, who were then prosecuted and jailed: between 1830 and 1836 over 800 people were prosecuted for selling unstamped papers, 219 of them in 1835. Trade union activity had increased rapidly after the repeal of the Combination Acts (declaring unions illegal) in 1824–25, and culminated in the Grand National Consolidated Trades Union which claimed to have a million members. In 1834 the employers moved against the new unionism, and the government made an example of the Tolpuddle Martyrs—six Dorsetshire laborers who were sentenced to seven years' transportation to Australia for administering an illegal oath in their newly formed trade union lodge. This severe check, soon to be followed by the economic recession of 1837–42, put an end to further union development until the return of prosperity in the 1840s. For the time being, Chartism seemed to offer a better hope of advancement than trade unionism. As movements faded into one another, a continuity was provided by the personnel. Many of the leaders, at both national and local levels, were active in all these movements. A working man of radical inclinations did not limit himself to one particular cause, but rather supported all types of social and political agitation in the belief that they were all part of a general movement for change. Nor was there much exclusiveness in acquiring a social philosophy. Ideas from all sources were welcome, and eclecticism was no bar.

The most fruitful of these sources was Owenite socialism. Robert Owen, a successful industrialist who made a fortune in cotton spinning, elaborated his plans for social reconstruction in the years after the Napoleonic Wars. His first followers were mainly radical philanthropists, but in the late 1820s Owenism attracted support among working men. The trade union ferment of 1829–34 was dominated by Owenite theories, and for a few months in 1833–34 Owen was the acknowledged leader of the working classes. After the collapse of the Grand National Consolidated Trades Union, the Owenites developed a national organization of agents and branches which carried on propaganda and social activities until about 1845. The institutions of Owenism, however, were never as influential as its social theories. Many working-class leaders, who criticized Owen and the Owenites in the 1830s, nevertheless acknowledged their debt to Owenite socialism. Owenism provided a kind of reservoir from which different groups and individuals drew ideas and inspiration which they then applied as they chose.

Essentially, Owenism was the main British variety of what Marx and Engels called "utopian socialism," but which is more usefully described as "communitarianism." The Owenites believed that society could be radically transformed by means of experimental communities, in which property was held in common and social and economic activity was organized on a cooperative basis. This was a method of effecting social change which was radical, peaceful, and immediate. Between 1825 and 1847 seven Owenite communities were founded in Britain, the largest ones being at Orbiston in Scotland and East Tytherly, Hampshire. But attractive as the sectarian ideal of withdrawal from society in order to get on with building the "new moral world" might have appeared in the grim years of the 1830s and 1840s, the communities did not flourish as had been hoped. Other Owenite institutions for changing society were scarcely more successful. Labor exchanges, where artisans could exchange the products of their labor through the medium of labor notes, did not spread beyond London and

Birmingham. Only the cooperative trading stores, some of which were established by working men to accumulate funds for starting a community, proved eventually to be viable; and the continuous history of the modern cooperative movement is usually traced from the foundation of an Owenite store in Rochdale in 1844.

If Owenism did not produce strong and stable institutions, it did provide a yeast of ideas which found their way into other movements. Communitarianism was a challenge to a society in which community values had been weakened by emphasis on individual enterprise, self-help, and competition. The Owenites called themselves "socialists" from the mid-1830s because they wished to emphasize a social, as opposed to an individual, approach in all fields of human endeavor, including economic organization. They formulated a critique of capitalism and an alternative theory to orthodox political economy which were echoed by many working-class leaders. The basis of the Owenite "economy of cooperation" was a general labor theory of value, derived partly from a doctrine of natural right (as found in the works of John Locke) and partly from the economic arguments of the contemporary political economist David Ricardo. If, as the Owenites maintained, labor is the source of all wealth, and men exchange their products according to the amount of labor embodied in them, little theory was needed to convince working men that they had a right to the whole produce of their labor—and, as a corollary, that if they were poor it must be because they were not receiving the full value of what they produced. In the bargain between capital and labor, it was argued, labor received only a part of the wealth to which it was entitled. Further, competitive commercial society was fettered by inadequate demand: the depression of wages to subsistence level destroyed incentive to higher production by laboring men, and the low level of their consumption caused by inadequate purchasing power put a ceiling on production.

A favorite starting point for Owenite discussions was the contrast between "wealth and misery" or the paradox of "poverty in the midst of plenty." Owen was one of the first men to realize the social significance of the great increase in productive power attained during the early years of the nineteenth century, and the potentiality of material abundance was fundamental to the Owenite case. Despite some elements of backward-looking agrarianism and paternalism in the communities, Owenism did not turn its back on the Industrial Revolution or try to take refuge in some premachine idyll. Owen, as one of the most successful industrialists of his age, believed that for the first time in human history the necessary material means were available to enable everyone to lead a good life, free from poverty and insecurity. Yet, in fact, he argued, society suffered from "the paralyzing effects of superabundance," which he traced in the short run to machinery. This was not inevitable but was solely the result of the competitive system, and given a "rational" arrangement of society machinery could be a blessing instead of a curse. In all Owenite plans for community, machinery was posited as the basis for reduced hours of labor and the elimination of heavy or disagreeable types of work. Under the competitive system, however, machinery led to a devaluation of human labor: some men were directly displaced by labor-saving machines, and the wages of those remaining in work were forced down by the reservoir of unemployed.

Some of the same qualities that made Owenism attractive were also found in other social movements. The need for community and the craving for fellowship were catered for in the Friendly Benefit societies, which were the oldest and most numerous of the truly indigenous institutions of laboring men. In return for a small weekly or monthly contribution paid into a common fund, they provided sickness and funeral benefits. The members met monthly in a local public house to transact business and, more interestingly, to drink beer and have a convivial time. An annual feast was held, and the funerals of deceased members were usually followed by a supper. Ceremony and ritual were an essential part of the societies' life. They held open-air processions with bands, banners, and uniforms on all possible public occasions. Indoors, they conducted secret initiation rites, using mystical symbols, grandiloquent titles, and regalia, mostly in imitation of the freemasons. Originally, friendly societies had been local institutions with seldom more than a hundred members. But in the 1830s and 1840s these were eclipsed by the growth of the affiliated orders, with their organization into a unity (headquarters), districts, and lodges. The oldest and largest of these was the Manchester Unity, Independent Order of Oddfellows. There were also the Ancient Order of Foresters, the Loyal Order of Ancient Britons, and the Antediluvian Buffaloes.

In point of numbers, the friendly societies far exceeded any other social organization except the churches. From an estimated 925,000 members in 1815, they grew to about 4 million in 1872 (compared with nearly 400,000 in the Cooperative Movement and 500,000 trade unionists in the same year). By 1842 the Manchester Unity of Oddfellows had 3,500 lodges with 220,000 members. The strongholds of the societies were the industrial North and Midlands, and the membership was mainly from the better-off sections of the working classes. Institutionally, the friendly societies were very close to trade unionism, and in some cases unions were registered as friendly societies to protect their funds. With the rise of the affiliated orders there was some friction between the lodges and the central body; and in true sectarian fashion the discontented members split off and formed a new society. In general, friendly societies were not agents of social change but rather of social adjustment. The middle classes (in contrast to their attitude toward trade unions) welcomed the friendly societies as institutions of working-class self-help, while regretting that they "wasted" time and money on conviviality. Yet without the opportunities for social intercourse which they provided, the friendly societies would not have flourished as they did. For many thousands of working men they satisfied a longing for membership in some institution to which they could feel they belonged, a place where they would be welcomed as a "brother," not treated as a "hand." Such opportunities, as we have already seen, were not too numerous in the new industrial society.

The movements so far considered were predominantly working class in orientation, although Owenites eschewed any class appeal and adopted the title Association of All Classes of All Nations. To complete our brief survey we need to refer to movements that originated with other groups and that had different aims and objectives. For obvious reasons, the aristocracy and gentry did not need to promote social movements to advance their interests; but the middle classes, who were by no means so content with the status quo, had both the incentive and the means to do so. Two movements illustrate the potentialities for change of middle-class efforts. The first, the Anti-Corn Law League, was an agitation to secure changes which benefited, in the first instance, the industrial middle class. The second, temperance, was pioneered by members of the lower middle classes but directed primarily at the working classes.

In many ways, the Anti-Corn Law League was the middle-class counterpart of Chartism. Beginning in September 1838 as the Manchester Anti-Corn Law Association, a group of Manchester radicals (led by J. B. Smith, George Wilson, and Richard Cobden) launched a campaign to secure the repeal of the taxes on imported corn (chiefly wheat), which they regarded as pernicious and obsolescent. They argued that the Corn Laws raised the price of food and contributed to the distress that followed the poor harvest and the onslaught of the depression in the winter of 1837–38. The Corn Laws, moreover, were designed to protect the agricultural interest at the expense of the rest of the nation and were a blatant piece of class legislation. Free trade, so the argument ran, was the one sure way to promote industry and reduce the cost of living (and also wages, added the Chartists); the Corn Laws were a symbol of the policy of protection and aristocratic privilege. As the movement grew, it became a rallying point for the whole panoply of middle-class grievances. The leaguers made strenuous efforts to present their case as a national and not simply a class interest. But they failed to convince any considerable part of the working classes, who agreed rather with the Chartists that repeal should follow universal suffrage. And Manchester talk of feudal tyranny in the countryside did nothing to mollify the suspicions of the gentry that the league was an attack on the traditional control of power by the landed interest.

During its first two years, the league was mainly a propagandist body. With a headquarters in Manchester and local associations in other northern and midland towns, it held meetings, employed lecturers, and distributed tracts. The impact of these activities was somewhat reduced by the greater excitement aroused by Chartism, which was then at its peak. Attempts to counter Chartist influence, either through a rival body (such as the Leeds Household Suffrage Association of 1840) or by direct alliance with the Chartists (as at Birmingham in 1841–42), came to nothing; but the lesson was drawn that propaganda was not enough and that political means would have to be employed. The political machine that the leaguers perfected between 1842 and 1846 was a model for the conduct of a campaign to win public support and bring pressure to bear on Parliament. A most efficient organization through a central and local associations, employing full-time agents and using the most up-to-date business methods, went into action. Public relations were skillfully cultivated by means of lectures, publications, well-advertised conferences, and the purchase of press support. Electoral registers were closely checked to get out the free trade vote, objections raised to the claims of possible protectionist voters, and the forty-shilling freehold franchise (retained, ironically, in the 1832 Reform Act as a concession to the landed interest) was exploited to create new free trade voters. The payoff came in 1846. Famine in Ireland followed the failure of the potato crop at the end of 1845, and with the urgent need for alternative cheap food, the leader of the Whigs, Lord John Russell, abandoned his opposition to further reform and supported repeal. As described earlier, Sir Robert Peel, the Conservative prime minister, had also been gradually moving toward a policy of repeal, and in 1846 was able to carry such a measure through Parliament, although only at the cost of splitting his party.

The good fortune of the leaguers in gaining their objective contrasted markedly with the failure of the Chartists to win universal suffrage. Both movements worked to apply political pressure for the remedy of economic grievances but were also prepared to try other methods too. The league at the time of the Plug riots in 1842 toyed with the idea of encouraging a little physical force to back up their demands. John Bright, the best-known Anti-Corn Law spokesman of the day, urged nonpayment of taxes; and the extremist wing of the repealers urged the adoption of "bold measures." But the leaguers had the great advantage over the Chartists of being the spokesmen for the dominant middle classes, backed by the power of industry, the vote, and the ideology of orthodox political economy. The friends of progress and morality, like G. R. Porter and Samuel Smiles, rallied to the support of the league. As Cobden wrote in a letter to Peel, the repeal of the Corn Laws was a logical result of the passing of the Reform Bill.

The temperance movement was a middle-class venture of a different kind. It arose after the passing of the Beerhouse Act of 1830, which was intended to reduce drunkenness by making it easier to buy beer than spirits. But the social and moral effects of drink were such as to convince many middle-class reformers that a campaign to wean laboring men from drinking habits was an imperative duty. There was a widespread belief among practical social reformers (especially those sympathetic to Owenism) that man was often the victim of circumstances, that his conduct and beliefs were to a large extent determined by his environment, and that consequently the most effective way to eradicate antisocial attitudes and behavior was to remove the obstacles to a happy social existence. Expenditure on drink reduced the amount of income available for other (socially preferable) activities; and excessive drinking produced social misery. Temperance was a method of tackling this social problem. For some reformers, however, the problem had another dimension: drinking was not only a social evil, it was a personal sin. The rescuing of the working classes from the demon of drink was a mission of salvation. An individualist appeal and a personal approach, culminating in signing the "pledge," were characteristic of this type of temperance reform. Together, the personal and social approaches constituted a powerful motivation for an antidrink movement.

The honor of claiming the first British temperance society is usually accorded to Bradford (June 1830), but the first national body seems to have been the British and Foreign Temperance Society, which held its inaugural meeting in Exeter Hall, London, in 1831. This was an upper middle-class organization, in favor of moderation (temperance) rather than abstinence. It was soon followed by a lower middle-class rival, the British Temperance Association, started by Joseph Livesey of Preston in 1835 and advocating complete abstinence (teetotalism) from all alcoholic beverages. Nonconformist religious influence was strong in the B.T.A., and its fanaticism offended more moderate men. Consequently, a third body, the National Temperance Society, sprang up in 1842 after disputes about the use of sacramental wine. It was middle class, interdenominational, and opposed to teetotalism. Until the formation of the United Kingdom Alliance in 1853, which rapidly became the leading British temperance organization, the movement lacked institutional unity, and its main strength, as with so many British social movements, was in the localities of the North and Midlands. The network of Bands of Hope, tract societies, and Young Men's Improvement associations built around the chapels soon became formidable auxiliaries in the battle to stamp out drink. Livesey's policy of "moral suasion" was a combination of self-help and evangelical conversion, replete with calls to "repent" and "root out sin." A vast propaganda through lectures, sermons, books, magazines, and tracts was commenced. Public debates with opponents, coffee stalls, and the encouragement of leisure-time activities as a counterattraction to the public house were all grist to the temperance mill. How many people were reached by the temperance cause is impossible to determine; certainly it made an impact on the respectable, self-help sections of the working classes and on the chapel-going lower middle classes. Compared with the Anti-Corn Law League, the temperance organization of the 1840s was much less professional and streamlined; but it was more deeply rooted, its objectives were much broader and far-reaching, and its campaign was more prolonged. Until 1853 the temperance movement as a whole did not seek legislation to outlaw or restrict the sale of drink; only later was the emphasis switched to political pressure for prohibition or a permissive bill.

Very few of the social movements of early Victorian Britain were successful in the sense that they attained their declared objectives. Only if their aims were limited to securing a particular reform or piece of legislation to outlaw or restrict the sale of drink; only later was the the abolition of the stamp duty on newspapers) did they attain any obvious victory. Nevertheless, the constant striving, the restless seeking for change, was in itself a significant social phenomenon, for it helped to change the prevailing sense of what was socially desirable and what was preposterous.

Church and Chapel

The forces of change which were at work so strongly in the political, economic, and social life of the nation are also observable in religion. The Victorian era was essentially a religious age. Whether it was also more spiritual than earlier or succeeding ages is by no means so clear. At any rate, the amount of outward religious observance was strikingly different from that in Britain today.

In 1851, for the first and only time, an official census of attendance at all places of religious worship was taken. It showed that on Sunday, March 30, 1851, over seven million of the eighteen million inhabitants of England and Wales attended public worship. After allowing for young children, invalids, and aged persons, and those who were occupied in household and other work on Sundays (totaling about 30 percent of the population who could not attend church or chapel) it was estimated that about 60 percent of possible worshipers attended and 40 percent did not. When these overall figures are broken down, they reveal something of the pattern of religious worship in 1851. Attendance in rural areas and small towns was noticeably higher than in towns of more than 10,000 people. Most of the absentees lived in the large towns of the industrial areas. The Church of England was shown to be strongest in the villages and country towns, the Nonconformists in certain of the recently expanded towns of the "chief manufacturing districts."

To a later generation, the high proportion of church and chapel attenders is most impressive, but contemporaries were worried by the nonattenders. The number of attenders at services seemed small when compared with the number of sittings available in the churches and chapels. Thus in Leeds (with a population of 172,270 in 1851), which had a total of 76,488 sittings in all its places of worship, the number of worshipers at the most numerously attended morning services was 39,392. In particular, the working classes were most obviously absent. "In cities and large towns," wrote

Horace Mann, the author of the official report on the census, "it is observable how absolutely insignificant a portion of the congregations is composed of artisans." In his report Mann mentioned several possible causes of this; but they were all only different facets of a central conviction, widely held among laboring men, that religious services were primarily for the middle classes, and that the churches by and large were basically middle-class institutions.

The indifference or hostility of working men toward the Church of England is not difficult to explain. Politically, the Anglican clergy were unpopular because they adhered more faithfully than any other group to the high Tory party in the days of its decline. Intellectually, the "Erastianism" of the Church (that is, its subordination to the state) aroused nothing but contempt in the minds of working-class reformers. Socially, the gulf between a vicar with an income of as much as £1,000 a year and a hand-loom weaver with 12s. a week, if he were lucky, was felt to be too great to allow of any common interests. At the other extreme were the 5,230 curates in England and Wales whose average annual stipend amounted to only £80. It was not necessary to be a Dissenter to feel repelled by the abuses within the Church. The main forms of Church of England Christianity did not make much appeal to ordinary working people in the 1830s. If the Church were to make any significant impact on the working classes—or on many of the industrial middle classes—it clearly required a new approach. Thomas Arnold, the famous headmaster of Rugby School, writing in 1832, commented: "Phrases which did well enough formerly, now only excite a sneer; it does not do to talk to the operatives about our pure and apostolic church,' and 'our glorious constitution'; they have no respect for either; but one must take higher ground. . . . The Church as it now stands, no human power can save."

The revival within the Church of England, which did much to strengthen its hold among the middle and upper classes if not among laboring people, came from its two opposing extremes. It will be recalled that the Church was a curious mixture of Protestantism and Catholicism, and from both of these elements came challenges which upset the comfortable inertia of the Establishment. First in time was the Protestant challenge. Contemporary with Wesley, and motivated, like the Methodists, by a desire to grapple with profound spiritual problems which the Church as a whole ignored, a group known as the evangelicals developed within the Church during the last quarter of the eighteenth century. Their best-known stronghold was at Clapham, then a suburban village near London. This "Clapham Sect" centered on the rector of Clapham, John Venn, and included Zachary Macaulay (a London merchant and father of the Whig historian), Henry Thornton (a rich banker and M.P.), William Wilberforce (an M.P. and close friend of William Pitt, the prime minister), James Stephen (a lawyer), and other prominent members of the middle class. At

Cambridge University the evangelicals counted scholars such as Isaac Milner and Charles Simeon. In the country they drew support from earnest clergymen and converted philanthropists like Hannah More, a notable bluestocking (or female intellectual) of the period.

The evangelicals, as was to be expected from such a strongly middle-class group, exerted a liberalizing influence. They cared little about the Church as an institution, but a great deal about the saving of souls. Theologically, they were mild Calvinists, who emphasized the need for personal salvation and the importance of good works. They were strongly antipapist, distrustful of high churchmen, and had little time for liturgy and ritual. Their concern was with "vital" or "true" religion, as opposed to the merely "nominal" Christianity which they observed all around them.

The outcome of these evangelical tenets was to be seen in various measures of fashionable philanthropy: schools for the poor, societies for the suppression of vice and the strict observance of the Sabbath, pressure for the "reformation of manners." Although they were always a minority in the Church of England and made many enemies by their apparent rigidity and kill-joy puritanism, the evangelicals scored some notable successes. Their twenty-year fight against slavery, led by Wilberforce, culminated in the abolition of the slave trade in 1807, and slavery in all British colonies was ended in 1833. At home they attacked ecclesiastical abuses such as nonresidence of clergy and founded Sunday schools and the Religious Tract Society. For work abroad they organized the Church Missionary Society (1799) and the British and Foreign Bible Society (1804). Within the Church of England they upheld standards of personal belief and piety that put to shame the laxity and worldliness of the majority of Anglicans; and in society at large their impact was responsible for the changes in morality which were obvious to contemporaries by 1830. They gave to the Victorians that strong ethical code which found its summation in the concept of duty.

The second challenge within the Church of England came from the opposite extreme, the High Church or Catholic wing. Sparked in 1833 by the Whigs' attempt to reform the Anglican Church in Ireland through the amalgamation of redundant bishoprics, a group of Oxford scholars and clerics launched what became the Oxford (or Tractarian) Movement. The leaders were John Keble, Dr. Edward Bouverie Pusey, and John Henry Newman, and they soon gained influential supporters. They emphasized the Catholic elements in the Church of England (the creeds, sacraments, liturgy, apostolic succession) and looked back to the teachings of the High Church Anglican divines of the seventeenth century. To spread their views, they published a series of *Tracts for the Times,* the first of which was written by Newman in 1833. From then until 1839 the Tractarians caused considerable controversy in the university; but after 1839 they were increasingly attacked and discredited by the authorities. Newman struggled for several years to prove to his own satisfaction that the Church of England was truly a part of the Catholic Church; but he finally despaired and in 1845 went over to Rome. His secession to the Roman Catholic Church was a blow to the movement, and others followed him. But the majority remained within the Church of England and continued to press for the changes they desired. During the years 1833–45 the Tractarians made a great impression as teachers in the university, and thereafter their influence was carried by the young men who had been their students into all parts of the country. "I believe in one Catholic and Apostolic Church," proclaimed the Tractarians; and they awakened in the Church of England a new awareness of its sacramental traditions and the richness of Catholic devotion. Like the evangelicals, the Tractarians were always a minority; but they similarly acted as a leaven in the lump.

The signs of change within the Church of England first became apparent about 1836. The Victorian Church which then began to emerge was marked by energy and strength. In rural areas a good deal of the old social tradition, shorn of its worst abuses, continued. But in the towns a new figure—the slum parson—began to emerge; and in the industrial areas Anglican champions of social reform appeared side by side with Chartists and radicals. New parishes, archdeaconries, and dioceses were created in industrial districts. By 1850 evidence of new life within the Church was abundantly clear. There was a veritable spate of repairing old churches and building new ones. School building and the formation of guilds, sisterhoods, and charities were indicative of a new fervor in parochial work. Perhaps of greatest significance in its social effects was the new conception of the role of the Church in the community. If this was interpreted by Thomas Arnold to mean a Christian scholar and gentleman in every parish, the other side of the medal was the emphasis on obligations toward the parishioners.

As Arnold's phrase suggested, the gulf between the rectory and the cottage was to remain as great as ever. What was new was the insistence that the middle classes, lay and clerical, had a duty toward the laboring population. Contemporaries never used the word "guilt," but the hum of evangelical fervor in a multitude of organizations for good works after 1836 suggests that some such feeling was perhaps subconsciously implicit in the relation between the middle classes and the poor. Clothing clubs, soup kitchens, parochial schools were alike products, in some degree, of this relationship.

It was in the industrial areas that the new type of Anglican, whether parson or layman, marked the greatest break with the immediate past. Richard Oastler, who campaigned against the brutalities of child slavery in Yorkshire mills, and urged fierce resistance to the New Poor Law, had left the Methodist church of his childhood to join the Church of England.

The Rev. George Stringer Bull, vicar of Bierley, championed the same causes throughout the 1830s. By far the most influential of the new type of Anglican clergyman in the North was the Rev. Dr. Walter Farquhar Hook, vicar of Leeds from 1837 to 1859. The fortunes of the Church in Leeds were at a low ebb when Hook began his ministry there. It was his achievement that he, a high churchman in the midst of a strongly evangelical community, rehabilitated the Church of England in the eyes of the middle classes and won the respect and even the affection of many of the working classes. That he earned the epithet of "the working man's vicar" was due largely to his obvious and sincere concern for projects of social reform. His open support of the factory reform movement, the early closing movement, and the development of public parks, together with his active work for popular education, ranged him on the side of working-class reformers. His social philosophy, like Oastler's, was Tory-radicalism, with its ideal of the well-being of the whole of society and not just of one class. It was a conscious attempt to make Christianity relevant to industrial society.

Nevertheless, even the most sympathetic "working man's vicar" was far removed socially from his working-class flock. No one ever suggested that a laboring man might become a vicar; the ideal of a scholar and gentleman in every parish made such an idea preposterous. If the working classes, or indeed many of the middle classes, desired a closer identification with the organization and control of the Church, they had to turn elsewhere. Hence it was in the various Nonconformist churches that many of them found a more congenial religious home. Despite the herculean labors of Hook in Leeds, the dominant religious ethos of the West Riding was essentially one of Dissent. Shortly after his arrival in Leeds in 1837 Hook perceived this clearly. "The real fact is," he wrote, "that the established religion in Leeds is Methodism, and it is Methodism that all the most pious among the Churchmen unconsciously talk. If you ask a poor person the ground of his hope, he will immediately say that he feels he is saved, however great a sinner he may be." It was then eighty-five years since Methodism had been first introduced into Leeds by John Nelson, a stonemason of Birstal, who had been converted after hearing John Wesley preach at Moorfields in 1739. By 1851, out of a total of 983,423 attendances made on census Sunday in Yorkshire, over 600,000 were at Dissenting places of worship, and of these 431,000 were at Methodist chapels of various sorts.

The Methodist body in the first half of the nineteenth century, however, was by no means homogeneous, and the social and political allegiances of Methodists were divided along the lines of Disraeli's "Two Nations," the rich and the poor. As long as John Wesley himself was alive, the Methodists generally took little active part in politics, but after his death in 1791 the official political neutrality of the central organization, the Wesleyan Conference, became increasingly, in effect, political conservatism. The growing wealth of many middle-class members of the societies, and the consequent desire to be considered respectable, naturally inclined them to shun anything that might carry the taint of radicalism or disloyalty, especially in the period after 1815. By the 1830s there was added to this negative instinct a positive desire to support the political and social programs of the middle classes, of which many of them were members. Wesleyan mill owners and businessmen were not prepared to remain neutral on social and political issues which affected them closely.

Underlying the dominant conservatism of official Methodism was a liberal and democratic spirit. From the time when John Wesley took to preaching salvation in the open air and humble men were converted, Methodism was a popular movement, and most of the schisms which rent the central Wesleyan body until 1849 were attempts, in one form or another, to reassert this basic characteristic. The breakaway churches, such as the Methodist New Connexion (1796), the Primitive Methodists (1811), the Bible Christians (1815), the Protestant Methodists (1827), the Barkerites (1841), and the Wesleyan Reformers (1849), were characterized by differences of organization and personalities, not of doctrine. Methodism, unlike the Church of England, was essentially a laymen's religion. In addition to the full-time ministers (who had the superintendence of a number of chapels in a circuit), there was an army of active lay helpers, numbering in 1850 some 20,000 local preachers, over 50,000 class leaders, together with trustees, stewards, prayer leaders, and Sunday school teachers. How many of these were working men is difficult to ascertain, and the class composition of Methodism differed between Connexions and between individual chapels in the same Connexion. At the two extremes of the social scale—among the aristocracy and the nonrespectable laboring poor—Methodism had little influence; but among the middle classes and some sections of the working classes it secured a firm hold. While the Wesleyan Methodists in most places were predominantly a middle-class body, the Primitive Methodists had a pronounced working-class flavor. In some of the industrial towns and villages of the Midlands, and in rural areas too, the Primitive Methodists successfully pioneered a type of religion adapted to the needs of laboring men and women. Farm laborers attended the "ranters" meetings, held in a crowded cottage or plain, humble village chapel, and listened to a local preacher who was himself a working man and spoke their idiom. They felt at home there in a way they seldom did in the parish church with its liturgy, ritual, and sermon by a middle-class parson.

There are other types of evidence of the impact of Methodism at a popular level. It is not an accident that almost every self-educated working man in early and mid-Victorian England, when he came to write his memoirs, paid tribute to the beneficial influences of Methodism in his youth. The accounts of self-educated men show a pattern of Methodist domestic piety, help in a local Sunday school, conversion, membership of a Methodist class, preaching, and then (usually) a progression beyond the original Methodism to some new intellectual position. Methodism for them was almost a natural stage in their educational and moral development; and for thousands of less distinguished laboring men and women it remained an intellectual and philosophical resting place.

The impact that Methodism made on working men was complex. Insofar as it inculcated the goals of respectability and hard work, it reinforced the puritan values of the middle classes. The convenience of religion as a work discipline was not lost upon contemporaries. But the popular roots of Methodism also meant that it could contribute to some of the working-class movements described earlier. The Methodist system of class meetings provided a useful model for Chartist and radical organization, and a class or band meeting could as easily study the works of Thomas Paine as the Old Testament. Camp meetings and chapels were institutions which could serve secular as well as religious purposes, and the eloquence and self-discipline acquired through preaching from a chapel pulpit was a useful training for addressing mass meetings of Chartists or factory reformers. As schools of practical democracy and self-government, the Methodist chapels rendered valuable service to popular movements. Not only did working men utilize directly Methodist forms and techniques for other causes, but they also assimilated Methodist thought and attitudes into movements for social and political reform.

No other group of Nonconformists had such a large following among the working classes as the Methodists. The Old Dissent (that is, the churches descended from the sects of the seventeenth century) was predominantly middle class in membership and outlook, with the exception of certain Baptist chapels in the industrial North and in Wales. When the Old Dissenters wished to establish contact with the working classes, they had to make a conscious effort to go out to them. The artisan who felt out of place, socially and spiritually, in an Anglican church was likely to feel scarcely less of a stranger in the company of wealthy industrialists in their large and fashionable downtown chapels. While the Old Dissent did not make the same type of direct appeal to sections of the working classes as did Methodism, its influence nevertheless was often in a direction sympathetic to working-class advance. An important minority in the leadership of the Old Dissenting bodies was radically inclined toward social and political change; and could usually be counted on to support specific demands on questions of popular education, extension of the suffrage, and attacks on ancient privilege.

Of growing importance was the Roman Catholic Church. Since the Reformation the Catholics in England and Scotland had been reduced to a small, sometimes persecuted group which had played little part in the national life, but with the constantly growing Irish immigration the situation in Great Britain was radically changed. Instead of a church composed of a few ancient landed families, mostly in the North, the Roman communion became a body catering to the needs of predominantly working-class congregations of Irish origin. So rapidly did the numbers grow that in 1850 the Roman hierarchy was reintroduced into Great Britain (amid enraged Protestant and Anglican protests at the "papal aggression"), and a small but highly distinguished flow of converts from the Tractarians added a leaven of English intellectual respectability.

Yet wider than all formal religious institutions, whether popular or respectable, was the influence of Nonconformist Christianity which colored the thinking of members of the middle and working classes. The desire for a religion free from credal beliefs, conceding the right of private judgment, and unconnected with any ecclesiastical hierarchy was widespread. Early Victorian Britain was the scene of many spectacular losses of religious faith in the literary world, of which George Eliot, James Anthony Froude, and Francis Newman (John Henry's brother) are the best-known examples; and among working-class reformers a strong anticlerical and Paineite tradition was preserved. Yet the ethical standards of unbelievers were the same as those of professed Christians. Their morality was as puritanical as that of strict church- or chapel-goers. They were models of rectitude in their devotion to duty. This code of beliefs and ethics, followed by Christians and unbelievers alike, was basically evangelical. In the previous generation the evangelicals had been a group of devout, Calvinist-minded reformers within the Anglican Church. But for the Victorians the values with which the evangelicals were associated became an orthodoxy, and evangelicalism (Christian or secular) part of the ideology of the age. When we say, then, that the early Victorian period was a religious age we do not mean that everyone went to church (though a large proportion of the population in fact did so), but that Protestant evangelicalism was a basic ingredient in the dominant ideology. Men's values and standards, their assumptions and attitudes, functioned within this context.

CHAPTER FIVE

The mid-Victorian years from 1848 to 1867 have been variously described as an age of compromise, balance, equipoise, or consensus. Behind these different appellations lies the common belief that Britain after 1848 entered a period of calm, in marked contrast to the events described in the previous chapter. Without seeking to exaggerate such contrasts or imply that after 1848 the country was a very different sort of place to live in, it is true that the mood and tone of the 1850s and 1860s seemed far removed from the anxieties and turmoil of the previous generation. For many millions of people the 1830s and 1840s had been times of unemployment, misery, frustration, and sheer hunger. But now the corner seemed to have been turned, and the long-promised "good time coming" to be within sight. The basis for such hopes was economic prosperity, some of which percolated down to most sections of the community. The returns for the grim decades of the second, intensive phase of the Industrial Revolution came to the mid-Victorians.

Symbolizing the new era was the Great Exhibition of 1851. There had been exhibitions before, but never one like this. It was in every way an enormous success, far exceeding the fondest hopes of its promoters, led by the prince consort. Designed by Joseph Paxton, who had previously built a great conservatory for his patron, the Duke of Devonshire, the huge

Victorian Prosperity:
1848-1867

building of glass and iron in Hyde Park captured the imagination of the nation. It was bigger than the largest cathedral and was visited by over six million people. The 100,000 exhibits covered every imaginable aspect of mid-nineteenth-century civilization; and though ingenuity and extravagance were perhaps more in evidence than good taste, the "visibility of progress," especially British progress, was plain for all to see. The themes of the Great Exhibition were moral as well as material. Particular emphasis was put on the gospel of work and self-help, and also on the promotion of international peace through commerce and free trade. These provided the keynotes of the period we have now to examine.

Bourgeois England

In every period the general social climate is largely set by one particular group or class; the others reluctantly or willingly adapt themselves to it. This dominant section of the community after 1848 was the middle class. Although they did not immediately rush forward after 1832 to seize the reins of political power, it became increasingly obvious that their interests, their ideas, and their habits were the dominant ones. Sometimes, this was concealed behind an aristocratic exterior, for it has always been a British characteristic to assimilate new wealth and power with the old. But the realities of the situation were tacitly acknowledged. No better example of this could be cited than Sir Robert Peel. His ancestors had been yeomen farmers, his father had made a fortune as a cotton spinner and had acquired a baronetcy, and Peel himself took over the leadership of the Tory party from the Duke of Wellington. Even at the very top of the social order, in the persons of Victoria and Albert, the nation saw not the apex of a feudal aristocracy but something quite new: a bourgeois family on the throne. This was a far cry from the days of George IV when the monarchy had become a symbol of extravagance, immorality, and aristocratic degeneracy. At the opposite end of the social scale many of the working classes developed bourgeois habits and aspired to a modest level of respectability. Confident of their economic strength and moral superiority, the middle classes could imagine no happier fate for the nation than that it should be made over in their own image. The lifestyle of the middle classes became the model to be emulated by the nation at large.

In Victorian Britain the definition of middle class was clearer than it is today, although the criteria of membership were not rigid or even definite. Income, occupation, education, religion, and type of home were all

The Great Exhibition, 1851: The Crystal Palace.

used in assessing a person's social status. Even so, there were wide differences between the upper and lower middle classes. At the top were wealthy London bankers and merchants who mixed with the aristocracy on terms of familiarity; in the North and Midlands were self-made industrial magnates; and everywhere there were the £10 householders—small manufacturers, shopkeepers, coal and corn merchants, master tailors, innkeepers, commercial travelers, dealers of all kinds. To these "tradesmen" should be added a growing army of clerks, office workers, teachers, officials, managers, and professional men at various levels. The growth in size, importance, and self-awareness of these sections of the community was a main feature of Victorian England.

A middle-class way of life had several distinguishing characteristics which marked it off from the aristocracy above and the working classes below. The basic requirement for middle-class status was a steady income derived from a nonmanual job in business or the professions. Three hundred pounds a year was frequently quoted as the minimum necessary for the satisfaction of normal middle-class expectations, but many people enjoyed three times that figure. On the other hand, clerks and teachers earned only £60–80 a year—less than a skilled artisan. A house of suitable size and location was next required. This could vary from a six-room terrace house to a substantial villa with ten or more rooms. The ideal was described by Dickens in *Pickwick Papers:*

> Everything was so beautiful! The lawn in front, the garden behind, the miniature conservatory, the dining-room, the drawing-room, the bed-rooms, the smoking-room, and above all the study, with its pictures and easy-chairs, and odd cabinets, and queer tables, and books out of number, with a large cheerful window opening upon a pleasant lawn and commanding a pretty landscape, just dotted here and there with little houses almost hidden by the trees; and then the curtains, and the carpets, and the chairs, and the sofas! Everything was so beautiful, so compact, so neat, and in such exquisite taste, said everybody, that there really was no deciding what to admire most.

A Victorian house today is usually regarded as uncomfortable and inconvenient. But this is largely because of the absence of servants. The typical nineteenth-century villa was designed vertically rather than horizontally, the servants occupying the basement and attics, the family living and sleeping on the floors between. Domestic service was a crucial factor in the middle-class standard of living. In 1851 domestic servants totaled more than one million and were the largest single group of employed persons in any occupation except agriculture. Thereafter, they continued to increase steadily; and at the end of the century, when he carried out his great survey of working-class poverty in York, the sociologist Seebohm Rowntree still took the keeping or not of domestic servants as marking the division between the working and middle classes. The middle class

A bourgeois monarchy: Queen Victoria and the Prince Consort, 1861. (Gernsheim Collection, The University of Texas at Austin.)

was defined essentially as the servant-keeping class. Even the humblest householders in the lower middle classes managed to keep a young servant girl who made the fires and helped with the washing and cleaning; and a minimum of three female servants (cook, housemaid, and nursemaid) was regarded as normal. Menservants were something of a luxury, and could be afforded only by richer householders. The emphasis in the Victorian home was on comfort, and in the absence of labor-saving appliances this was most easily obtained by a plentiful use of servants. Mrs. Isabella Beeton's *Book of Household Management* first appeared in 1861 and went through numerous later editions. "Mrs. Beeton" became a household name as the standard English cookbook, but in fact the early editions were not merely recipe books but complete guides to all aspects of housekeeping. Detailed instructions on the duties of each type of servant were given (how to make a bed, clean a grate, dust a room), for middle-class domestic economy became an elaborate ritual presided over by the wife and mistress of the household.

Central to all aspects of middle-class life was the cult of home and the sanctity of the family. The image of the cosy hearth, round which the family gathered regularly, was repeated endlessly in poems and magazine articles. Home was especially a private place, where the individual could retire from the stresses and strains of the busy world. Windows were heavily curtained to frustrate the prying eyes of strangers; gardens were surrounded by high brick walls to preserve privacy from neighbors. Such was the dominance of the cult of home that domestic virtue extended to literature and the fine arts. Novels and plays had to be such as a father could read aloud to his wife and daughters without embarrassment—following the example of the egregious Dr. Thomas Bowdler, who in 1818 had published a *Family Shakespeare* from which all "improper" passages had been removed. Paintings were expected to be didactic and, above all, moral. Favorite artists were those who painted warm, sentimental subjects with great attention to realistic detail, such as Edwin Landseer, whose animal scenes were highly admired by the queen and Prince Albert.

The middle-class family was a strictly hierarchical group with the

Middle-class domesticity: Bringing in the Christmas pudding, 1849. (Alexis Soyer, *The Modern Housewife or Menagère*, Science and Technology Research Center, The New York Public Library.)

husband at its head. His authority over all other members—wife, children, servants—was virtually absolute and was supported by the whole weight of social, legal, and religious approval. For women the middle-class family could be an unsatisfactory institution, since the wife was so completely subjected to her husband; and for unmarried daughters and rebellious sons it could be equally oppressive. Divorce, although legalized in 1857, was unspeakably disgraceful and was not much used. Contraception was not practiced at all, and the burden of successive (and unwanted) pregnancies was heavy. Sex was unmentionable in the Victorian home, and children's questions about it were turned aside, so that they grew up puzzled, ignorant, and resentful. The ideal of chastity and the practice of prudery were the defenses of the middle-class family against the pressures of sexuality. One of the least attractive features of Victorianism was this treatment of sexual relationships, with its double standard (one for men and another for women) and its hypocrisy in the face of unpleasant realities. But before condemning the middle-class Victorians out of hand, it is well to remember that "respectability" was a bulwark against the great underworld of prostitution and crime which lay at their doorstep and which they feared might one day engulf them.

A good deal of middle-class social philosophy was embodied in the doctrine of self-help and the closely related gospel of work. Samuel Smiles, a Scottish doctor, published his *Self-Help* in 1859, and it immediately became a best seller. This famous self-help manual was a series of potted biographies of men who had risen from poverty and obscurity to affluence and success by their own efforts, interspersed with proverbial sayings and moral comments. Its enormous popularity came from its success in presenting the dominant social values of the time in simple, acceptable form. Smiles claimed no originality for *Self-Help*, and the period was in fact flooded with books of advice about how to get on through self-improvement.

It was widely agreed that the foremost quality necessary for success in life was industry, the capacity and willingness for hard work. This, not genius, was the secret of most successful men. "The qualities necessary to ensure success," Smiles assured his readers, "are not at all extraordinary. They may, for the most part, be summed up in these two—common sense and perseverance." Such effort was necessary in the first place to earn a socially adequate income; and such an income was the basis of independence, without which a man could not be considered free. In relation to this central aim of independence, the lesser virtues of frugality, self-denial, and thrift stood as means to an end. Thrift appeared to Smiles as an effective agency for working-class betterment precisely because it would make the working man independent; it would enable him to become a truly free man instead of a wage slave. The power of a penny a day saved, he

The ideal of self-help: Title page of a temperance journal, *British Workman*, January 1859. (J. F. C. Harrison, *Learning and Living*, Routledge & Kegan Paul, Ltd.)

argued, was potentially a greater force for working-class emancipation than Chartism, universal suffrage, or strikes.

Besides thrift, there were numerous ancillary aids to success. Punctuality and early rising were essential in young people. So also were habits of orderliness, for just as genius seldom dispensed with the need for hard work, so success was seldom attained by accident. Leisure was not to be wasted but used. A concern for the little things in life was not to be despised; positively, because if one takes care of the pence the pounds take care of themselves, and, negatively, because a little sin leads to a big one. More important still was a "prudent" marriage in accordance with Malthusian precepts. "Marriage without means is like a horse without beans," repeated the manuals on happy homes; "Before you marry be sure of a home wherein to tarry," advised the writers of moral stories in the family magazines. There were also other desirable, although not strictly essential, ingredients. Piety and religious observance, adherence to temperance principles, and avoidance of bad temper had obvious material value. Conversely, "sensual" amusements, religious "infidelity," trade disputes, and political agitation were to be avoided. Contemporaries felt that the combination of certain moral qualities with a few simple techniques of living would produce those habits most conducive to success. The pedigree of these ideas of social morality was puritan, transmitted through the dominant evangelicalism of the middle classes.

Underlying all middle-class ideas of man and society were the basic assumptions of liberalism. The term derived from *liber*, meaning a free man; and liberalism for the Victorians was synonymous with freedom, in the philosophic, religious, economic, and political spheres. At the center of the universe, they argued (echoing the American transcendentalist, Ralph Waldo Emerson), stood the individual, whose needs and interests were paramount and against whom all the institutions of the world were secondary. Philosophically, liberals subscribed to the view (expressed in the American Declaration of Independence) that all men had an inalienable right to "life, liberty, and the pursuit of happiness." In religion, liberalism meant the assertion of the individual conscience, and the freedom of individual interpretation, against the claims to authority of the Church of England or the Roman Church. Liberals tended therefore to be Nonconformists or evangelical Anglicans. Politically, liberals championed attacks on privilege and corruption, especially aristocratic exclusiveness, and their watchword was reform.

Liberal economics was the most powerful orthodoxy of the nineteenth century, and under the name "political economy" was fiercely attacked and skillfully defended. Its central tenet was laissez-faire, or the "leave-alone" principle. Since the operation of a free market economy was declared to be in accordance with "natural" laws, it followed that there should be as little interference with economic activity as possible. Perfect competition and pursuit of individual self-interest would result in the maximum benefit to the whole community. The role of the state was to stay out of economic (and, indeed, of most other) affairs and merely hold the ring for competing interests. A distrust of state action and a preference for individualism wherever it could be encouraged was deeply ingrained in the mid-Victorians. Not all of them of course were prepared to press their belief in universal laissez-faire and individualism to extremes. But many of the middle classes found these doctrines sufficiently to their liking to press for free trade not only in business but in religion and education as well. Competition in all areas of life, advised Smiles, was necessary for "the advancement of individualism and through that of society at large."

That liberalism appealed to the middle classes is hardly surprising. It was essentially their ideology. The great success of the middle classes, however, was the extent to which their ideology penetrated other classes and created an essentially bourgeois nation. With the aristocratic culture liberalism made only modest inroads. But with sections of the working classes the impact went deeper. The cooperative and trade union movements became models of working-class, collective self-help.

Trade unionism in Britain originated with the trade clubs of the eighteenth century. These were associations of journeymen (that is, wage workers) in the skilled handicrafts—hatters, compositors, woolen workers. They usually met in a tavern, and their object was to have a convivial evening and discuss the affairs of the trade. Soon they gained control of the initiation of apprentices, organized benefit funds for sickness and burial, and operated as an employment bureau for masters seeking skilled workers. A trade union was originally a federation of these clubs, on a local or temporary basis. From 1799 to 1824 unions were outlawed by the Combination Acts, the government fearing that they might foster revolutionary and seditious schemes and the employers hating them for interfering in wages and working conditions. But in 1824, largely through the efforts of Francis Place, the radical tailor of Charing Cross, London, the Combination Acts were repealed; and trade unionism grew rapidly in the late 1820s and early 1830s. A climax came with the formation of the Owenite Grand National Consolidated Trades Union (1833–34), which was the first attempt at a national union embracing all trades throughout the country. After its collapse working-class energies were channeled into other movements, notably Chartism. When this in turn began to lack momentum in the 1840s, trade unionism revived and thereafter grew steadily.

The New Model unionism of the 1850s (as it was called by the pioneer labor historians, Sidney and Beatrice Webb) differed from earlier efforts in several important respects. Unlike the unions of the 1820s and 1830s, with their secrecy, millennialism, and revolutionary goals, the new unions were sober, respectable, and stable. The Amalgamated Society of

Engineers (1851) was a model for the future. Consisting of highly skilled men, it was able to exact high dues of a shilling a week, and offered a full range of friendly benefits. It was run by a small staff of full-time officials, publicized its activities to enlist wide sympathy for its case, and generally sought to promote an image of reasonableness and respectability. The new spirit of unionism is well conveyed by the advice of the *Flint-Glass Makers Magazine* in 1850: "If you do not wish to stand as you are and suffer more oppression, we say to you get knowledge, and in getting knowledge you get power. . . . Let us earnestly advise you to educate; get intelligence instead of alcohol—it is sweeter and more lasting." Instead of trying to overturn the capitalist system, mid-Victorian trade unions concentrated their efforts on gaining material benefits by bargaining and strengthening their own and their members' position in society. Because they were confined to the better-paid workers (the aristocracy of labor), they were able to adopt some of the Smilesian precepts of self-help. By the 1860s they were sufficiently powerful to agitate for changes in the law respecting unions and to play a part in the movement for the 1867 Reform Bill.

The cooperative movement was a similar example of successful working-class self-help. In 1844 a small band of Owenites founded a cooperative trading store in Rochdale, Lancashire. Their original hopes of a community gradually faded, but their store prospered. The Rochdale principle of paying an annual dividend to each member according to the amount of his purchases soon spread, and after a slow start in the 1850s the movement grew steadily. By the end of the century the "co-op" and the "divi" had become established institutions of working-class life in all the industrial towns of the North and Midlands. The movement extended beyond consumers' stores to a national Cooperative Wholesale Society, which supplied the stores and had its own factories. As with trade unionism, cooperation chiefly benefited the better-off sections of the working classes, those with a fairly steady income and aspirations to respectability. For the poor, who needed weekly credit and who could afford only goods of inferior quality, the cooperatives had little to offer. Originating as an Owenite socialist challenge to the capitalist system, the cooperative movement was converted into a great mutual thrift organization, basking in the approval of bourgeois society.

Propagation of the values of self-help, improvement, and respectability was largely an educational process. Industrial society, to a far greater extent than any previous age, was based on the written word. Literacy had a socializing function: it broke down the traditional, preindustrial, folk culture of the people and helped to spread the new ideology of the middle classes. The creation of a fully literate society was an imperative in the dominant philosophies of the Victorian age. The illiterate man could be a good evangelical Christian, but it was a definite advantage if he could read the Scriptures. A rational appeal was extremely difficult to communicate to working men who could not read. Victorian society therefore developed a network of educational institutions, catering to the needs of different groups and classes.

That fairly widespread illiteracy amongst the working classes existed in early Victorian England and Wales, despite a considerable amount of voluntary educational effort of various kinds, is clear from the statistics of the marriage registers, where brides and grooms who could not write their names signed with an "X." Joseph Brook, a weaver who gave evidence before the Assistant Handloom Weavers Commission in 1839, estimated that two-thirds of the adult weavers in Bradford could read but that not above a quarter could write. In general, the figures for the 1840s show that about two-thirds of the males and half the females were literate, at any rate to the extent of signing their names. But there were considerable regional differences in literacy rates which are not very easy to explain. After 1840 the percentage of literate persons increased, although for some time there was also an absolute increase in illiterates because of the growth in population. The root cause of the illiteracy was inadequate elementary education. In 1851 there were nearly five million children of school age, that is, between the ages of three and fifteen. Of these, 600,000 were at work, over two million were in school, and the remainder were neither at work nor in school.

For the children of the working classes, three main types of educational institution existed: the private day school (including the dame school), the Sunday school, and the factory school. The great majority of working-class pupils in common day schools were under the age of ten, and many attended for only two or three years. The quality of education in such schools was low, for the teachers were unqualified and the charge per head (school pence) was under 6d. per week. Dame schools, intended for the youngest children, were usually little more than baby-minding establishments. Factory schools, established under the educational clauses of the 1833 Factories Act, were not much better than the private day schools. The Sunday schools, which had grown rapidly since their foundation in the 1780s, were handicapped by the part-time basis of their operation and were perhaps mainly useful in giving able boys a start from which they could go on to educate themselves. Even when the school pence were forthcoming and parents were willing and able to forego their children's earnings for some years, the restricted curricula and haphazard organization of primary education were such as to provide at best a certain amount of "instruction" and seldom a genuine education. With limited facilities for primary education, the educational aspirations of the working classes tended to be kept low.

The existence of perhaps a quarter or a third of the laboring poor who were totally illiterate, and a further percentage whose literacy was only rudimentary, constituted a barrier to the spread of middle-class ideology. An increase in the provision of elementary school facilities was the main response to this challenge. Encouraged by a modest annual grant of £20,000 from the government in 1833 (increased to £30,000 in 1839) and by the setting-up of a small central administration and inspectorate, the voluntary religious school societies built a network of elementary schools across the country. Thanks to the religious rivalry between the two main providing bodies—the British and Foreign School Society (Nonconformist) and the National Society (Church of England)—a system of public elementary education was established. Throughout the 1850s and 1860s this system of competition between the Anglicans and Nonconformists (free trade in education) continued to spread; but by 1870 it had failed to provide schooling for more than half the children in London and for only a third to a fifth of the children elsewhere. State intervention thus became inescapable if adequate provision was to be made, and in 1870 the Education Act began the process of supplementing and, ultimately, replacing the voluntary schools with state schools.

The institutions of education for the middle and upper classes were a strange assortment of ancient privilege and recent innovation. In the cities and market towns the old grammar schools offered a traditional, classics-based curriculum for the sons of local tradesmen and businessmen. For the aristocracy, gentry, and wealthy middle classes the Public Schools provided an education for leadership, which successfully integrated the old and new wealth into a ruling elite. These Public Schools were in fact anything but public: some were ancient foundations which had transformed themselves by taking fee-paying pupils, others were new schools built specially for the children of the middle classes. All were expensive, exclusive, and (usually) run as boarding, not day, schools. The pace-setter was Rugby School, which, under the headmastership of Dr. Thomas Arnold from 1828 to 1842, soon transformed the tone and content of Public School education. Arnold's ideal was to turn out Christian gentlemen. He introduced "modern" subjects (French, history, mathematics) into the old classical curriculum, emphasized the value of team games, and gave responsibilities of leadership to the older students as prefects. The ideal of "clean living and high thinking" was inculcated in the future leaders of Britain and her empire and immortalized in Thomas Hughes's novel of Rugby life, *Tom Brown's Schooldays* (1857).

Higher education proved more resistant to middle-class demands for reform. The universities of Oxford and Cambridge survived as archaic, eighteenth-century institutions throughout the first half of the nineteenth century, but were forced by pressure from outside to begin modernizing themselves in the 1850s. The first of the new universities was London, founded in 1828, and followed shortly by Durham (1832) and Owens College, Manchester (1851). But a university education, unlike a Public School education, was not regarded by many middle-class industrialists and businessmen as essential for their sons unless they had political or professional ambitions for them.

Critics of Victorian Society

Despite the affluence, optimism, and complacency of much of mid-Victorian life, there were always those who doubted and questioned the assumptions and values of Victorian society. Most of these critics attacked the commercialization of life, to which they attributed the social evils of big cities, the bad taste in art and architecture, and the false values of the middle classes. Behind these criticisms was a fundamental doubt about the desirability of the competitive, industrial society which the Industrial Revolution had produced.

The attack was well and truly launched in the 1830s and 1840s by Thomas Carlyle, who was listened to by his contemporaries as an Old Testament prophet of the age. He thundered against "mammon worship" and condemned the "cash nexus" to which the relationship between human beings had been reduced. "We call it a Society," he wrote in *Past and Present* (1843), "and go about professing openly the totalest separation, isolation. Our life is not a mutual helpfulness; but rather, cloaked under due laws-of-war, named 'fair competition' and so forth, it is a mutual hostility." The new industrial order in England was not a true society because it lacked the necessary characteristics of wholeness, unity, and stability. Instead it offered only fragmentation, loneliness, and strife. Karl Marx, the great German socialist who came to live in London from 1849, described much the same phenomena as "alienation." Carlyle attacked the morality of industrial capitalism and insisted that human, not cash, values should be paramount. He protested against the degradation of labor under industrialism and proclaimed that work should be man's highest calling: "All work, even cotton-spinning, is noble; work is alone noble."

The doctrine of the dignity of all labor—which contrasted so strikingly with the realities of working-class life—could become little more than a pious platitude in the pages of Samuel Smiles; or it could be the beginning of a vision of a new society. John Ruskin in *The Stones of Venice* (1853) made it the latter, and his widely admired writings made him the most influential critic of Victorianism before the socialists of the 1880s. "The great cry that rises from all our manufacturing cities," he wrote, "louder than the furnace blast, is . . . that we manufacture everything there except men." Ruskin began with a criticism of the arts, but soon developed a theory of economics which was opposed to orthodox political economy. His stance was basically moral. In *Unto This Last* (1862) he elaborated on Carlyle's strictures on the worship of money-making and pleaded that men should be treated as more important than things. "There is no wealth but life," he concluded; riches and wealth were to be assessed not in material goods but in the number of "noble and happy human beings." In these respects he found Victorian England sadly lacking.

Ruskin and Carlyle were largely negative critics, and it was left for William Morris, an ardent disciple of Ruskin in the 1850s and 1860s, to find a positive solution to these problems in socialism. But Morris did not reach this position until the 1880s, and in mid-Victorian England he could only give vent to his hatred of middle-class values. His rebellion was that of a poet, artist, and craftsman, and he turned, like Carlyle and Ruskin, to the Middle Ages for an alternative social ethic. Toward the end of his life Morris recalled how he felt in the 1860s about Victorian civilization:

> What shall I say concerning its mastery of, and its waste of mechanical power, its commonwealth so rich, its stupendous organization—for the misery of life! Its contempt of simple pleasures which everyone could enjoy but for its folly? Its eyeless vulgarity which has destroyed art, the one certain solace of labour? . . . Was it all to end in a counting-house on the top of a cinder-heap, with Podsnap's drawing-room in the offing, and a Whig committee dealing out champagne to the rich and margerine to the poor . . . ?

Like many of his contemporaries, Morris was impressed by Dickens's brilliant characterization of the middle classes in *Our Mutual Friend* (1864–65). In the person of Mr. Podsnap, Dickens exposed the hollowness and shallowness of much bourgeois life. Podsnap was a self-satisfied, narrow, and eminently respectable businessman. For him, "the world got up at eight, shaved close at a quarter past, breakfasted at nine, went to the City at 10, came home at half-past five, and dined at seven." He was extremely self-righteous: "He always knew exactly what Providence meant. Inferior and less respectable men might fall short of that mark, but Mr. Podsnap was always up to it." He had an incomparable capacity for not seeing the things he considered disagreeable—such as poverty and starvation: "I don't want to know about it; I don't choose to discuss it; I don't admit it." His taste was abominable: "Hideous solidity was the characteristic of the Podsnap plate. Everything was made to look as heavy as it could, and to take up as much room as possible." "Podsnappery" was a powerful indictment of the false values and pretensions of middle-class philistinism.

The term "philistine" was used most effectively by another critic of Victorianism, Matthew Arnold, son of Dr. Thomas Arnold, the headmaster of Rugby School. In *Culture and Anarchy* (1869), Matthew Arnold presented the case for humanism (especially, "sweetness and light") as an alternative to the unloveliness, bigotry, and crude individualism of English society. Arnold was deeply disturbed by the insufficiency of that combination of nonconformity and industrialism (which he equated with liberalism, and which he saw as the dominant influence of the time) for the attainment of the good life. It seemed to him that liberalism, with its "faith in machinery," its definition of freedom as "doing as one likes," and its ignoring of the state (that is, the nation in its collective, corporative character), resulted in spiritual impoverishment and ultimately anarchy. In a famous chapter he characterized Victorian society as divided into three categories: the philistines, the barbarians, and the populace. The philistines were the middle classes, "stiff-necked and perverse in [their] resistance to light," whose horizons were bounded by "business, chapels [and] tea-meetings." Barbarians was the most suitable name for the aristocracy, whose main concern was with field-sports and the cultivation of "outward gifts and graces," to the exclusion of any inward culture. The populace was the great mass of the working class, which, thanks to its middle-class mentors, "is now issuing from its hiding-place to assert an Englishman's heaven-born privilege of doing as he likes, and is beginning to perplex us by marching where it likes, meeting where it likes, bawling what it likes, breaking what it likes." England, argued Arnold, was suffering from an overdose of Hebraism, with its emphasis on doing, duty, sin, and the teachings of St. Paul. The remedy was a return to Hellenism, or the Greek values of thinking, spontaneity, and beauty, as found in the writings of Plato.

Arnold, Dickens, Morris, Ruskin, and Carlyle protested against the ugliness, stuffiness, insensitivity, and hypocrisy of mid-Victorianism. They were concerned about the quality of life. From a different angle they were joined by the greatest of the philosophers of liberalism, John Stuart Mill. He had been brought up by his father, James Mill, in the Benthamite tradition, and became the leader of the Benthamites (or "utilitarians," as they were called). His essay *On Liberty* (1859) is the classic statement of the case for liberal freedom and is devoted to an analysis of "the nature and limits of the power which can be legitimately exercised by society over the individual." In the course of this analysis he warned against the "tyranny of the majority." Whereas in the past, he argued, the danger to the liberty of the individual had come from despots and tyrannical governments, in mid-Victorian England the danger came from society itself—a tyranny "more formidable than many kinds of political oppression, since . . . it leaves fewer means of escape, penetrating much more deeply into the details of life, and enslaving the soul itself." The pressures to conform to the "prevailing opinion and feeling" of society—which in fact meant the ideas and practices of the middle class—were so strong as to be well nigh irresistible. In a remarkable passage he exposed the dangers of what today we call "keeping up with the Joneses":

> In our times, from the highest class of society down to the lowest, everyone lives as under the eye of a hostile and dreaded censorship. Not only in what

concerns others, but in what concerns only themselves, the individual or the family do not ask themselves what do I prefer? or, what would suit my character and disposition? or, what would allow the best and highest in me to have fair play and enable it to grow and thrive? They ask themselves, what is suitable to my position? what is usually done by persons of my station and pecuniary circumstances? or (worse still) what is usually done by persons of a station and circumstances superior to mine? I do not mean that they choose what is customary in preference to what suits their own inclination. It does not occur to them to have any inclination except for what is customary. Thus the mind itself is bowed to the yoke: even in what people do for pleasure, conformity is the first thing thought of; they like in crowds; they exercise choice only among things commonly done; peculiarity of taste, eccentricity of conduct are shunned equally with crimes, until by dint of not following their own nature they have no nature to follow: their human capacities are withered and starved; they become incapable of any strong wishes or native pleasures, and are generally without either opinions or feelings of home growth, or properly their own. . . .

So deeply did Mill fear this tendency that he advocated eccentricity for its own sake: "in this age . . . the mere refusal to bend the knee to custom is itself a service." Only thus could the "tyranny of opinion" (which was always the tyranny of "collective mediocrity") be opposed.

To the open critics must be added those who expressed doubts about certain fundamental assumptions of Victorian society. The conflict between science and religion raised doubts of this nature. In the same year (1859) that Smiles's *Self-Help* and Mill's *On Liberty* appeared, Charles Darwin published his *Origin of Species*. Darwin's hypothesis was described succinctly by his great apologist, T. H. Huxley, as follows:

All species have been produced by the development of varieties from common stocks by the conversion of these first into permanent races and then into new species, by the process of *natural selection*, which process is essentially identical with that artificial selection by which man has originated the races of domestic animals—the *struggle for existence* taking the place of man, and exerting, in the case of natural selection, that selective action which he performs in artificial selection.

The Darwinian theory of evolution was fiercely attacked, both by outraged churchmen and by scientists who feared that it undermined the idea of moral purpose in nature. The publication of the *Origin* brought to a head an intellectual conflict which had been growing steadily during the previous decades. Already the "higher criticism" of the Bible on historical grounds and the researches of geologists had challenged any literal acceptance of the Genesis story of the creation or any fundamentalist belief in the Bible as God's actual words. Now Darwin's work contradicted the idea of man being specially created at all. The *Origin* presented a mass of data that could be explained only by a theory of evolution that seemed to destroy many traditional Christian doctrines.

Darwin's *Origin of Species* was an epoch-making book, in the sense that it altered irrevocably the direction of men's thought. After its publication it was no longer possible for intelligent men to go on thinking in the same way as they had done previously. This, of course, was profoundly disquieting, and its implications were at first resisted. By the end of the century it was apparent that what had begun as an intellectual, scientific revolt against traditional authority had become part of a challenge to the moral, religious, and social bases of Victorian England.

That mid-Victorian society could produce its own critics and doubters of the stature of Mill, Arnold, and Darwin is a testimony to the greatness of the age. But, inevitably, many of the problems they posed were insoluble within the framework of Victorianism itself. Only when the certainties of Victorian society began to crumble in the 1880s could the logic of the working-out of their ideas be seen.

Pax Britannica

For most Britons the nineteenth century was a time of peace. Between 1815 and 1914 Britain took part in no major war. With the exception of the Crimean episode (1854–56), her wars were confined to imperialist adventures in remote parts of the world and against industrially backward peoples. It was an article of faith with middle-class politicians and theorists that free trade was a powerful force for international peace: men and nations who traded together, it was argued, had too many common interests to fight one another. That the lion's share of the benefits from a system of worldwide free trade would fall to Britain makes this argument today seem somewhat less than disinterested. Nevertheless, the British interest in preserving peace was not without its benefits to other nations, including the United States. Britain was never in a position to impose peace as the Romans had done with their Pax Romana. But British influence in international affairs was so great after 1815 that it is no exaggeration to speak of a "Pax Britannica," or British peace.

This influence was based on the British navy, by which means Britain was able to act as the policeman of the world, ensuring for herself and others the freedom of the seas. She had emerged from the Napoleonic Wars with a huge and victorious fleet, and although much of it was subsequently put into cold storage and the remainder somewhat neglected, it remained larger and more effective than that of any other nation. It protected a great merchant marine and the bases and colonies of the British empire through which the workshop of the world carried on a large part of its trade. Because of her unique and early industrialization, Britain developed a peculiarly strong international trade, based on the exchange of her manufactured products for raw materials and food. By 1870 this foreign trade was more than that of France, Germany, and Italy combined. British exports, which in 1850 had been at the rate of £71 million a year, by 1870 were nearly £200 million, and imports increased in the same period from £100 million to £300 million a year. The difference between the value of imports and exports (usually referred to as the "balance of payments") was made up by "invisible exports," such as shipping, banking, and income from overseas investments. These "invisible" earnings were very large and of crucial importance to the Victorian economy. The tonnage of British shipping was between a third and a half of the world total. British investment abroad in 1850 was about £250 million; by 1873 it was nearly £1,000 million. This massive export of capital went to build railways, bridges, and harbors in Europe, America, and the empire. British economic interests—trade, shipping, and investments—were thus worldwide and gave rise to a complex pattern of international relations. The Pax Britannica stemmed from a need for open overseas markets and the preservation of stable conditions in territories where British capital was invested.

Given this overall commitment to maritime power for the protection of trade and the maintenance of peace, British national interests had to be defined more exactly in the different parts of the globe. In Europe the operative concept in British foreign policy was the balance of power. Put quite simply, this was the belief that it was in Britain's interest to prevent any one European state from becoming so powerful that it might dominate the continent, as France had done under Napoleon. Because of her geographical separateness and her worldwide economic interests, Britain considered herself to be in, but not of, Europe. She had no territorial ambitions in Europe, and her reliance on sea power rather than armies made it difficult for her to prevent sudden military actions by great land powers such as Russia or France. Nevertheless, under a succession of able foreign secretaries—Castlereagh, Canning, and Palmerston—Britain exerted her influence by a mixture of adroit diplomacy, threats, bluff, and (in 1854–56) military intervention. Ideologically, Britain preferred to support liberal, constitutional regimes against absolutist monarchies and dictatorships; but as always in such cases, the ultimate consideration was her own national interest.

After the peace of 1815 British policy in Europe was to continue only enough commitment to prevent the resurgence of French aggression. Castlereagh, who had no sympathy with liberalism, nevertheless refused to join with the autocratic powers (Russia, Prussia, and Austria) in the Holy Alliance; and his successor, Canning, pursued an independent line which involved championing the freedom of the South American colonies from Spain and Portugal and the Greeks against the Turkish empire. From 1830 until his death in 1865 the most important figure in determining British foreign policy was Lord Palmerston, who was for long periods foreign secretary and later prime minister. An aristocrat of Regency vintage at home, he identified Britain with liberal causes abroad and asserted a

Changing the face of the land: Crimple Valley viaduct, Harrogate, on the York and North Midland Railway, 1847. (Science Museum, London.)

John Bullish aggressiveness which has seldom been equaled. In the infamous Don Pacifico affair in 1850, he championed the claims of a Portuguese Jewish money-lender, whose property had been destroyed by a Greek mob in Athens, on the grounds that Don Pacifico had been born in Gibraltar and could therefore claim British citizenship. An ultimatum was sent to Greece and backed up with a naval blockade. Defending his actions in the House of Commons, Palmerston claimed that "as the Roman in days of old held himself free from indignity when he could say *civis Romanus sum* ["I am a Roman citizen"], so also a British subject, in whatever land he may be, shall feel confident that the watchful eye and the strong arm of England, will protect him against injustice and wrong."

Threats to the equilibrium of Europe could come from various quarters. In 1830 the Belgians revolted against the Dutch, and the danger was that France would intervene on behalf of the Belgians while Holland appealed to Russia, Prussia, and Austria. It had long been British policy to prevent the channel ports from falling into the hands of a major European power. Palmerston skillfully negotiated recognition of the new independent state of Belgium by the great powers, coerced the Dutch into accepting the settlement, and in 1839 secured a guarantee of Belgian neutrality.

143

In the same year (1839) Palmerston scored another diplomatic success in a different area of traditional British concern, the Near East. Here the problem was to check Russian ambitions and shore up the declining Ottoman (Turkish) empire, which dominated the Arab and south East European worlds. Britain felt that Russian expansion into the area would jeopardize control of communications with India and the Far East. The obvious policy for Britain was to strengthen Turkey as a bastion against Russia. Unfortunately, the Turkish empire was too weak internally to be a very reliable force, and the sultan was beset by revolts from his vassals, especially the Egyptians. France also had ambitions in the Arab world, and was prepared to exploit rebellions against the sultan. Palmerston, therefore, had a very difficult task to make British interests prevail while averting war between the European powers. The issue came to a head in 1831–32 when the pasha of Egypt, Mehemet Ali, declared war on the sultan and invaded Palestine and Syria. To put down the rebellion the sultan entered into an alliance with Russia, which greatly alarmed Palmerston. When, therefore, war between Turkey and Egypt broke out again in 1839, Palmerston joined Russia, Prussia, and Austria in support of the sultan. France, who had backed Mehemet Ali, was isolated. Egyptian (and French) ambitions to take over parts of the Ottoman empire were thus frustrated; Turkey ("the sick man of Europe") was kept intact; and Russian designs were contained within a great power concert.

The settlement of the Near East question in 1841 was not final. In 1853 it erupted again. This time the issue was over who should control the holy places (associated with Christ's birth and crucifixion) in Palestine. The Tsar of Russia backed the claims of the Greek Orthodox monks; Napoleon III of France supported the Roman Catholics. Behind this relatively trivial issue was Russia's desire to exert paramount influence in the Ottoman empire, whose dismemberment she looked forward to. The Turks, however, strengthened by British sympathy, resisted the Russian demands. The tsar then sent his troops into the Danubian provinces (Rumania) of the Turkish empire, and the British and French retaliated by dispatching naval forces to protect Constantinople. After a Turkish naval squadron had been destroyed by the Russian fleet at Sinope on the Black Sea, the British and French fleets were ordered to the Black Sea, and in March 1854 war was declared against Russia.

The Crimean War (1854–56) was not a major confrontation between the great European powers but a limited action to check Russian expansion in one part of the world. The Allied (that is, British, French, Turkish) plan was to capture Sebastopol, a naval base in the Crimean peninsula, as a means of destroying Russian naval power. Sebastopol eventually fell, but only after a long siege and two costly battles at Balaclava and Inkerman. In 1856 Russia agreed to the Allied terms, which included relinquishment of her ambitions to control the Danubian provinces, recognition of the

The Crimean War: An early photograph by Roger Fenton, showing fraternization between British and French soldiers, 1855. (Gernsheim Collection, The University of Texas at Austin.)

continuing independence of Turkey, and the neutralization of the Black Sea. Thus, for the time being Russia was effectively checked, and the dissolution of the Turkish empire was postponed. But the Near Eastern question was by no means settled, and a few years later it was to plague William Gladstone, the great Liberal prime minister.

At home, the Crimean War was initially very popular. It aroused patriotic sentiment, and there was much talk of the need to prove that forty years of peace had not made the nation soft. Russia had long been hated by liberals as the archetypal despotism of Europe, and a strong feeling of "russophobia" was present by the 1850s. The first excitement, however, soon turned to criticism of the government when the incompetency of the army and the suffering of the troops became known—as it soon did, thanks to the reports of newspaper correspondents, who for the first time were able to send their reports by telegraph. As a military machine, the British army was far from impressive. Its commander-in-chief was Lord Raglan, one of Wellington's officers at Waterloo. He was personally very brave, but at the age of sixty-five quite unsuitable to command an army (he embarrassed his staff by still referring to the enemy as "the French," although in fact the enemy were the Russians and the French were allies). Hence, it is hardly surprising that the best-known episode in the war, the Charge of the Light Brigade (immortalized in Tennyson's poem), was the result of a tactical blunder; and the heroine of the war, Florence Nightingale, was a nurse who battled against the bureaucracy to establish decent conditions in the hospitals of the Crimea. The army was officered by out-of-date, aristocratic veterans, and the inadequacy of the supply system resulted in a grim winter in which food, fuel, equipment, and hospital services were sadly lacking. As the news of this state of affairs became known, criticism grew and turned into a radical attack on the whole aristocratic influence in government. The radicals were divided over the war: a majority welcomed it as an attack on the greatest tyranny in Europe; a vocal minority, led by the freetraders John Bright and Richard Cobden, opposed it on the grounds of pacifism and internationalism. The war cost Britain 25,000 lives and £70 million; in return, she had managed to prop up the Turkish empire for a few more years and had set back Russian influence in Europe.

Beyond Europe, the maintenance of a Pax Britannica was associated with a policy of imperialism. It is convenient to make a distinction between the formal empire (those areas in which the British flag was flown) and the informal empire, where British influence was exercised by other means such as economic penetration. In the mid-Victorian period there was greater enthusiasm for the latter type of expansion than for the former. After the loss of the first (American) empire in the eighteenth century, there was little enthusiasm for acquiring another. The usual view, as expressed by Benjamin Disraeli, was that colonies were "a millstone round our necks." Trade was one thing; political control and responsibility for overseas territories quite another. Far from being aggressive imperialists, most mid-Victorians were, at heart, "little Englanders." However, they did not find it easy to escape from the imperial entanglements of the past, and in fact they were drawn by the logic of the situation step by step into ever greater commitments overseas. To say that the British empire of the mid-nineteenth century was acquired by accident or in a fit of absentmindedness would be an exaggeration. But it was certainly not a planned, nor even a logically thought-out venture. Rather was it the result of a series of responses to problems and pressures of the day; a decision once taken limited the options for the future; one thing simply led on to another.

The nature of this process becomes clear when we look at specific examples. The formal empire consisted partly of small bases, partly of larger areas of white settlement, and partly of subject kingdoms ruled by a minority of British administrators. Sea power was dependent on strategically placed ports which could provide protection, refitting, and replenishing of supplies as required. At the Congress of Vienna in 1815, Britain provided herself with an ample supply of such bases: Heligoland, Malta, Mauritius, the Ionian Islands, the Cape of Good Hope, and islands in the Caribbean. These, together with older possessions such as Gibraltar and the West Indies and newer ones to come (Singapore, 1819; Hong Kong, 1842), provided a string of harbors around the world.

The second type of British colony—the area suitable for large-scale white settlement—was found in North America, South Africa, and Australasia. Throughout the nineteenth century Britain exported not only her manufactures and capital, but also her people. Between 1815 and 1914 nearly seventeen million persons emigrated from the United Kingdom, about 80 percent of them to North America. Yet the total population of the United Kingdom in 1821 was less than twenty-one million and only forty-five million in 1911. Although the United States received the largest share of this emigration, and a great many of the emigrants were from Ireland, there still remained an impressive departure of Britons to the colonies. Over three-quarters of a million people left the United Kingdom for Canada and close to a million for Australasia in the years between 1837 and 1867. In the peak year 1852, after the discovery of gold in Australia, over 80,000 persons emigrated there from Britain. The result of this huge emigration was to diffuse British culture widely throughout the world. Emigrants took with them the language, attitudes, assumptions, institutions, and discontents of the "old country." The social, political, and constitutional problems of early and mid-Victorian Britain had to be worked out anew in strange new environments. Among the most pressing issues was the colonists' demand for self-government.

In British North America this problem became urgent in 1837, when rebellions broke out in Upper Canada (now Ontario) and Lower Canada (Quebec). The settlers in Upper Canada were mainly loyalists who had left the United States after the American Revolution; Lower Canada was predominantly a colony of French farmers in settlements along the St. Lawrence River. The Whig government sent out Lord Durham ("Radical Jack") in 1838 to look into the situation, and his report formed the basis of the Canada Act of 1840. The two provinces of Upper and Lower Canada were united, and shortly afterward "responsible" (that is, local) self-government was granted. In 1867 the process was taken a stage further by the British North America Act, which created a virtually self-governing Dominion of Canada. The dominion was a federation of provinces, including, in addition to Ontario and Quebec, the maritime provinces of New Brunswick and Nova Scotia. In Australia similar developments toward self-government took place in the 1850s. New South Wales and Van Dieman's Land (later

Tasmania) had been founded as penal colonies, to which convicts were transported from Britain. After 1840 convicts were no longer sent to New South Wales, nor to any of the eastern colonies in Australia after 1853 (although the transportation system lasted in Western Australia until 1868). The discovery of gold in 1851 brought an influx of free settlers, which strengthened the demand for self-government. Separate colonies were founded across the continent: Western Australia in 1829; South Australia, 1836; Victoria, 1850. New Zealand was declared an independent colony in 1840 and granted responsible government in 1853. Emigration to the Cape Colony in South Africa was much smaller than to North America or Australasia; but the same principle of representative institutions was applied, and in 1853 self-government was thrust upon the somewhat reluctant colonists.

The third type of British colony is best exemplified by India. Here the problems were of an entirely different order. Reflecting the original commercial interest in India, the huge subcontinent was ruled not directly by the British government but by the East India Company, under the direction of a board of control which sat in London. The combination of trading and government functions became increasingly unsatisfactory, and the company's monopoly of trading activities was first modified (1813) and then abolished (1833). The chief executive officer in India was the governor-general, usually a member of the aristocracy and appointed by the government of the day. He received his orders from London, but the slowness of communications and the complexity of Indian problems meant that in a real sense he made policy. Developments in mid-Victorian India illustrate the nature of British imperialism at this time.

First and foremost were economic interests. India in the nineteenth century became an increasingly crucial part of the British economy. Until 1850 the largest market for British cotton goods was Latin America, but in the second half of the century its place was taken by India and the Far East. After the Napoleonic Wars, India's share of British cotton exports grew steadily, until by the mid-1870s it was 40–45 percent. In the days of the East India Company's monopoly Indian cottons and silks had been exchanged for British woolens and hardware. But after 1813 India's cotton exports to England ceased, and her native textile industry was largely destroyed by the influx of Lancashire cotton goods. The prosperity of the staple British export industry thus became directly tied to the Indian market. Again, India became a vital area for the export of British capital. In the 1850s, with the building of railways and public utilities, 20 percent of the total British investment abroad went to India. Lastly, India's trading position with other countries in the Far East helped to solve Britain's balance-of-payments problem. For instance, India had an export surplus (largely derived from the opium trade) with China and the Far East and a trade deficit with Britain. The British had difficulty in their trade with China, from whom they imported tea and silk, because of the reluctance of the Chinese to take British exports in exchange, and the Indian export of opium was a convenient way of balancing the British account. To maintain this arrangement in the face of Chinese government opposition and to force trading concessions from China, Britain went to war with China in 1839–42, in 1856–58, and again in 1859–60. With so much at stake it is not difficult to see why control of India was such an important part of British foreign and naval policy right up to the First World War.

The economic interest largely determined other aspects of Indian policy. In the eighteenth century, although Englishmen went to India openly to make profits, they largely accepted Indian culture and institutions as they found them. But in the Age of Reform, and with the contemporary passion for improvement, this gave way to a policy of westernization. The Victorians were convinced of the superiority of their civilization over all others, and genuinely felt that they were conferring a great benefit on India by imposing British values and institutions on the ancient, decadent cultures of the inhabitants. As Macaulay, who advised on legal and educational reform, put it, "A single shelf of a good European library was worth the whole native literature of India and Arabia." Reform of the material conditions of life was carried through energetically: legal, administrative, and educational systems were set up; commerce was expanded; railways, canals, and telegraphs were built. The same combination of evangelical and utilitarian energy that had put Britain on the path of progress was set to work in India. However, the British were not loved for all this. They were respected for some of their qualities, especially their sense of justice, but, in comparison with the Englishmen of the eighteenth century, the Victorian rulers seemed cold and aloof. As the British tightened their hold on India, the gulf between an Eastern and a Western culture became harder to bridge.

It was a proud boast of the British that they brought peace and order to the vast territories of India on a scale never known before. The Pax Britannica, however, was achieved only by the maintenance of a considerable army and by fighting a series of annexationist wars. Once it was decided that India should be a part of the formal empire, the logic of maintaining stable frontiers led to the eventual acquisition of almost the entire subcontinent. Throughout the first half of the nineteenth century each decade saw some new territory annexed by war or treaty or some frontier campaign to repulse a threatened attack: in 1814–16 it was war against the Gurkhas of Nepal, in 1816–18 against the Pindaris in north-central India, and in 1817–18 against the Mahrattas. The coastal parts of Ceylon had been occupied between 1803 and 1814; in 1815 the interior was annexed after a campaign to restore peace between the King of Kandy and his rebel subjects. War against Burma in 1824–25 arose out of the need to protect the eastern border of Bengal and resulted in the annexation of more territory. On the northwest frontier, fear of Russian influence led to interference in Afghanistan and a costly, nearly disastrous, war in 1839–42. The next year, 1843, Sind was conquered and annexed. Then came the conquest of the Punjab after wars against the Sikhs in 1845–46 and 1848–49. A second Burmese war in 1852 added more territory. In some instances, British control was extended without recourse to war. Under the doctrine of "lapse and adoption," the governor-general could annex native states whose rulers died without natural heirs and who were denied the usual Indian right of adoption. In this way four states were annexed between 1848 and 1854; and in 1856 the kingdom of Oudh was taken over, even though the corrupt nawab did have heirs. By the 1850s about two-thirds of India was under direct British rule, and the remainder was governed by independent princes who were bound to Britain by separate treaties.

The British policies of reform and territorial annexation caused a good deal of unease among Indians. Westernization implied a denigration of Hindu customs and procedures, and British rule, however paternal, was alien and imposed by force of arms. Grievances under such a system were bound to be many, and in 1857 the various discontents and fears came to a head in the great Indian Mutiny. The immediate cause of the mutiny was a rumor among the sepoy (native) troops that the cartridges for a new rifle were greased with animal fat; since the cartridges were bitten before being put into the rifle, this caused offense to both Hindus and Muslims, who would be defiled. The army at this time consisted of some 40,000 British troops and 230,000 sepoys. In the Ganges Valley, where most of the action took place, the sepoy regiments killed their British officers and marched to Delhi, where they proclaimed the old king as Moghul Emperor of all India. For some months British power seemed to be shaken; but the rebels were unable to take advantage of their overwhelming numbers, and by the early months of 1858 British troops and loyal Sikh allies had crushed the mutiny. The fighting was conducted with great savagery on both sides. Sepoy massacres of British women and children were met by harsh reprisals from the English regiments. The memories of these atrocities and reprisals lasted long in India, and British-Indian relations were never the same again. In 1858 the East India Company was finally abolished, and the governor-general became the viceroy. The power of the British raj was reinforced, but the pace of reform slowed and Indians and Britons drew further apart, each retreating into his own separate culture.

India however, in the mid-Victorian period was an anomaly. For the most part, Britain did not need formal colonies, since her interests could be just as well served by an informal empire. There was no necessity to try to conquer Latin America or China or Southeast Asia; a little judicious gunboat diplomacy was usually all that was required to secure favorable conditions for British trade and investment. All underdeveloped countries were a potential part of Britain's worldwide informal empire. As the workshop of the world Britain could undersell all competitors, provided she could operate in conditions of free trade. Her navy was designed to uphold such conditions. In the last quarter of the century these halcyon days were to disappear. But until then British prosperity flowed from the Pax Britannica.

Select Bibliography

General works, 1714–1867

The standard works in the Oxford History of England series are: Basil Williams, *The Whig Supremacy, 1714–60* (1939); J. Steven Watson, *The Reign of George III, 1760–1815* (1960); and Sir Llewellyn Woodward, *The Age of Reform, 1815–1870* (2nd ed., 1962). All these have full bibliographies and are particularly strong on the political side. An excellent survey, with more attention paid to the interaction of social and cultural factors, is Asa Briggs, *The Age of Improvement* (Harper Torchbook, 1959). R. K. Webb, *Modern England* (1968) is a well balanced history from the early eighteenth century to the present and contains a great many valuable references in the footnotes. An older work, still of some interest for its liberal social and economic approach, is G. D. H. Cole and Raymond Postgate, *The Common People, 1746–1946* (1938; 2nd ed., 1946). The Pelican History of England series (paperback) has two first-rate volumes which are relevant: J. H. Plumb, *England in the Eighteenth Century* (1950) and David Thomson, *England in the Nineteenth Century* (1951).

Volumes X, XI, and XII of the *English Historical Documents* series contain useful collections of primary material, mainly of a political and institutional kind: D. B. Horn and Mary Ransome, eds., *E.H.D., 1714–1783* (1957); A. Aspinall and E. A. Smith, eds., *E.H.D., 1783–1832* (1959); and G. M. Young and W. D. Handcock, eds., *E.H.D., 1833–1874* (1956). These volumes have full introductions and bibliographies. A shorter collection of documents, intended for use with a text such as the present one, is J. F. C. Harrison, ed., *Society and Politics in England, 1780–1960* (1965).

An indispensable work of statistical information of all kinds is B. R. Mitchell and Phyllis Deane, *Abstract of British Historical Statistics* (1962).

Chapter One

The essential reading on the structure of eighteenth-century politics and administration are the pioneer works of L. B. Namier, *The Structure of Politics at the Accession of George III* (1929; 2nd ed., 1957) and *England in the Age of the American Revolution* (1930). These should be supplemented with Richard Pares, *King George III and the Politicians* (1953); H. Butterfield, *George III and the Historians* (1957); Robert Walcott, *English Politics in the Early Eighteenth Century* (1956); J. H. Plumb, *Sir Robert Walpole* (1960). For details of the working of the parliamentary system, see E. and A. G. Porritt, *The Unreformed House of Commons*, 2 vols. (1903), and also

Elie Halévy, *England in 1815*, vol. I *History of the English People in the Nineteenth Century* (1924; repr., 1961).

A useful social survey is M. Dorothy George, *England in Transition* (1953); also, Dorothy Marshall, *English People in the Eighteenth Century* (1956). The standard work on landed society is G. E. Mingay, *English Landed Society in the Eighteenth Century* (1963). On the Church of England, the definitive work is Norman Sykes, *Church and State in the Eighteenth Century* (1934). There is no good, modern history of Methodism. The standard account is W. J. Townsend, H. B. Workman, and George Eayrs, *A New History of Methodism*, 2 vols. (1909). To this should be added Maldwyn Edwards, *John Wesley and the Eighteenth Century* (1955); R. F. Wearmouth, *Methodism and the Common People of the Eighteenth Century* (1945); and Leslie F. Church, *The Early Methodist People* (1948). Wesley's *Journal* is a fascinating contemporary document which provides insights into many aspects of life and thought in the eighteenth century. The definitive edition is edited by Nehemiah Curnock (1960); but there are also other versions, such as the Everyman edition. Two other contemporary sources which give firsthand accounts of everyday life are James Woodforde, *The Diary of a Country Parson, 1758–1802*, ed. John Beresford (1949), and Daniel Defoe, *A Tour Through the Whole Island of Great Britain* (1724–26; repr., Everyman ed.).

Chapter Two

Of the great number of books on the Industrial Revolution, the most suitable for introductory reading are T. S. Ashton, *The Industrial Revolution 1760–1830* (1948) and Phyllis Deane, *The First Industrial Revolution* (1965). A stimulating and controversial interpretation is W. W. Rostow, *The Stages of Economic Growth* (1960). Important works on the subject are David S. Landes, *The Unbound Prometheus* (1969), which sets British development in a European context; E. J. Hobsbawm, *Industry and Empire* (1968), which continues the story down to the present; M. W. Flinn, *Origins of the Industrial Revolution* (1966); and (rather more technical) R. M. Hartwell, ed., *The Causes of the Industrial Revolution in England* (1967) and *The Industrial Revolution and Economic Growth* (1972). Neil J. Smelser, *Social Change in the Industrial Revolution* (1959) is a case study of the Lancashire cotton industry, 1770–1840, which attempts to apply sociological methods to social history.

Among older works, Paul Mantoux, *The Industrial Revolution in the Eighteenth Century* (1928; rev. ed., 1962) is well worth reading; as also are the pioneer works of J. L. & Barbara Hammond, *The Rise of Modern Industry* (1925; repr., 1969), *The Village Labourer* (1911), *The Town Labourer* (1917), and *The Skilled Labourer* (1919) —all reprinted many times since. Two useful selections of readings, which introduce the various conflicting interpretations by historians of the Industrial Revolution, are Philip A. M. Taylor, ed., *The Industrial Revolution in Britain* (Heath Problems in European Civilization series, 1958) and C. Stewart Doty, ed., *The Industrial Revolution* (Holt, Rinehart European Problem Studies, 1969).

The main articles relating to the debate among historians about population changes are contained in the very important volume edited by D. V. Glass and D. E. C. Eversley, *Population in History* (1965). Shorter treatment of the subject can be found in D. V. Glass, *Introduction to Malthus* (1953), which also reprints two of Malthus's smaller works, and H. J. Habakkuk, *Population Growth and Economic Development Since 1750* (1972).

On agricultural changes, the most useful work is J. D. Chambers and G. E. Mingay, *The Agricultural Revolution, 1750–1880* (1966). The standard history of English agriculture is still Lord Ernle, *English Farming, Past and Present* (1912; new ed., ed. O. R. McGregor, 1961). A delightful contemporary account is William Cobbett, *Rural Rides* (1830; repr., Penguin Books, 1967).

Chapter Three

Further reading on these topics should begin with some of the works mentioned at the beginning of this bibliography, especially Watson, *Reign of George III*. For general imperial history, see C. E. Carrington, *The British Overseas* (2nd ed., 1968). A standard work is V. T. Harlow, *The Founding of the Second British Empire, 1763–93* (1952); and for India, Edward Thompson and G. T. Garratt, *The Rise and Fulfillment of British Rule in India* (1934) is useful. A stimulating book which deals with the attitudes of imperialists toward the outside world is V. G. Kiernan, *The Lords of Human Kind* (1969); and for the British in India in the eighteenth century, see Percival Spear, *The Nabobs* (1932; 2nd ed., 1963).

Foreign policy and the French wars are best followed in R. W. Seton-Watson, *Britain in Europe, 1789–1914* (1937) and in H. W. V. Temperley and Lilian M. Penson, eds., *Foundations of British Foreign Policy from Pitt, 1792, to Salisbury, 1902* (1938). A very readable account of the Irish rising of 1798 is Thomas Pakenham, *The Year of Liberty* (1969). Of books on the romantics and their reaction to the events of their time, one of the best is David V. Erdman, *Blake: Prophet Against Empire* (1954; rev. ed., 1969). For radicalism of the 1790s, see E. P. Thompson, *The Making of the English Working Class* (1963).

Chapter Four

There are several excellent (primarily social) histories covering this period. G. M. Young, *Victorian England: Portrait of an Age* (1936; 2nd ed., 1953) is a minor classic, although not always easy to appreciate on first reading because of its erudite allusions. G. Kitson Clark, *The Making of Victorian England* (1962) and J. F. C. Harrison, *The Early Victorians, 1832–51* (1971) are easier reading. Useful for the period after the Napoleonic Wars is R. J. White, *Waterloo to Peterloo* (1957). An old-fashioned social history, which nevertheless has much interesting and not-easy-to-find material, is G. M. Young, ed., *Early Victorian England, 1830–1865*, 2 vols. (1934). The first four volumes of Elie Halévy, *A History of the English People in the Nineteenth Century* (repr., 1961) are very useful, especially volume I, *England in 1815*, which is a masterly survey of the political, economic, religious, and cultural institutions at the beginning of the century. This is also the place to introduce two excellent interpretative works: S. G. Checkland, *The Rise of Industrial Society in England, 1815–1885* (1964) and Harold Perkin, *The Origins of Modern English Society, 1780–1880* (1969). The novels of Charles Dickens (*Oliver Twist, Dombey and Son, Little Dorrit, Bleak House, Hard Times*) and Mrs. Gaskell (*Mary Barton, North and South*) provide an incomparable introduction to the tone and temper of early and mid-Victorian society.

The standard work on the Reform Bill of 1832 is J. R. M. Butler, *The Passing of the Great Reform Bill* (1914); and Charles Seymour, *Electoral Reform in England and Wales* (1915) has additional material. Essential reading on this topic is Norman Gash, *Politics in the Age of Peel* (1953), which can be usefully supplemented with his other works: *Mr. Secretary Peel* (1961) and *Reaction and Reconstruction in English Politics, 1832–1852* (1965). On Peterloo, see Donald Read, *Peterloo* (1958) and Joyce Marlow, *The Peterloo Massacre* (1969). Two useful collections of readings are W. H. Maehl, ed., *The Reform Bill of 1832* (Holt, Rinehart European Problem Studies, 1967), and Gilbert A. Cahill, ed., *The Great Reform Bill of 1832* (Heath Problems in European Civilization series, 1969).

The economic and social history of the period is authoritatively set out in J. H. Clapham's great (and eminently readable) work, *An Economic History of Modern Britain*, 3 vols. (1926–38). The first volume, *The Early Railway Age, 1820–1850*, is particularly recommended. If a more concise account is required, J. D. Chambers, *The Workshop of the World* (1961) is most useful; and W. W. Rostow, *The British Economy of the Nineteenth Century* (1948) should also be consulted. Much of the controversy among historians on aspects of social and economic history is carried on in articles in academic journals. Thus the debate about the standard of living of the working classes has to be pursued in various places. A convenient list of the relevant articles and chapters is given in Webb, *Modern England*, p. 234. There are two contemporary works which all students should be familiar with: F. Engels, *The Condition of the Working Class in England in 1844* (1845) and Edwin Chadwick, *Report on the Sanitary Condition of the Labouring Population of Great Britain* (1842; repr., ed. M. W. Flinn, 1965).

Chadwick's career can be studied in S. E. Finer, *The Life and Times of Sir Edwin Chadwick* (1952). On the poor laws, see J. R. Poynter, *Society and Pauperism* (1969); and for the Benthamite background, Elie Halévy, *The Growth of Philosophic Radicalism* (1928) and Mary Peter Mack, *Jeremy Bentham, an Odyssey of Ideas* (1963). The best study of the anti-poor law movement is in Cecil Driver, *Tory Radical: The Life of Richard Oastler* (1946); and for the closely connected factory movement, see J. T. Ward, *The Factory Movement, 1830–1855* (1962).

There is a considerable body of work on the social and working class movements of the first half of the nineteenth century, and some guidance may be welcomed by beginners. Everyone will wish to read E. P. Thompson's brilliant study, *The Making of the English Working Class* (1963), which has done much to set the tone of subsequent research and writing in the field of labor history. If a simpler and more institutional approach is required, then the older work of G. D. H. Cole, *A Short History of the British Working Class Movement, 1789–1947* (2nd ed., 1948) is very useful. Important books in this area are: Asa Briggs and John Saville, *Essays in Labour History* (1960); E. J. Hobsbawm, *Labouring Men* (1964); George Rudé, *The Crowd in History, 1730–1848* (1964). A useful collection of documents is G. D. H. Cole and A. W. Filson, *British Working Class Movements: Select Documents, 1789–1875* (1951; repr., 1965). Two older biographies are valuable: G. D. H. Cole, *The Life of William Cobbett* (1924; 3rd ed., rev., 1947) and Graham Wallas, *The Life of Francis Place, 1771–1854* (1898; repr., 1951).

Although there are many works on Chartism, there is no comprehensive, general history of the movement. It is therefore best to start with Mark Hovell, *The Chartist Movement* (1918; repr., 1966) and follow this with A. R. Schoyen, *The Chartist Challenge* (1958).

The best collection of essays on Chartism is Asa Briggs, ed., *Chartist Studies* (1959; repr., 1965); and a useful collection of documents, together with an introductory essay, is Dorothy Thompson, *The Early Chartists* (1971). Important as the only history of Chartism written by a participant is R. G. Gammage, *History of the Chartist Movement, 1837–1854* (1854; 2nd ed., 1894; repr., 1969).

For early English socialism, the best introduction is still Max Beer, *A History of British Socialism* (1919; repr., 1940). On Owen and Owenism, see J. F. C. Harrison, *Quest for the New Moral World* (1969), which has a full bibliography, and the two biographies: Frank Podmore, *Robert Owen: A Biography* (1906; repr., 1923) and G. D. H. Cole, *Life of Robert Owen* (1925; 3rd ed., 1965).

On other social movements, the following provide good starting points: Joel H. Wiener, *The War of the Unstamped* (1969) and Patricia Hollis, *The Pauper Press* (1970)—both studies of the unstamped press movement; P. H. J. H. Gosden, *The Friendly Societies in England, 1815–1875* (1961); Malcolm I. Thomis, *The Luddites* (1970);

Norman McCord, *The Anti-Corn Law League, 1838–1846* (2nd ed., 1968); Brian Harrison, *Drink and the Victorians: The Temperance Question in England, 1815–1872* (1971).

On religion, the best general survey is Owen Chadwick, *The Victorian Church*, vol. I (1966); but the older survey, S. C. Carpenter, *Church and People, 1789–1889* (1933), is still very useful. For the Evangelicals, see Ford K. Brown, *Fathers of the Victorians* (1961). The Oxford Movement is best studied in Y. T. Brilioth, *The Anglican Revival* (1925) and in Dean Church's classic account, R. W. Church, *The Oxford Movement: Twelve Years, 1833–1845* (1891; repr., 1971). An excellent introduction is the essay in Owen Chadwick, *The Mind of the Oxford Movement* (1960), which reprints some of the writings of the Tractarians. John Henry Newman's *Apologia pro Vita Sua* (1864), his spiritual autobiography, is one of the key books of the nineteenth century. For Methodism, see Maldwyn Edwards, *After Wesley* (1935) and R. F. Wearmouth, *Methodism and the Working-Class Movements of England, 1800–1850* (1937).

Chapter Five

In addition to the various general histories which extend into this period, two excellent interpretations of mid-Victorian Britain should be consulted: W. L. Burn, *The Age of Equipoise* (1964) and Geoffrey Best, *Mid-Victorian Britain, 1851–1875* (1971). The following works cover a fascinating range of literary, cultural, religious, social, and political topics: Walter E. Houghton, *The Victorian Frame of Mind, 1830–1870* (1957); Jerome Hamilton Buckley, *The Victorian Temper* (1951); *Ideas and Beliefs of the Victorians* (1949; repr., 1966); Philip Appleman, William A. Madden, Michael Wolff, eds., *1859: Entering an Age of Crisis* (1959); Basil Willey, *Nineteenth Century Studies: Coleridge to Matthew Arnold* (1949) and *More Nineteenth Century Studies: A Group of Honest Doubters* (1956); Robert Robson, ed., *Ideas and Institutions of Victorian Britain* (1967); Asa Briggs, *Victorian People* (1954) and *Victorian Cities* (1963).

Aristocratic England is well described in F. M. L. Thompson, *English Landed Society in the Nineteenth Century* (1963). For the Great Exhibition, see Christopher Hobhouse, *1851 and the Crystal Palace* (1950 ed.) and Yvonne Ffrench, *The Great Exhibition 1851* (1950). On self-help, the essential reading is Samuel Smiles, *Self-Help* (1859; ed. and with introd. by Asa Briggs, 1958). There is also a chapter on self-help in J. F. C. Harrison, *Learning and Living, 1790–1960* (1961). No history of the family in England has yet appeared, but in the meantime the best introduction to the Victorian family is chapter 3 of O. R. McGregor, *Divorce in England* (1957). Family planning among the Victorian middle classes is dealt with in J. A. Banks, *Prosperity and Parenthood* (1954). Of the large number of books on Darwin and the impact of scientific theory, the following will be found useful: Philip Appleman, ed., *Darwin* (1970), which reprints a selection of Darwin's works and essays about him, and William Irvine, *Apes, Angels and Victorians* (1955). The standard history of education (with a full bibliography) is J. W. Adamson, *English Education, 1789–1902* (1930); but this should be supplemented with Brian Simon, *Studies in the History of Education, 1780–1870* (1960). On the ideal of the Victorian Public School, David Newsome, *Godliness and Good Learning* (1961) is to be recommended.

Just as Newman's *Apologia* documents one important strand in the complex web of Victorian intellectual and spiritual history, so John Stuart Mill's *Autobiography* (1873) is essential for an understanding of nineteenth-century liberalism. To this should also be added his famous essay, *On Liberty* (1859). The best biography is Michael St. John Packe, *The Life of John Stuart Mill* (1954). Political liberalism is analyzed in John Vincent, *The Formation of the Liberal Party, 1857–1868* (1966).

The Crimean War is presented in a very readable study: Cecil Woodham-Smith, *The Reason Why* (1953). The political aspects are examined in Olive Anderson, *A Liberal State at War* (1967). Also by Cecil Woodham-Smith, and equally readable, is her study of the Irish famine, *The Great Hunger* (1962).

Social movements after 1848 were much less stormy than in the previous twenty years. Much the most important development was the emergence of a strong, stable trade union organization. This is best studied in the classic work of the Webbs: Sidney and Beatrice Webb, *The History of Trade Unionism* (rev. ed., 1920). Likewise, the growth of the cooperative movement is a characteristic of the period of Victorian prosperity. For this, see G. D. H. Cole, *A Century of Cooperation* (1944). Labor politics are dealt with in Frances E. Gillespie, *Labor and Politics in England, 1850–1867* (1927) and Royden Harrison, *Before the Socialists* (1965). For vivid descriptions of working-class life, see Henry Mayhew, *London Labour and the London Poor*, 4 vols. (1861–64; repr., 1969), and E. P. Thompson and Eileen Yeo, eds., *The Unknown Mayhew* (1971), which reprints Mayhew's articles in the *Morning Chronicle* of 1849–50.

A useful bibliography is Josef L. Altholz, ed., *Victorian England, 1837–1901* (1970), which has some 2,500 entries covering all aspects of Victorian history, except literature as such.

Kings and Queens of England

Important Kings Before the Norman Conquest

Bretwealdas
c.	477–491	Aelle, King of the West Saxons
c.	560–584	Caelwin, King of the West Saxons
	584–616	Aethelbert, King of Kent
c.	600–616	Raedwald, King of East Anglia
	616–632	Edwin, King of Northumbria
	633–641	Oswald, King of Northumbria
	654–670	Oswiu, King of Northumbria

King of Mercia
758–796   Offa

Kings of the West Saxons
802–839	Egbert
866–871	Aethelraed
871–899	Alfred
899–925	Edward the Elder

(Beginning in Egbert's time the West Saxon kings exercised authority over most of southern England, and Edward the Elder and his successors exercised a varying amount of control over the Scandinavian kingdoms in the north. In 954 this control became permanent and from then onward the kings of the West Saxons ruled all England.)

Rulers of England
959–975	Edgar the Peaceable
979–1016	Aethelraed the Redeless
1016–1035	Cnut
1042–1066	Edward the Confessor
1066	Harold Godwinson

Normans
1066–1087	William I
1087–1100	William II
1100–1135	Henry I
1135–1154	Stephen

Angevins-Plantagenets
1154–1189   Henry II

1189–1199	Richard I
1199–1216	John
1216–1272	Henry III
1272–1307	Edward I
1307–1327	Edward II
1327–1377	Edward III
1377–1399	Richard II

Lancastrians

1399–1413	Henry IV
1413–1422	Henry V
1422–1461	Henry VI

Yorkists

1461–1483	Edward IV
1483	Edward V
1483–1485	Richard III

Tudors

1485–1509	Henry VII
1509–1547	Henry VIII
1547–1553	Edward VI
1553–1558	Mary (I)
1558–1603	Elizabeth I

Stuarts

1603–1625	James I
1625–1649	Charles I
1649–1660	Commonwealth and Protectorate
1660–1685	Charles II
1685–1688	James II
1688–1702	William III and Mary (II)
1702–1714	Anne

Hanoverians

1714–1727	George I
1727–1760	George II
1760–1820	George III
1820–1830	George IV
1830–1837	William IV
1837–1901	Victoria
1901–1910	Edward VII
1910–1936	George V
1936	Edward VIII
1936–1952	George VI
1952–	Elizabeth II

Prime Ministers of England

1721	Sir Robert Walpole
1742	Earl of Wilmington
1743	Honorable Henry Pelham
1754	Duke of Newcastle
1756	Duke of Devonshire
1757	Duke of Newcastle
1762	Earl of Bute
1763	George Grenville
1765	Marquis of Rockingham
1766	William Pitt, Earl of Chatham
1768	Duke of Grafton
1770	Lord North
1782	Marquis of Rockingham
1782	Earl of Shelburne
1783	Duke of Portland
1783	William Pitt, the Younger
1801	Henry Addington
1804	William Pitt, the Younger
1806	Lord Grenville
1807	Duke of Portland
1809	Spencer Perceval
1812	Earl of Liverpool
1827	George Canning
1827	Viscount Goderich
1828	Duke of Wellington
1830	Earl Grey
1834	Viscount Melbourne
1834	Sir Robert Peel
1835	Viscount Melbourne
1841	Sir Robert Peel
1846	Lord John Russell
1852	Earl of Derby
1852	Earl of Aberdeen
1855	Viscount Palmerston
1858	Earl of Derby
1859	Viscount Palmerston
1865	Lord John Russell
1866	Earl of Derby
1868	Benjamin Disraeli

Index

Act of Settlement, 2
Adams, John, 56, 58, 60
Addison, Joseph, 18
Advowsons, 14
Afghanistan, 150
Africa, 65
Agriculture, 44–48, 84, 86–87, 97, 99, 102, 127
  Board of, 46
Albert, Prince Consort, 126, 128, 129
Alienation, 137
Alleghenies, 55, 57
Amalgamated Society of Engineers, 133–34
American Declaration of Independence, 132
Ancient Order of Foresters, 112
Andover, 101
Anne, Queen, 10, 27
Antediluvian Buffaloes, 112
Anti-Corn Law League, 84, 104, 106, 108, 113–14, 115
Anti-poor law agitation, 103, 104, 109, 119
Appalachians, 55
Apprenticeship, 41, 133
Architecture:
  cottage, 97–98
  Georgian, 16–18
  Gothic, 68
  Victorian domestic, 127
Aristocracy, 3–11, 49, 68, 80–82, 113, 139, 146
Arkwright, Richard, 34, 40
Arnold, Matthew:
  Culture and Anarchy, 138–39
Arnold, Thomas, 117, 119, 136, 138
Artisans, 77, 91, 94, 107, 108, 117, 133–34
Ascendancy, the, 72
Ashworth, Messrs., 89

Assistant Handloom Weavers Commission, 135
Association of All Classes of All Nations, 113
Athens, 143
Attwood, Thomas, 81
Aurangzeb, 61
Australia, 61, 73, 110, 147–48
Austria, 69, 79, 142–43

Baines, Edward:
  History of the Cotton Manufacture in Great Britain, 1835, 35, 36
Baker, Robert, 94, 96
Bakewell, Robert, 45
Balaclava, 144
Balance of power, 142
Ballast-heavers, 102
Bamford, Samuel:
  Early Days, 32–34
Band of Hope, 115
Banks, 40
Baptists, 122
Barkerites, 121
Bastille, 66
Bath, 81
Bedford, Duke of, 52
Beerhouse Act, 114
Beeton, Isabella:
  Book of Household Management, 128
Belgium, 143
Bengal, 62, 65, 150
Bentham, Jeremy, 67, 100
Berkeley, George, 14
Berkshire, 98
Bethnal Green, 95
Bible Christians, 121
Bible criticism, 140
Bierley, 120

Birmingham, 4, 8, 37, 38, 39, 77, 83, 87, 106, 107, 108, 111, 114
Birmingham Political Union, 81
Birstal, 120
Bishops, 11
Black, Dr., 40
Black Sea, 144–45
Blades, William, 97
Blake, William, 67
Blanketeers, 77
Blenheim, 6, 54
Blücher, General, 70
Bluebooks, government, 91
Board of Trade, 79, 85
Bombay, 62
Boroughs, 8–10, 76, 82, 83
Boston, 55, 58
Boston Tea Party, 58
Botany Bay, 73
Boulton, Matthew, 37, 39, 40
Bourbons, 66
Bowdler, Thomas, 129
Bradford, 32, 87, 88, 115, 135
Brahmins, 65
Bridgewater, Duke of, 39
Bright, John, 114, 146
Brighton, 61
Bristol, 4, 55, 82
British and Foreign Bible Society, 118
British and Foreign School Society, 136
British and Foreign Temperance Society, 115
British North America Act, 147
British Temperance Association, 115
Britons, Loyal Order of Ancient, 112
Brook, Joseph, 135
Brougham, Henry, 81
Buffaloes, Antediluvian, 112
Bull, Rev. George Stringer, 120
Bull, John, 2, 52, 143
Burdett, Sir Francis, 80
Burgoyne, General, 60
Burke, Edmund:
    Reflections on the Revolution in France, 67–68
Burma, 150
Burns, Robert, 67
Bute, Earl of, 52, 53

Cabinet, 7
Calcutta, 62

Calvinism, 118, 123
Cambridge, 8, 50, 88, 118, 136
Camp meetings, 122
Canada, 60, 147
Canada Act, 147
Canals, 38–39
Canning, George, 79, 80, 142
Cape of Good Hope, 70, 147, 148
Capital, 39–40, 44, 49, 142, 147, 148
Capitalism, 47–49, 111, 134, 137
Carlyle, Thomas, 91, 100, 104, 137–38
    Past and Present, 137
Carnatic, 62
Cartwright, Major John, 67, 76, 77
Castle Howard, 6
Castlereagh, Viscount, 79, 142
Cato Street Conspiracy, 78
Ceylon, 70, 149–50
Chadwick, Edwin, 95–96, 100–04
    Report on the Sanitary Conditions, 96
    Poor Law *Report,* 99–100
Chandernagore, 62
Chandos Clause, 82
Charles II, 62, 80
Charles X (of France), 81
Charleston, 55, 58
Chartism, 104–10, 113–14, 122, 132, 133
Chelsea, 94
Chester, 88
China, 61, 64, 148–49
Cholera, 96
Church Missionary Society, 118
Church of England, 10, 14–16, 19–21, 76, 79, 116–20, 132, 136
Churchill, John, 54
Cities. *See* Urbanism
Clapham Sect, 117
Class, 3–4, 43, 48, 102, 108, 112–13, 120, 127–28
Clive, Robert, 62, 64
Coal industry, 36–37, 44, 85, 86
Coalbrookdale, 36
Cobbett, William, 27, 48, 77, 81–82, 83, 88
    Political Register, 77, 82
Cobden, Richard, 113, 114, 146
Coke, Thomas, 46
Coleridge, Samuel Taylor, 67
Colonies, American, 54–61, 146
Combination Acts, 109, 133

Common lands, 47–48
Commons, House of, 7–11, 42, 76, 81–85, 105, 143
Communitarianism, 110–12
Community, 48
Complete Suffrage Union, 108
Concord, 58
"Condition-of-England question," 91, 98
Congregationalists, 50
Congress of Vienna, 70, 147
Connaught, 73
Connecticut, 56
Conservatism, 84
Constantinople, 144
Continental system, 69–70, 71
Conversion, 19
Convicts, 61, 73, 110, 148
Cook, James, 61
Cooperation, 104, 111, 112, 134
Cooperative Wholesale Society, 134
Corn Laws, 84, 113–14
Cornwall, 8, 9
Cornwallis, General, 60
Coromandel coast, 62
Corporation Act, 80
Corresponding Societies, 67, 77, 104, 106
Cort, Henry, 37
Cotswolds, 98
Cotton industry, 32–36, 50, 65, 86, 148
Counties, 8–9
Coventry, 95
Crompton, Samuel, 34
Crop rotation, 45

Dale, David, 41, 42
Darby, Abraham, 36, 40
Darwin, Charles:
    Origin of Species, 140–41
Death, 27
Declaration of Independence, 60
Deference, 12
Defoe, Daniel:
    Tour Through the Whole Island of Great Britain, 31–32
Deism, 17–18
Delaware, 56
Delhi, 61, 150
Democracy, 75–85, 121–22, 139–40
Demography, 26–29, 87–88
Derby, 82

Derbyshire, 34, 42, 77
Devon, 8
Devonshire, Duke of, 52–53
Dickens, Charles, 88
    Hard Times, 85
    Our Mutual Friend, 138
    Pickwick Papers, 127
Disease, 27, 96
Disraeli, Benjamin, 85, 120, 146
Dissenters, 49–50, 80, 84, 120, 122
Divorce, 130
Dodd, William:
    Factory System Illustrated, 89–90
Domestic economy, 128–29
Domestic system, 30–34, 42–43, 89
Don Pacifico, 143
Dorset, 8, 97, 109
Dublin, 73
Durham, 136
Durham, Lord, 81, 147

East Anglia, 30, 32
East India Company, 58, 62–65, 148, 150
East Tytherly, 110
Economic growth, 29–43, 50, 85–87
"Economic man," 43
Economy, fluctuation of, 86–87, 91, 103, 107
Edinburgh, 39, 50, 92
Education, 43, 50, 135–36
    adult, 104
    self-, 121–22
Education Act (1870), 136
Egypt, 144
Elba, 70
Eldon, Lord, 79
Eliot, George, 123
Emerson, Ralph Waldo, 132
Emigration, 27, 147
Empire, British, 54–65, 141–51
Enclosure, 46–48, 98
Engels, Friedrich, 88, 91, 107, 110
    Condition of the Working Class in England in 1844, 94
Engineering, 37
Enthusiasm, 17, 19
Epworth, 19
Erastianism, 117
Evangelicalism, 65, 115, 117–18, 123, 132, 149

Evolution, theory of, 140–41
Exeter, 88
Exeter Hall, 115

Factory Acts, 88–89, 135
Factory reform, 104, 109, 119–20
Factory system, 34, 36, 42, 88–91
Family, 129–30
Famine, Irish, 84, 114
Far East, 144, 148
Flint-Glass Makers Magazine, 134
Food production, 44
Foresters, Ancient Order of, 112
Forty-shilling freeholders, 9, 72, 82, 114
Fox, Charles James, 67
Fox hunting, 14
Framework knitters, 107
France, 25, 29, 49, 50, 53–55, 60, 62,
    65–73, 141, 142, 144–46
Franchise, parliamentary, 8–10, 76–83,
    113–14. *See also* Chartism
Free trade, 79, 84, 113–14, 141
Friendly benefit societies, 104, 112–13
Froude, James Anthony, 123

Gage, General, 58
Gainsborough, 39
Gammage, R. G., 108
Ganges, 62, 150
Gentry, 12–14
George I, 7, 52
George II, 7, 52
George III, 46, 52–53
George IV, 52, 80, 126
Georgia, 19, 55
Gibraltar, 147
Gin drinking, 4
Gladstone, William Ewart, 85, 145
Glasgow, 50, 87, 94, 95
Goa, 62
Gold, discovery of, 147, 148
Gott, Benjamin, 39
Gradgrind, Mr., 85
Grand National Consolidated Trades
    Union, 104, 109, 110, 133
Great Exhibition, 87, 124–25, 126
Great Industry, the, 86
Greece, 79, 142–43
Grenville, George, 57
Grey, Earl, 81, 82

Gurkhas, 149

Habeas corpus, 67, 77
Halévy, Elie, 76
Halifax, 32, 109
Hall, Edward, 92–93
Hampden clubs, 77
Hampshire, 110
Handloom weavers, 30–34, 42, 89, 94,
    107, 135
Hanover, 2, 7, 52
Hardy, Thomas, 67
Hargreaves, James, 34
Hastings, Warren, 62, 64
Heligoland, 147
Hindus, 150
Hogarth, William, 4–5
Holbeck, 92
Holland, 25, 29, 51, 69, 143
Holy Alliance, 142
Home, cult of, 129
Hong Kong, 147
Hook, Rev. Walter Farquhar, 120
Houses:
    of aristocracy, 6
    of artisans, 94
    cellar dwellings as, 94
    middle-class, 127–28
    of operatives, 89–90
    of poor, 16, 32–33, 92–98
    rural, 96–98
Howe, General, 60
Hudson Bay, 55
Hughes, Thomas:
    Tom Brown's Schooldays, 136
Hungry Forties, 87
Hunslet, 92
Hunt, Henry, 77
Huntsman, Benjamin, 36
Huskisson, William, 79
Huxley, T. H., 140
Hyde Park, 125

Ideology:
    of evangelicalism, 123
    of imperialism, 65
    of liberalism, 66, 132–33
    middle-class, 125–33
Illiteracy, 135–36
Imperialism, 54–55, 61, 64–65, 69, 146–
    50

Improvement, 74, 79, 84, 85, 115
    agricultural 46–47
Income, national, 85, 86, 91
Incomes, individual, 4, 91, 117, 127
Independent Order of Oddfellows, 112
India, 61–65, 144, 148–50
India Act (1784), 62
Indians (American), 57
Individualism, 132–33, 138–40
Industrial Revolution, 2, 7, 22–51, 65–
    66, 71, 74, 85–104, 111
Industrialization, 24–25, 44, 50, 87
Inkerman, 144
Insurrection, 106, 108
Intellectuals, 66, 67
Interests, 76
Inventions, 34–38, 44–45
Investment, 40, 44, 64, 86, 87, 142, 151
Ionian Islands, 147
Ireland, 27, 50, 72–73, 79–80, 84, 98,
    114, 147
Irish, in England, 94, 123
Irish Rebellion (1798), 54, 72–73
Iron industry, 36–37, 86
Islington, 94

Jacobins, 66, 67, 77, 78
Jacobites, 10, 54
James II, 10
Justices of the Peace, 12–14, 98

Keble, John, 118
King, Gregory, 26
    Natural and Political Observations,
        3–4

Labor, 40–43, 111–12
    child, 42, 90, 119
    discipline of, 43
    market, 99
    theory of value of, 111
Laborers, rural, 47–48, 98–104, 121
Laissez-faire, 49, 100, 132–33
Lake District, 68
Lancashire, 32–34, 42, 65, 79, 89, 98,
    107, 108, 134
Land, 5–6
Landseer, Edwin, 129
Latitudinarianism, 19

Leeds, 8, 32, 39, 83, 87, 92–96, 106,
    107, 116, 120
Leeds Household Suffrage Association,
    114
Leeds Working Men's Association, 106
Leicester, 32, 107
Less eligibility, 99, 103–04
Lexington, 58
Liberalism, 66, 79, 132–33, 139
Light Brigade, charge of, 146
Lincolnshire, 19
Literacy, 134–35
Little England, 146
Liverpool, 4, 87, 88, 94, 95
Liverpool, Lord, 79, 80
Livesey, Joseph, 115
Locke, John, 17, 111
Lodging houses, 95
London, 4, 8, 9, 27, 38, 39, 40, 42, 55,
    71, 77, 80, 83, 87, 88, 94, 106,
    107, 110, 115, 127, 133, 136,
    137, 148
London Corresponding Society, 67
London Working Men's Association,
    106
Lords, House of, 3, 7, 11, 30, 62, 80–83
Louis XIV, 54
Louis XVI, 77
Louis Philippe, 81
Louisiana, 57, 60
Lovett, William, 106, 107, 108
Loyal Order of Ancient Britons, 112
Luddism, 77

McAdam, John Loudon, 38
Macaulay, Thomas Babington, 81, 149
Macaulay, Zachary, 117
Machinery, 34–38, 88, 90, 111–12
Mackintosh, James, 67
Madras, 62
Mahrattas, 149
Malta, 70, 147
Malta, 70, 147
Malthus, Rev. Thomas:
    An Essay on the Principle of Popula-
        tion, 28–29
Malthusianism, 28–29, 85, 104, 132
Manchester, 4, 8, 33–34, 36, 39, 77, 83,
    87, 94, 95, 96, 106, 112, 113, 136
Mann, Horace, 117
Marlborough, Duke of, 54

Marshall, William, 46
Marx, Karl, 88, 107, 110, 137
Maryland, 56
Massachusetts, 58
Mauritius, 70, 147
Mayhew, Henry, 102, 103
Mehemet, Ali, 144
Melbourne, Viscount, 84
Mercantilism, 56, 57, 60, 72
Merchants, 3, 7, 56
Metcalf, John, 38
Methodism, 19–21, 43, 120–22
Methodist New Connexion, 121
Mexico, 60
Middle classes, 43, 50, 76, 81, 82, 84,
        106, 112–13, 114, 117, 119, 121,
        125–37, 138–39
Midlands, 76, 77, 85, 98, 107, 112, 121,
        127, 134
Migration, 87
Mill, James, 139
Mill, John Stuart, 139–40
    On Liberty, 139
Milner, Isaac, 118
Mississippi, 57
Moghuls, 61, 150
Monarchy, 5, 7, 52, 128
Moorfields, 120
Moral force, 105
Moravians, 19
More, Hannah, 118
Morris, William, 138, 139
Mortality, 26–27, 96
Municipal Corporations Act, 84
Muslims, 150
Mutiny, Indian, 62, 150

Nabobs, 64, 65
Nafferton, 97
Napoleon I, 66, 69–72, 142
Napoleon III, 144
Nasmyth, James, 86
National Society, 136
National Temperance Society, 115
National Union of the Working
        Classes, 81
Navigation Acts, 56, 57
Navy, 49, 69–70, 71–72, 141, 144, 151
Near East, 144–45
Nelson, John, 120

Nelson, Lord, 71
Nepal, 149
Netherlands, 54, 60, 70
New Brunswick, 147
New England, 60
New Hampshire, 55
New Lanark, 41, 42
New model unionism, 133
New Orleans, 57
New South Wales, 147, 148
New York, 55, 58, 60
New Zealand, 61, 148
Newcastle, Duke of, 6, 9–11, 52–53
Newcomen, Thomas, 37
Newman, Francis, 123
Newman, John Henry, 118–19
Newton, Sir Isaac, 16–17
Nightingale, Florence, 146
Nonconformity, 49, 115, 116, 120–23,
        136, 138–39. *See also* Meth-
        odism
Nore, 71
Norfolk, 14
Norfolk system, 46
North, Lord, 53, 57, 58, 60
Northern Star, The, 106
Norwich, 4, 24, 32, 87, 88
Nottingham, 32, 82, 95
Nova Scotia, 147

Oastler, Richard, 119, 120
O'Connor, Feargus, 107, 108
Oddfellows, Independent Order of, 112
Ohio, 55
Old Corruption, 83
Old Sarum, 8
Oligarchy, 5–11
Ontario, 147
Open fields, 46–47
Operatives, factory, 89–90, 103
Opium, 64, 148–49
Orbiston, 110
Orders in council, 70, 71
Ottoman empire, 144–46
Oudh, 150
Owen, Robert, 40, 41, 110–11
Owenism, 104, 106, 110–12, 113, 114–15,
        133, 134
Owens College, 136
Oxford, 8, 19, 50, 100, 118, 136
Oxford Movement, 118–19

Paine, Thomas, 122, 123
  Common Sense, 60
  Rights of Man, 67–68
Palestine, 144
Palmerston, Viscount, 142–45
Papal aggression, 123
Parish, 13, 38, 41
Parliament, 7–11, 12, 47, 64, 73, 76, 81–83, 114
  Irish, 72–73
Parsons, 14–16
Paternalism, 42, 111
Patronage, 7–11, 53, 64
Paupers, 42, 101
Paxton, Joseph, 124
Peace, international, 141
Peasantry, Irish, 72–73
Peel, Sir Robert, 79, 84–85, 114, 126
Peerage. *See* Aristocracy
Pennsylvania, 56
Pentridge, 77
Peterloo, 77–78, 81, 106
Philadelphia, 55, 58
Philanthropy, 110, 118
Philistinism, 138–39
Phrenology, 104
Physical force, 105, 114
Pindaris, 149
Pitt, William (Earl of Chatham), 53–55, 67, 68
Pitt, William (the Younger), 69, 76, 79, 117
Place, Francis, 133
Places, 8
Plassey, 62
Plug riots, 107, 114
Poaching, 13
Podsnappery, 138
Police Force, Metropolitan, 79
Political economy, 98, 100–01, 111, 114, 132–33
Pondicherry, 62
Poor, laboring, 3–4, 15–16, 43, 47–48, 91, 99
Poor Laws, 84, 98–104
  as relief, 41, 98–100, 102–03
  Report (1834), 99, 100, 103
Pope, Alexander:
  Essay on Man, 10, 17
Population, 3, 25–29, 40, 50–51
Porter, George Richardson, 85, 86, 87, 91, 114

Progress of the Nation, 85
Portugal, 62, 70, 79, 142–43
Poverty, 98–104, 111
Power looms, 34
Preaching, 20
Presbyterians, 50
Preston, 115
Price, Richard, 67
Priestley, Joseph, 67
Prime minister, 7, 79
Primitive Methodists, 121
Primogeniture, 6–7, 12
Prince Regent, 61
Professions, growth of, 127
Progress, 74, 125
Property, 5–6, 8, 49, 76
Prostitution, 130
Protestant Methodists, 121
Prussia, 69, 79, 142–43, 144
Punjab, 150
Puritanism, 40, 43, 50, 118, 122, 132
Pusey, Edward Bouverie, 118
Putting out. *See* Domestic system

Quakers, 36, 50
Quebec, 147

Racialism, 65, 149
Radicalism, 67, 73, 76–78, 80–81, 84, 104–15, 121, 146
Raglan, Lord, 145–46
Railways, 85, 87
Reason, 16–18
Reform:
  parliamentary, 74–85, 104
  in India, 149
Reform Act (1832), 75–76, 81–83, 106, 108, 114
Regency, 52, 74, 94
Religion, 116–23
  and census of worship, 116
  and science, 140–41
Religious Tract Society, 118
Report from the Select Committee appointed to consider the state of the Woollen Manufacture in England (1806), 31
Repression, 77
Respectability, 92, 94, 115, 122, 126, 130, 134

Revolution:
American, 56–61, 72, 76
French, 65–73, 74
Glorious, 2, 10, 66
July (France), 80–81
possibility of, in England, 108
Rhode Island, 56
Ricardo, David, 111
Roads, 38
Robinson, Frederick (Viscount Gode-rich), 79, 80
Rochdale, 111, 134
Rockingham, Marquis of, 57
Roman Catholicism, 15, 72, 119, 122–23, 144
and Catholic emancipation, 79–80
Romanticism, 68
Rostow, W. W., 29
Rowntree, Seebohm, 127
Royal Society, 16
Rugby School, 117, 136, 138
Rumania, 144
Ruskin, John, 137–38, 139
Stones of Venice, The, 137
Unto This Last, 137
Russell, Lord John, 80, 82, 84, 114
Russia, 69, 70, 79, 142–46, 150
Rutland, 9

St. Helena, 70
St. Lawrence River, 57, 147
St. Monday, 42
Sanitation, 93–96
Sanskrit, 65
Saratoga, 60
Schools, 118, 135–36
Science, 16–17
Scotland, 8, 27, 32, 41, 42, 50, 67, 68, 73, 89, 98, 110, 122
Scott, Sir Walter, 68
Sebastopol, 144
Sectarianism, 110
Secularism, 104
Self-government, colonial, 147–48
Self-help, 21, 104, 107, 111, 115, 130–32, 133, 134
Senior, Nassau, 100
Servants, domestic, 127–28
Seven Dials, 95
Sewerage, 95–96
Sexuality, 90, 130

Sheep, 45
Sheffield, 36, 37, 87, 107
Shelburne, Earl of, 60
Shelley, Percy Bysshe:
England in 1819, 78
"Shopkeepers, nation of," 71
Short Time Committees, 109
Shropshire, 36
Shuttleworth, James Kay, 90
Sidmouth, Viscount, 79
Sikhs, 150
Simeon, Charles, 118
Sin, 115
Sind, 150
Singapore, 147
Six Acts, 78
Slavery, 55, 65, 118
Slums, 94–96
Smallpox, 96
Smiles, Samuel, 114, 133, 134, 137
Self-Help, 130–32, 140
Smith, Adam, 90
Wealth of Nations, 27
Smith, J. B., 113
Social change, 87, 107–08
Social mobility, 7, 23, 55
Social policy of, 100
Social structure, 3–4
Socialism, 104, 137–38. *See also* Owen-ism
Society for Constitutional Information, 76
Society for the Defense of the Bill of Rights, 76
Society of the Friends of the People, 77
Society of United Irishmen, 72
Somerset, 8
South Africa, 70, 147, 148
South America, 79, 142, 148
Spa Fields, 77
Spain, 54, 56, 60, 67, 69, 70, 142
Speenhamland, 98, 102
Spithead, 71
Sport, 14–15
Squatters, 47
Squires. *See* Gentry
Stamp Act, 57
Standard of living, debate on, 91
Statistical enquiries, 91, 92
Steam engines, 34, 37
Stephen, James, 117
Sterne, Lawrence, 14

Strutt, Jedediah, 42
Stukeley, William, 14
Suffrage. *See* Franchise, parliamentary
Swing riots, 99

Tasmania, 148
Taxation, 57
Taxes on Knowledge, 109
Taylor, William Cooke:
    Notes of a Tour in the Manufactur-
      ing Districts, 89
Teetotalism, 115
Telford, Thomas, 38, 67
Temperance movement, 104, 114–16
Ten-pound householders, 82, 127
Test Act, 80
Thornton, Henry, 117
Thrift, 130–32
Tolpuddle martyrs, 109–10
Tories, 10–11, 12, 68, 77–85, 99, 108,
    117, 126
Tory radicalism, 120
Townshend, Charles, 52, 57
Townshend, Viscount ("Turnip"), 46
Tractarians, 118–19, 123
Tracts for the Times, 118
Trade:
    colonial, 56, 146
    foreign, 49, 50–51, 54, 141–42, 151
    Indian, 62–65, 148–50
    patterns of, 70, 71
    rivalry in, 69
Trade unions, 100, 104, 109–10, 112,
    133–34
Trafalgar, 69, 72
Transport, 37–39
Tull, Jethro, 44
Turkey, 142, 144–46
Turton mills, 89
Treaty of Paris, 61
Turnpike Acts, 38
Typhus fever, 95

Ulster, 72
Unemployment, 87, 91, 98, 100, 103
Unitarians, 50, 67, 92
United Irishmen, Society of, 72
United Kingdom Alliance, 115
United Kingdom of Great Britain and
    Ireland, 73, 79

United States of America, 60, 141, 147
Universities, 8, 50, 118–19, 136–37
Unstamped press, 104, 109
Urbanism, 34–35, 44, 87–88, 92
Ure, Andrew:
    Philosophy of Manufactures, 91
Utilitarianism, 139, 149

Van Dieman's Land. *See* Tasmania
Vaughan, Rev. Robert:
    Age of Great Cities, The, 88
Venn, John, 117
Victoria, Queen, 126, 128, 129
Virgin Islands, 55

Wales, 8, 21, 50
Walpole, Sir Robert, 11, 16, 54
War:
    of American Independence, 50, 58–
      61, 69, 72–73
    Crimean, 141, 144–46
    with France (1793–1815), 54, 66, 69–
      73, 77, 98
    in India, 149–50
    of Jenkins's Ear, 54
    Opium, 149
    Seven Years, 53–55, 57
    of Spanish Succession, 54
Washington, George, 58
Waterloo, 54, 70, 71, 80, 145
Water power, 34, 41–42
Watt, James, 37, 39, 40
Webb, Beatrice, 133
Webb, Sidney, 133
Weber, Max, 49
Wellington, Duke of, 70, 71, 80–83,
    126, 145
Wentworth Woodhouse, 6
Wesley, Charles, 19
Wesley, John, 19–21, 117, 120–21
Wesleyan Reformers, 121
Wesleyanism. *See* Methodism
West Indies, 55, 56, 70, 147
Westminster, 9
Whigs, 10–11, 12, 49, 52–53, 60, 67,
    71–85, 99, 108, 114
White, Gilbert, 14
Whitefield, George, 19

Whitworth, Joseph, 86
Wilberforce, William, 117, 118
Wilkes, John, 76
Wilkinson, John, 40
William III, 7, 54
Wilson, Benjamin, 109
Wilson, George, 113
Wiltshire, 8
Women, position of, 130
Woodforde, Rev. James, 14–16
Woolen industry, 30–32
Worcester, 81
Wordsworth, William, 66, 67
  Lyrical Ballads, 68–69
Work:
  ethic, 43, 49–50, 122
  gospel of, 130, 137

habits, 42–43
hours of, 42, 90
Workhouses, 100–04
Working class, 43, 76, 81, 82, 89–91,
    108, 112–13, 115, 117, 120, 121–
    22, 133–36, 139
Wyvill, Rev. Christopher, 76

York, 24, 38, 95, 127
Yorkshire, 9, 30–32, 89, 97, 98, 107,
    109, 119, 120
Yorkshire Association, 76
Yorktown, 60
Young, Arthur, 46, 48
Young Men's Improvement associa-
    tions, 115

A 3
B 4
C 5
D 6
E 7
F 8
G 9
H 0
I 1
J